Reporting for Journalists

Second Edition

Chris Frost

Routledge
Taylor & Francis Group

LONDON AND NEW YORK

First published 2010
by Routledge
2 Park Square, Milton Park, Abingdon, Oxon OX14 4RN

Simultaneously published in the USA and Canada
by Routledge
270 Madison Ave, New York, NY 10016

Routledge is an imprint of the Taylor & Francis Group, an informa business

Typeset in Goudy and Scala Sans by
Florence Production Ltd, Stoodleigh, Devon
Printed and bound in Great Britain by
CPI Antony Rowe, Chippenham, Wiltshire

British Library Cataloguing in Publication Data
A catalogue record for this book is available from the British Library

Library of Congress Cataloging in Publication Data
Frost, Chris, 1950–.
    Reporting for journalists/by Chris Frost. – 2nd ed.
        p. cm. – (Media skills)
        Includes bibliographical references and index.
    1. Reporters and reporting.   I. Title.
    PN4781.F74 2010
    070.4′3 – dc22   2009048987

ISBN10: 0–415–55319–9 (hbk)
ISBN10: 0–415–55320–2 (pbk)
ISBN10: 0–203–87197–9 (ebk)

ISBN13: 978–0–415–55319–3 (hbk)
ISBN13: 978–0–415–55320–9 (pbk)
ISBN13: 978–0–203–87197–3 (ebk)

Reporting for Journalists

Reporting for Journalists explains the key skills needed by the twenty-first-century news reporter. From the process of finding a story and tracing sources to interviewing contacts, gathering information and filing the finished report, it is an essential handbook for students of journalism and a useful guide for working professionals.

Reporting for Journalists explores the role of the reporter in the world of modern journalism and emphasises the importance of learning to report across all media – radio, television, online, newspapers and periodicals. Using case studies, and examples of print, online and broadcast news stories, the second edition of *Reporting for Journalists* includes:

- information on using wikis, blogs, social networks and online maps
- finding a story and how to develop ideas
- researching the story and building the contacts book, including crowd sourcing and using chatrooms
- interacting with readers and viewers and user-generated content
- making the best use of computer-aided reporting, newsgroups and search engines
- covering courts, councils and press conferences
- reporting using video, audio and text
- preparing reports for broadcast or publication
- consideration of ethical practice, and cultural expectations and problems
- an annotated guide to further reading, a glossary of key terms and a list of journalism websites and organisations.

Chris Frost is Head of Journalism at Liverpool John Moores University, UK. A journalist and teacher for almost 40 years, he chairs the National Union of Journalists' ethics council and is a member of the NUJ Professional Training Committee. He is the author of *Journalism Ethics and Regulation* (2007); *Media Ethics and Self Regulation* (2000); and *Designing for Newspapers and Magazines* (2003).

Media Skills

EDITED BY: RICHARD KEEBLE, LINCOLN UNIVERSITY
SERIES ADVISERS: WYNFORD HICKS AND JENNY MCKAY

The *Media Skills* series provides a concise and thorough introduction to a rapidly changing media landscape. Each book is written by media and journalism lecturers or experienced professionals and is a key resource for a particular industry. Offering helpful advice and information and using practical examples from print, broadcast and digital media, as well as discussing ethical and regulatory issues, *Media Skills* books are essential guides for students and media professionals.

English for Journalists
3rd edition
Wynford Hicks

Writing for Journalists
2nd edition
Wynford Hicks with Sally Adams, Harriett Gilbert and Tim Holmes

Interviewing for Radio
Jim Beaman

Web Production for Writers and Journalists
2nd edition
Jason Whittaker

Ethics for Journalists
2nd edition
Richard Keeble

Scriptwriting for the Screen
2nd edition
Charlie Moritz

Interviewing for Journalists
2nd edition
Sally Adams, with Wynford Hicks

Researching for Television and Radio
Adèle Emm

Reporting for Journalists
2nd edition
Chris Frost

Subediting for Journalists
Wynford Hicks and Tim Holmes

Designing for Newspapers and Magazines
Chris Frost

Writing for Broadcast Journalists
Rick Thompson

Freelancing for Television and Radio
Leslie Mitchell

Programme Making for Radio
Jim Beaman

Magazine Production
Jason Whittaker

Production Management for Television
Leslie Mitchell

Feature Writing for Journalists
Sharon Wheeler

*To the women in my life:
my mother, wife, daughters and sister.*

Contents

1	Introduction	1
2	The role of the reporter	6
3	Finding a story	22
4	Researching the story	41
5	Office procedures	76
6	On the road	85
7	Making contact	98
8	Getting the story	115
9	Interviewing	143
10	Production	164
11	And finally ...	183
	Glossary and acronyms	188
	Further reading	191
	Internet sites of interest	194
	Bibliography	197
	Index	204

1
Introduction

Some people want to become reporters for the glamour; some want to change the world. But I've always thought the best reporters do the job because they're just plain nosy. Wanting to know what people are up to, and to be the first to tell others about it, is what drives many reporters. Holding up a mirror to society in order to present the truth is a laudable aim, but it is not always top priority when trying to satisfy a **newsdesk** with limited resources and seemingly endless space to fill. The daily grind of filling pages is not always glamorous. But finding out what your community is up to because you can't stand not knowing, and then passing that knowledge on to help others manage their daily lives a little bit better, is rewarding – and can be fun.

This is the second edition of this book, and it's amazing to see how much has changed in the reporter's life since the first edition. When I was writing the first edition in 2001, websites were useful research tools, e-mail was a major form of communication and social networking was just getting started. Now all news outlets have an associated website, which means reporters must now consider how best to communicate their story; e-mail is now the most common means of communication; and social networking is becoming a clear alternative to the traditional media. In 2001, satellite navigation (satnav) was for the very rich, and wi-fi was yet to be a significant carrier. Broadband, wi-fi and satnav are now terms with which we are very familiar, and for most of us they are an integral part of our lives.

These changes have led many to believe that **citizen journalism** and **blogging** mean we are all journalists now, and that the professional journalist will eventually become a thing of the past – but that seems unlikely to me. We have always been able to share our writing, yet we have continued to queue to snap up the latest writings from our favourite authors. Similarly, while wider access to democracy will become available with blogs and network sites offering unusual and differing viewpoints, we will still want to access good quality, trustworthy news about our social and geographical communities – and that will need to be collated by professional journalists, people who gather news from all sources (including bloggers) and present it in a way that is easily digestible, but also informative. This may require fewer journalists than in the past, although I doubt it, but it will also require even higher professional standards. It also involves a change in the perception of journalism. This developing collaboration in journalism has meant a seismic and probably permanent shift in approach. No longer do journalists pass down the word 'from on high', accessing information that only journalists can reach and offering the distillation of this wisdom to others. All can now access the information, and all can take part in the debate. Interactivity and the involvement of readers and viewers is now all-important. From responses to articles in blogs or comments and e-mails sent to TV and radio news programmes, to web statistics on who is reading what, journalists now have a much closer link to readers and viewers than ever before. It's an exciting challenge, and brings methods of working that are different from those of journalists 20 years ago, but it should result in a better service to, and a better relationship with, the readers and viewers.

Writing this second edition has been a welcome opportunity to revisit basic skills. I'd like to thank those reviewers who looked at the first edition, offering praise when they thought I'd got it right and making valuable suggestions for improvement when times had changed or the text needed a different emphasis.

Journalism is the 'exercise by occupation of the right to free expression available to every citizen' (Robertson 1983: 3). There is nothing to stop anyone being a journalist, but in order to be paid for it, you need to be able to do it better than most. Citizen journalism, blogs and social networking allow anyone to publish stories and opinion, but as the world becomes awash with websites riding the publisher's favourite hobbyhorse, being a good journalist means finding stories people want to read, researching them as fully as possible, gathering information, views and opinions, and then getting the finished result back to the newsroom accurately and without delay. It's a tough brief, but an exciting one.

There can be few work-day thrills to match chasing the emergency sirens to a major fire or terrorist attack, gathering the story and then seeing your work broadcast or published in print or on the web, complete with your **byline**. The job satisfaction to be gained from spending days building a case against a corrupt politician, with all the careful meetings and research that involves, must also be hard to match in other careers.

For someone who *needs* to know what is going on – who is endlessly fascinated by the doings of fellow humans – being a reporter is the perfect job. You are actually paid to gossip in pubs with shady characters, meet the rich and famous in an effort to find out how they got to be like that with only a little discernible talent, or expose the dirty doings of lowlifes and criminals. It means that days are rarely the same, and many lead to anecdotes that can keep veteran colleagues talking for hours in a cosy pub with the help of a few beers.

Of course, not all reporters start as, or want to be, general news reporters, and there are a number of specialists who get the same thrill from reporting on sport or cars or fashion, or whatever it is that gets them excited.

Nearly every reporter in the UK these days starts his or her career on a journalism course. This will either be a one-year diploma course straight from school, or more likely a journalism degree or a postgraduate course following a degree in almost any subject. English, politics and history are popular and appropriate choices. There are advantages to each type of course and every college varies in what it has to offer.

Those with a particular desire to be a political reporter, for instance, might be better off studying politics and then taking a postgraduate course in either broadcast or newspaper journalism. Those who are less certain where their future lies might prefer a journalism degree that will allow them to learn the business inside out.

Journalism is often thought of as being both a glamorous and a well paid job. While there are certainly some journalists who are extremely well paid, who inhabit a very glamorous world, for the majority the pay is low and the work is not always glamorous. However, the work is usually interesting, and promotion to an executive position or as a correspondent for a major network can mean good money. And the training journalists receive, both at college and on the job, can lead to other, more lucrative careers both within and outside the media, so training as a journalist can be a sound starting point to an interesting and varied working life.

It is probable that if you are reading this book, you are already on some sort of journalism course, so it is not my intention to explain in detail what is available. If you want to know more, the National Council for the Training of Journalists, the Broadcast Journalism Training Council, the National Union of Journalists and the Association for Journalism Education all offer sound advice. Their contact details, together with web addresses for some of the key courses in the UK, are at the back of this book.

I do think I should explain the range of jobs available within journalism. Most journalists start as reporters for local newspapers, radio stations, news websites or magazines. They cover general news, which means everything from police calls and chasing fire engines through to local sport, politics, business and crime. After a couple of years, a reporter usually will either start to specialise in a certain type of reporting, or will seek a news job on a larger paper or broadcast station, or both. It is also possible to move into production or management and become a content manager, news editor or producer. Promotion or career development usually involves moving to another paper or station, often in a major city where a large number of the better paid and more prestigious jobs are on offer.

This book is intended to guide student journalists towards good practice as they take their early steps towards becoming reporters. I have tended to assume that your first job is, or will be, working for a local newspaper and its associated news website or a radio station, so the advice is tailored to a local approach, although most of it applies to reporting at any level.

The chapters follow each other in much the same way as the various stages of a reporter's job. I deal with the key practicalities and ethical issues of each stage in the appropriate chapter, so that, for instance, alongside discussion about finding and fostering contacts sits ethical advice about how to deal with such sources, the problems the reporter often faces, and how to overcome them. I have also identified a number of terms that you might need to check. These are identified in **bold italic**, and you can find their meaning in the glossary in Chapter 12.

Chapter 2 starts by looking at what a reporter is and what his or her role should be. It tries to explain what news is, and the distinction that is made between news and feature material. Chapter 3 begins the process of finding a story and examines where reporters get stories from.

Chapter 4 gives advice on how to research the story. It looks at the sources reporters rely on and how to get in touch with them. It also considers ways to use the web and other computer tools to aid reporting. In Chapter 5, the would-be reporter is shown how to work in a modern newsroom, while Chapter 6 considers how best to cope out on the road in an environment where self-reliance and initiative are the key to doing a great job. Going out on the road is a waste of time unless you are contacting people, so Chapter 7 is all about who to see and how to deal with them. Chapter 8 takes us inside the door to get the story, whether in court, council or press conferences; dealing with a wide range of contacts and considering who to see, where to go and what to do.

Having arranged your interview, you need to question your source, and Chapter 9 covers the important points of carrying out a good interview for news reporting. Chapter 10 looks at producing the story. This includes filing copy but also producing a news package. For broadcast reporters and a growing number of newspaper and magazine reporters, the performance interview is a vital part of this process. Whether on video or audio, this public interview of a source, either live or as part of a pre-recorded package, is a central part of the story, and its special problems need particular consideration. Chapter 10 examines this process and explains how best to use sound and pictures, actuality and interviews, and how to think about location/studio links and pieces to camera. Chapter 11 adds additional information about useful addresses, codes of conduct and ethics, and a glossary; and Chapter 12 provides a bibliography, reading references, and information on how to contact useful journalism organisations.

I hope you enjoy the book, and that it helps you to go on to work at something that you will find to be worthwhile, lots of fun, and that offers much career satisfaction.

2

The role of
the reporter

What is a reporter, and how does a good reporter relate to the world? A good reporter is unavoidably linked with what society sees as important about journalism. Many claims are made about the importance of journalism in a modern democracy. That great *Times* editor Delane believed:

> The duty of the journalist is the same as that of the historian – to seek out the truth, above all things, and to present to his readers not the truth as statecraft would wish them to know, but the truth as near as he can attain it.
>
> (cited in Williams 1957: 8)

Without good reporters to investigate and point the spotlight of truth into the dark recesses of business corruption, political double dealing or government incompetence, ordinary citizens would find it much more difficult to influence their world, and would have limited opportunities to understand and make decisions on such important issues as how to vote, where to live, what career path to follow, how to invest their life savings, and how to bring up their children. We need good quality, up-to-date information if we are going to be well enough informed to make the best of our opportunities, and we rely on journalism to get us that information.

Randall sums it up by saying that good journalists, wherever they are, will be attempting the same thing: 'intelligent fact-based journalism, honest in intent and effect, serving no cause but the discernible truth, and written clearly for its readers whoever they may be' (Randall 1996: 2).

But we need to understand that the perfect reporter, as identified by Randall, is as much fantasy as mild-mannered Clark Kent with his alter-ego Superman. The modern reporter lives in a world of 24-hour news, incessant deadlines and profit-hungry employers, making it difficult to live up to the ideal identified by Randall, and most observers see a very different reality, summed up by Professor Bob Franklin in a dismissive critique: 'These are giddy claims which will doubtless trigger incredulity among many readers of the contemporary British press' (Franklin 1997: 29). Franklin believes that the view of journalists as fearless crusaders and journalism as an investigative activity requires qualification. He also points out that, willingly or not, journalists do occasionally print untruths or half-truths.

This is the reporter's dilemma. We know that much is expected of us in terms of gathering the truth and presenting it to a public that supports the ideals of individual liberty and democratic government, but we also know that the reality is usually driven by circulation, ratings or profit. A journalist who wants to keep on working is constantly balancing the search for truth with the search for a story that will have readers or viewers queuing up to learn more.

It's like confusing politicians with politics. Politics is about power, and in the west we control that through democracy, giving people the right to have their views considered by those in power. Most politicians support this view – they probably even believe it – but when it comes to actually putting it into practice, things are rarely so high-minded.

Politicians are ambitious and human, just like everyone else, and just like everyone else they want to be popular and they also want to be re-elected. This means they often try to hide their mistakes or prevent us making full and informed choices by limiting the information they make available to the democratic process – just witness the uproar over the redactions of MPs' expenses claims as journalists tried to expose abuses. We all try to get by as honestly as we can, but the need to make a living can tempt us all to bend our principles.

Much of journalism is the routine gathering of information, most of it predictable and based around such events as court hearings, council meetings, sporting events and parliament. These days, with the pursuit of media consumers more crucial than ever before, the journalist has also had to become entertainer, finding stories and features that will delight the audience rather than inform, titillate rather than educate. With ever-increasing media output from a huge growth of sources, such as digital TV and the internet, tempting audiences to spend less and less time with any individual provider, persuading readers to spend a little longer with your news outlet has become one of the critical performance measures for the media. Consequently journalists rarely get the time or the encouragement for the big investigation to expose corruption or right wrongs. They are required to find entertaining and exciting stories quickly and with minimum research. Rather than investigating the detailed rights and wrongs of a major political debate, they will report only the 'row' between the major protagonists. This kind of reporting has the confrontation, drama and, of course, entertainment value of the gladiatorial contests of the Roman era without the blood and gore, but helps no-one to understand the issues in what might be an important political debate.

The move of advertising revenues from TV and newspapers to the internet and direct mail advertising means that all the traditional news media have been finding it difficult to keep profits up, and in a continuing pursuit of shareholder cash have been offering bigger dividends at the expense of the ability to deliver quality news. The credit crunch has put this process into overdrive, with much of the regional press responding to a crash in revenue caused by the evaporation of advertising in areas such as jobs, homes and motors by laying off staff, many of them from editorial. Commercial TV and radio have fared no better, with the fall in advertising revenue speeding up as fewer people advertise and ever fewer of them with local TV or radio. Media outlets that had already seen year-on-year reductions in circulation or ratings as their news services failed to offer consumers what they needed responded by reducing the level of service still further. At the time of writing whole sections of the industry, the regional press in particular, seem set to nosedive into terminal decline.

Profits may have stayed up during the nineties and noughties as services reduced, but that is unlikely to continue, with many companies warning of huge losses to come. Newsdesks are now constantly forced to seek the lowest common denominator with stories that consumers will follow but that are cheap to produce. The death of Jade Goody in 2009 is a prime example, with copy and research provided by Max Clifford Associates, the PR company. This story has been a guaranteed circulation-builder for many of the national newspapers and celebrity magazines but effectively the whole thing has been PR; a manufactured tale of trial and adversity ending in tragedy designed to tug our heartstrings and keep us reading. It is in this world that the reporter battles, trying on the one hand to remain honest to the readers, listeners and viewers, who rely on careful research and honest reporting to shape their world, while on the other hand pleasing an employer or editor who needs to report good profits to the next shareholders' meeting.

Reporting in different media

A reporter of 50 years ago started his or her working life in newspapers and, after a career of several years in weekly and daily journalism, chose either to move into the growing area of broadcast, or to stay in newspapers.

It is no longer such a straightforward decision. Broadcasting, online media and print are now melding into one, with reporters being expected to produce reports in text, video and/or audio as appropriate. Newspapers are likely to be published into the foreseeable future and magazines will be with us for a long time to come, but electronic publishing, online and by terrestrial and satellite broadcasting, is how most reporters will be working in the next ten years. Most modern reporters need to learn a range of skills that will allow them to work in different media throughout their career. No-one works in just one medium any more, and even a reporter on a small local weekly paper needs to understand how to produce text, video and audio for the paper's website.

There are obvious differences in working in the different media, although these seem to be reducing all the time as technology brings the various media platforms closer together – but there are more similarities than might be supposed.

All media require reporters with the same basic qualifications:

- an overwhelming curiosity about people and events;
- dogged determination to find out what is going on;
- an ability to mix with people, charm them and persuade them to tell you things;
- an ability to come up with interesting and original ideas for news stories and features;
- the initiative and cunning to get to places and people;
- the ability to present the information gathered in a way that suits the medium and the target audience.

While the technology for the different media separates the practitioners, the common elements listed above mean that, whatever the discipline, a reporter feels a common bond with other reporters. Learning to work with a camera team; coming to terms with the limitations of text; presenting stories that do not allow you to use any pictures; or, indeed, working with a medium that allows you to use text, sound, pictures and video but that places impossible demands in terms of a deadline and the breadth of material it will swallow, are all problems that the reporter must come to terms with.

Television

TV reporters need to have a real awareness of image and the way in which pictures will affect the story. They are less concerned with literature, and are more concerned with emotion and good pictures. This can mean they are often more concerned with the way sources present the material than what is actually said, but it can also mean putting over powerful messages.

Radio

Radio journalists do not need to think in pictures, but they do need to be able to paint pictures with sound. Sound is a very important medium because its approach is much more direct. We can concentrate on driving, for instance, but still listen to a radio broadcast. We can't (or most of us can't) concentrate on reading a newspaper and still do other tasks. Radio is a very immediate medium and is probably the best at alerting the public to a news story. Presentation is important in radio because vocal tone is very important in radio work. Someone with an irritating voice or a strong accent or dialect would not find radio work easy.

Print

Print journalists are able to gather more on a story and are generally able (or often required) to gather more stories. The newspaper together with its online partner, is still the medium with the largest amount of space to lavish on appropriate stories. Filling space is much more likely to be a problem for the newspaper reporter than for broadcasters. Many a district office reporter on one of the big evening papers faces the daily task of filling two pages of news on his or her own. This leaves little time for investigation or thinking about presentation. The newspaper reporter still needs to be creative about stories, however, and needs to think about picture ideas.

Online

Most reporters, whatever the company that employs them, will also work for an associated website. Some will work only to a website. These reporters need to think about presenting their work in a number of ways. They need to be aware of the technological limitations of their medium, but they don't need to be technicians. They need to think in depth as well as about immediacy, and they can use video, audio, pictures and text to tell the story. Many will also be providing material for a traditional news output, whether that is a newspaper, magazine or broadcast.

News: what it is and how to identify it

The media are there to present the consumer with information, whether through a review, news report, feature, profile, or listings of forthcoming events. Even adverts contain some information. You need to understand what it is that people want to read or hear on their news bulletins if you are to become a good reporter.

Although many reporters write news and features, you need to have a clear awareness of the difference so that you can understand how to use different techniques in different types of story.

As human beings, we all require information in order to function, and there seem to be two types of information that we are particularly interested in. The first tells us about our surroundings and environment: information that we need in order, at the basest level, to ensure our survival. We need to predict where we are likely to find food and safe shelter. Of course, in a modern world, our methods of fulfilling these desires are much more sophisticated, and so our intelligence-gathering is directed towards our pockets, our jobs, our comfort and our security – it has been interesting to note that reports presented during the credit crunch of 2008/09 concentrated on where to get cheap food and energy prices, and on worries about jobs and homes. Our security is identified by many commentators (see Venables 1993) as a prime quality of news. This includes health, food, safety and shelter.

The second type of information is about ourselves and, by extension, our fellow human beings. Most people want to be considered normal members of their society (or subset of society) – to fit in and be accepted, and they are prepared to modify their behaviour to do this. In small communities, hundreds of years ago, we could do that by observation. But in large, educated, metropolitan, even global communities, it is much more difficult. It is even possible to be a member, or want to be a member, of a subset of society where your physical contact with similar members is limited to two or three people in the local community. The traditional media have always been a normalising influence, allowing *Telegraph* readers (for instance) to commune with other *Telegraph* readers and accept and adjust shared values, no matter where they live in the country. The internet is able to play an important role here, with the rise of interactivity around stories and opinion. Letters pages, always a popular part of newspapers, have been expanded in all media to allow interaction and group activities. The internet has proved to be a powerful force in normalising such small subsocieties, and it is likely that this development will continue. Social networking is already one of the most successful phenomena on the net, and it is directly related to this desire to be part of a community: a group of people with whom we can share common feelings.

As the world has become more sophisticated, so it has become more difficult to align such shared values, and it is here that the media have played an important part. We now get our views about society from sources such as soap operas, dramas, the news, news features, and true-life tales in magazines and website fanzines.

One of the difficulties we have is separating fact from fiction. We need to be able to work out that our favourite soap opera might well have something to say about how British society works, whereas a drama such as *Heroes*, popular though it may be, perhaps doesn't. This is even more important in news, where we are relying on accurate, timely information for more immediate support in areas such as our comfort and security. We need to be able to separate fact from rumour, truth from propaganda.

The communities to which we belong are very important to us because we like to belong and we enjoy the companionship of those with whom we feel comfortable. Most of us belong to a number of overlapping social groupings in which we hold greater or lesser positions of social status, such as:

- family
- friends (often based around school, social network site or work)
- local special interest group
- school, college or work
- home town
- hobby or leisure activity
- profession, work group or trade union
- nation.

Many of these groupings hold their community interest with gossip – most social network websites are little else. So we should not be surprised that gossip plays an important part in news reporting, particularly in newspapers, which have been overtaken by radio and TV as an alerting medium. No-one really uses newspapers nowadays to follow a breaking story. TV, the internet and, best of all, radio are far better at it. But newspapers and websites are good at gossip, which relies on small but significant details.

Gluckman says that gossip can also be used by social groups to preserve their exclusiveness by closing the doors to parvenus (Gluckman 1963). Many of the society gossip columns use this effect to be open enough to allow readers to understand, but not be part of an exclusive set that they wish to join. Gossip is often condemned as being part of the dumbing down of news outlets; it is seen as lacking the intellectual importance of hard news.

In fact 'soft news' – news about people and their relationships – is very important. This human interest news, which is about people, their communities and relationships, tells us about who we are. Our ability to relate to others, to understand their problems, to sympathise and empathise underpins much of our understanding of key social issues. Soft news is at the heart of good reporting and often brings us the best and most widely read stories.

'Hard news', on the other hand, is about issues, and often concerns more urgent and critical matters. Hard news is more likely to be about facts and figures than people's feelings. Hard news is often the starting point for a run of stories giving the facts and setting the agenda. Soft news will help us understand how it affects people and how they feel about it. It is often easier to present the hard news story that a factory is closing down as more important than the soft news story that a worker at the factory will have to give up their home because they can no longer afford their mortgage and must send their children to live with parents-in-law, yet the one is the cause of the other, and the effect is more likely to chime with us as individuals than the cause. The reality of closing a factory is that people will lose their homes, and perhaps their families.

Any new or threatening situation may require us to make decisions, and this requires information – hard news. So important is communication during a disaster that normal social barriers are often lowered. We will talk to strangers in a way we would never consider normally. Even relatively low-grade disruption of our life, such as a fire drill or a very late train, seems to give us the permission to breach normal etiquette and talk to strangers. The more important an event to a particular public, the more detailed and urgent the requirement for news becomes. Without an authoritative source of facts, whether that is a newspaper or trusted broadcast station, rumours often run riot; something that is frighteningly easy with the internet there to lend a hand. Rumours start because people believe their group to be in danger and so, although the rumour is unverified, feel they should pass it on. For example, if a worker heard that their employer's business was doing badly and people were going to be made redundant, they would pass that information on to colleagues completely unverified.

According to Tamotsu Shibutani (1966), rumour is a group process. Groups of people discuss a piece of information one of them has heard and then pass it on to others, together with their own interpretation. That interpretation might include their own knowledge, their own fears and their own concerns. All these might alter the rumour, changing it from the original story. Journalists are often dragged into the rumour machine and this could be when a story first claims a reporter's attention.

A reporter always needs to play the sceptic, listening but demanding proof and seeking sources. Sometimes a story is too good to risk not using it as quickly as possible. This means checking as much as possible and then following up the detail for later editions or bulletins.

Tamotsu Shibutani (1966) hypothesises that if the demand for news by the public exceeds the supply made available through institutional channels, rumour construction is likely to occur. We see this happening when a big story breaks and demand for news exceeds its supply because reporters simply cannot gather enough material quickly enough to satisfy demand and interest (Frost 2007: 81). This certainly happened following the death of the Princess of Wales in 1997. Social barriers were lowered and strangers talked openly about the death in trains and buses. People were desperate to find out more information and rumours ran riot.

At its most simple, news is information we were unaware of until we read it or saw it in the media. However, much news is predictable, keeping us up to date with stories we know to be happening. News can be said to be a *factual* (the reporter should have gone to considerable pains to ensure the material is truthful), *topical* event that is *of interest to the target group* of the media outlet producing it. The Royal Commission on the Press (1949) (The Ross commission) said about news:

> There are, however, certain elements common to all concep-
> tions of news. To be news an event must first be interesting
> to the public, and the public for this purpose means for each
> paper the people who read that paper, and others like them.
> Second, and equally important, it must be new, and newness
> is measured in newspaper offices in terms of minutes.
> (Royal Commission on the Press 1949: 103)

The commission went on to identify items of interest as being: sport; news about people; news about strange or amusing adventures; tragedies; accidents; crimes; 'News whose sentiment or excitement brings some colour into life' (*ibid.*: 104).

The commission used *new* in the sense in which I use *topical*: it has happened within the frequency of the medium in which it appears. So for a weekly paper, it is anything that has happened within that week; for a radio bulletin, it is anything that has happened since the last bulletin. This should also include an element of novelty. By its nature as something topical, it will introduce an element that is new or novel to the audience. Nowadays we talk about target groups to mean what the Ross commission described as 'the people who read that paper and others like them' (*ibid.*).

Which stories interest a target group is a matter of judgement. Alastair Hetherington, editor of *The Guardian* in the 1960s, drew up a list of priorities for new staff:

- significance: social, economic, political;
- drama: excitement, entertainment;

- surprise: unpredictability, newness;
- personalities: royalty, showbiz;
- sex, scandal, crime;
- numbers: scale of the event;
- proximity: its geographical closeness (cited in Venables 1993: 3).

Johan Galtung and Mari Ruge were among the first academics to try to understand news decision-making in a study first published in the 1960s examining international news. They saw news as broken down into two categories: general news value, and news values of particular importance to western media. They identified the time elements and the need to coincide news choices with the perceived audience. They also identified that the media favoured news that directly affected the target audience (*meaningfulness*) or was easy for the target audience to understand; that there tended to be a news *threshold*; and that space limitations varied that threshold (*composition*) (Galtung and Ruge 1997).

Harcup and O'Neill examined Galtung and Ruge's research from the perspective of a new millennium and came up with a different list. It's worth noting that their survey took place almost 40 years later, and it only looked at UK national newspapers. Like Galtung and Ruge, they found that stories about the *power elite* or celebrities were favourites. *Relevance* to the target audience was still important, as was *magnitude*, both of the size of the event (either good or bad) or of the *surprise* within the story (Harcup and O'Neil 2001).

Journalists tend to use stories with clear time frames (disasters, crime, political rows), and if a story is about important issues but has no clear start time and no clear development highlights, they will try to provide them. So, for instance, rather than carry a story about hospital waiting lists and what is being done (or not done) about them, it is easier to print stories about the government's latest claim to be doing something or the opposition's claim that they are failing, as this gives a clearly identifiable time frame.

Hetherington identifies news from experience, while Galtung and Ruge identify it from observation, but they were not able to give clear rules that we could apply in any situation. Philip Schlesinger (1978: 51) reminds us that the problems of *time constraints* and *logistics* will also have an effect on whether a story makes it to the news bulletins. Logistical problems may, for instance, lead journalists to produce stories closer to home rather than spend time, money and effort taking a film crew abroad. If they do need to go abroad, they are more likely to justify the expense by filing stories that are well below the normal threshold. Did you notice, for instance, how many stories we got from China while all those media people were in Beijing to cover the Olympics? The western media are inevitably drawn towards covering elite nations because of the ability to travel quickly and easily and use the fast communication methods in the west.

John Venables is another thinker about news. He comes to the conclusion that *change* and *security concern* are 'two fundamental factors which motivate attentiveness in an audience' (Venables 1993: 34). He goes on to describe the importance of change: 'Without change, information cannot be interpreted as news. Change is important because it involves uncertainty, which in turn generates attention and concern' (*ibid.*). Change is undoubtedly a defining parameter of our lives. We measure time by changes. We wake up and go to work (a change); we stop work for lunch (a change); and so on. This is why some days seem boring and others fly by – it all depends on the amount of change. Change also explains why we choose a particular time to write about a certain story. The events roll like a river, but there has to be a reason why we build the news story at a particular point on the bank. That point is usually a change where a definite action may have been made, a decision taken. This change turns the otherwise continuously flowing story into news. It is worth noting that journalists and PR people often 'manufacture' stories by artificially inserting a change, such as ringing a source and then leading on the comments that source made. Venables also identifies *familiarity* (*ibid.*) as an important constituent of news. Galtung and Ruge (1997) before him saw *unambiguity* and *consonance* as important components of news. These terms mean that news stories will have a cultural basis that is understood by the audience so that explanation is kept to a minimum. Reporters covering the US 2008 presidential elections for the UK had to spend much time explaining the US electoral system so that the UK audience could understand how Obama was swept to power. If the election had been from a country of lesser significance, they probably would not have bothered.

So any news editor making a choice of news stories will be looking for stories that are:

- *topical* (fit within the time frame and involve a *change*);
- *true* (or at least have some basis in truth);

- are fit for the *target* group – they need to be *familiar*, but involve *change*, and be of interest to the group.

These may, of course, be constrained by *logistics* and possibly *composition*. Composition was identified by Galtung and Ruge (1997) and suggests that a story might be used because of the type of news elsewhere on the page or in the bulletin. One would not want a news bulletin that was all politics, for instance, and so a crime story might make it into the bulletin even though it is not very strong. ITN's 'and finally' stories were ideal examples of composition. The stories were set to a pattern and designed to end the bulletin on a positive note. They were not chosen for their news value, but to fit into the composition structure of the bulletin. And, of course, this is where entertainment fits in. We forget at our peril that people watch the news and read newspapers to be entertained as much as to be informed, so much of what we produce also needs to be entertaining.

Personal qualities

Working as a reporter requires some basic personality traits as well as a number of learned skills. Each reporter can learn how to develop their qualities, but if you are not naturally curious, for instance, there's not much point in being a reporter; there are plenty of other media jobs that require other attributes. If you start off with an overwhelming curiosity about people and events, this can be developed and honed to make the best use of it. Combine this with a dogged determination to find out what is going on, and you can become a superb reporter. Alastair Campbell, the former 10 Downing Street Communications Director, was interviewed on radio about his appointment to the post before Labour gained office in the nineties. He said that he and Tony Blair wondered who would be the first to contact him to discuss one of the several 'skeletons' in his closet: his mental breakdown and his writing for *Forum* magazine being two for which he is now widely known. He said the *News of the World* phoned within eight minutes of receiving the press release announcing his new post to ask about his writing for *Forum*. This quick response shows that at least one reporter had been interested enough in a former colleague to have found out about his early writing career – an inquiry that returned the dividend of a good story. Curiosity means that you gather a lot of snippets of information that can be used as the basis of good stories, often by linking or synthesising otherwise disparate pieces of information to produce interesting and original ideas for news stories and features. This means that good reporters need to read a lot, talk to people and ask questions.

Good reporters are also gregarious and enjoy meeting and talking to others. If you prefer your own company, then again, reporting may not be the life for you. A good reporter must be able to talk their way into places and find out who to interview to get the story, and where to go to get the right information.

Specialist reporting

A number of people become reporters for the consumer and trade magazine industries because they are specialists in their fields, rather than because they are journalists. They work with journalists and what they produce can be considered journalism, but they might still describe themselves as something else. Academics and some other professionals are particularly prone to follow this route. Whether they are lawyers, doctors, technologists, engineers or chemists, they are writing about their subject, popularising for ordinary people. Sports personalities and entertainers also join this throng of writers producing specialist columns, often for a specialist press market.

But there are also a number of journalists who, having served their apprenticeship as a news reporter, want to move on to specialist areas of writing. Sport is always a popular choice, but showbiz, motoring, crime, politics and fashion are other areas that attract enthusiastic specialists who write with deep knowledge for their newspapers or broadcast with passion for TV or radio. These specialists need all the basic skills of the reporter. They must be able to identify a good story. They need to be able to develop ideas to create further news stories or features. They must be able writers or broadcasters. In addition, they must have a passion for their chosen specialism and a desire to learn much more about it. That desire usually turns them into considerable experts after a few years.

Many specialists have their own clubs – the wine writers' circle, a motor writers' guild, a football writers' association, and so on.

Freelances

Not all reporters are employed by large media companies. Some are self-employed, gathering stories for specialist markets or a number of different media outlets. There are two types of **freelance**. Some choose to be freelance, often specialising in a particular area such as finance or sport. Their expertise means they can get regular work from a number of employers, none of whom needs their expertise permanently, but who are willing to pay by the day or by the article. The second group are freelance because they do not have a staff job. Often during an economic downturn reporters are laid off and then have to find work where they can. Many become freelance, digging up stories and selling them where they can, or seeking other work involving their skills of research and communication.

Freelances have particular requirements when it comes to developing stories. Not only do they need to think of good ideas for stories in the first place, but they also need to consider where they are going to sell the story. Some freelances specialise in an area of reporting and already have key markets lined up. This can be a good way to earn a freelance living. Perhaps you specialise in social work, for instance. This means finding news and feature stories in this field and sending them to the specialist magazines in the area. After a while, these magazines will come to recognise the expertise of such a freelance and may offer commissions or ask the freelance to cover conferences or special events. Other non-specialist publications often have specialist pages. *The Guardian*, for instance, has its weekly education supplement, and the editor of this will publish appropriate education pieces and will also come to trust regular freelances with suitable expertise. Read the *EducationGuardian* and you will see certain bylines appearing regularly. These are almost certainly freelance contributors whose work is being used or has been commissioned because of their expertise.

General freelances have more opportunities for a wider range of writing, but will often have to deal with news editors they don't know. Having written a story, it is even more important for such freelances to ensure the story is written in a way that suits the market of the target paper, magazine or broadcast station. This could mean writing the same story in a dozen different ways. A good freelance could sell a basic news story – for example about a woman protester fined for criminal damage after breaking into a local army base and painting a tank bright pink in protest at arms sales to Indonesia – to a number of outlets: the BBC, all the nationals, the local dailies and some of the foreign agencies. An interview with the protester would also be of interest to some of the women's magazines: 'How I stood up to be counted' or 'Women in the front line'. Some alternative lifestyle magazines might also be interested in the story on the basis of why she did it. It's probably stretching things a bit to try to sell the story to trade mags such as *Paint World*, but only because their budget may not be big enough to pay for 'Dulux puts tank in the pink'. Stories about how she broke into an army base, or the practical problems of painting a tank, might also appeal to some specialist mags (although probably too specialist to be able to pay much). They would need to be handled with care because of the security implications, but it would certainly be possible to build the story into a fun feature on 'Five crazy things to do after a night of lager' for *FHM* or *Loaded*.

A different approach, a new introduction and a new writing style can change an idea radically enough to allow the thinking freelance to sell the same basic story to a dozen different markets.

3
Finding a story

Mrs Beeton's nineteenth-century recipe famously began 'first, catch your hare'. The reporter's task is: first, find your story. No newspaper or news bulletin would sell without stories, and it is the reporter's job to find them. Much news can be anticipated and is the routine of daily life. These *diary stories*, as they are called, are tracked by the newsdesk as part of their forward planning and allocated to the reporter. They can be anything from a flower show to a United Nations press conference. Whatever the event, they all share one thing in common – someone wants you to cover the event and publish or broadcast stories about it. The flower show organiser wants local people to know about the show and its winners; the United Nations conference wants to tell the world of some new initiative and enhance the reputation of the UN. Stories that are not pre-ordained are often more interesting. The *off-diary story* is one discovered by the reporter on his/her own initiative, and is often a story someone, somewhere, doesn't want covered – whether the local MP's expenses scandal or the local mayor's illegal drug habit. Diary stories are the bread and butter of most local newspapers and radio stations – but it is the off-diary story, particularly if it is exclusive, that interests the good reporter, and it is a mark of status within the newsroom to be taken off the diary and allowed to work completely on one's own initiative investigating stories.

Market considerations

The first thing a reporter needs to consider when searching for a story is the market. If you are working for a local weekly paper then the stories you choose, how you approach them, and how you write them will be very different from those on the local radio or the national TV news.

The audiences of Radio 4, *The Daily Telegraph* and *The Sun* are all different, as are the audiences of *Cosmopolitan* and the *Keighley Times*, although with the right presentation all those publications might be interested in the same story. Who consumes the media you work for is important for two reasons: it identifies who you are writing for; and it identifies who is likely to advertise with your outlet. For most commercial media, advertising is the vital element that pays the bills and makes the profit, so attracting it is of prime concern to the journalist's employer and a major concern for the journalist, since without advertising the newspaper or broadcaster might go bust. So, once again, we return to the age-old dilemma of the reporter. While the good reporter is working hard to produce quality journalism that will interest and inform the consumer for whom he or she is writing, the editor is busy selecting material to print or broadcast that will produce a large audience of the type that the advertiser is seeking, to make it worth the advertisers' while to buy space or time. Watch afternoon TV, and the adverts are all for funeral insurance, stair lifts and accident compensation because afternoon audiences have a high proportion of the elderly and those off sick; adverts in *The Sun* are often for pay-as-you-go phone contracts and van insurance, as this paper is the first choice for 'white van man'.

A reporter needs to know the target audience well to make decisions about the use of a story. Consideration needs to be given to their age, sex, social class, background, occupation and earning power, because the more interested the target audience is, the keener the editor will be to use the story (because it will sell more and so attract more advertisers), and the more copy he or she will require. Newspapers, in particular, like to develop the feeling of belonging among readers by developing 'we groups' (Paine 1967: 278–285). This is often done by identifying groups to vilify, from teenage knife gangs (Boy falls to his death fleeing knife gang – *Daily Express* 22/8/09, www.dailyexpress.co.uk/posts/view/58013) to asylum seekers (Adult asylum seeker 'raped girl, 13, after he lied about age and was placed in children's home' – *Daily Mail* 11/05/09, www.dailymail.co.uk/news/article-1180151/Adult-asylum-seeker-raped-girl-13-lied-age-placed-childrens-home.html).

By identifying groups that can be 'exposed' as being of less worth than those reading the paper, a feeling of belonging to a 'we group' can be developed. This can then be augmented to produce an aspirational desire among readers to belong to a more exclusive social group – a 'we group within a we group' – with the appropriate lifestyle. This can be fostered by providing gossip about exclusive groups, and is one of the reasons why so many of us are so fascinated by celebrity. We require celebrities to live a lifestyle we can't afford with a social set we can't join so that we can live it by proxy. The long-running TV series about the lives of Jordan (Katy Price) and her ex-husband Peter Andre is one such example. They are paid to live a celebrity lifestyle (by selling their TV show, which follows their lives) so that those who aspire to such a lifestyle themselves can enjoy it by proxy. Of course, this means the downs as well as the ups, and many may watch simply to convince themselves that there is a horrific price to pay for celebrity. This aspirational nature of gossip is a well understood effect: the idea that the more exclusive the group, the greater the amount of gossip was first identified by Gluckman back in the 1960s (Gluckman 1963: 309).

While a good reporter should have a clear understanding of the nature of the audience, such understanding of different audiences is even more important for a freelance. A good freelance knows at a glance which publication/broadcast outlet will be interested in which story, how much material they would want on it, and how to angle the story. If you produce stories suitable for *The Sun* but try to sell them to BBC national news, or *vice versa*, you will soon go broke.

Most national newspapers, magazines and broadcast outlets these days have very clear ideas about their audience. This is a little more difficult on the local scene, where the temptation is to aim at everybody in the geographical area. However, most newspapers and local radio stations have a type of person in mind when writing or broadcasting. Local independent commercial radio, for instance, often tries to attract the 15–30-year-old market with short news bulletins and the latest pop music, while BBC local radio, with its greater emphasis on talk, is more likely to aim at the 50-year-old+ audience. Radio and particularly TV have relatively short bulletins and so can choose only the most important news for the audience. A national TV news bulletin can carry only the amount of news that would fit on a national newspaper's front page, and the choice and presentation order are often determined by the quality of the supporting video. Newspapers need to attract on the news-stand, and so will attempt a unique selling point if possible. The *Daily Mail*, for instance, aims at middle-class, middle-aged women with aspirations. Much of its news concerns issues that are directly connected with its readers' lives, such as education (most have children at school or college), the workplace or crime, or is lifestyle-based, looking at fashion, consumerism and the lives of the rich and famous. This *ethnocentric* nature of news (Watson 1998: 106) means that news is never the direct reflection of society that some commentators, such as Randall, would have us believe, when he wrote of holding 'up a mirror to society, reflecting its virtues and vices and also debunking its cherished myths' (Randall 1996: 2). A more accurate description might be the mirror of the fairy-tale evil stepmother: 'Mirror, mirror on the wall, who is the fairest of them all?' It is not a mirror at all, but wish-fulfilment. The media, all too often, are there to tell people what they want to hear.

News is aimed at an audience – an audience that, in most cases, has to be persuaded to buy the product. Audiences do not passively lap up all they are given – they are selective and choose which items of media they buy according to their enjoyment or need for what is on offer. This means that news is bound to follow certain patterns that the good reporter learns to identify: 'all news is reported from some particular angle' (Fowler 1999: 10).

Diary stories

Diary stories (or on-diary stories as they are sometimes known) are notified to the newsdesk from a number of external sources and are entered in the diary. A show here, a press conference there, everything from a local council meeting to a charity ball will be entered into the diary and may be allocated to a reporter to cover. It is important that any event you learn of is entered in the diary so that the news editor is also aware of it. It may well be an event you are unable to cover personally. You should also note follow-up ideas in the diary. For instance, if a local school is campaigning to build a new sports hall, then you should note all the key dates of the campaign in the diary to remind yourself and the newsdesk to follow up their progress. Local courts and council meetings are still a staple of the local paper. But there are plenty of other routine events that are entered in the diary year after year. Much diary work these days is organised through a forward planning service. As well as receiving information from PR companies and organisations, a forward planning service is able to update the newsdesk on what is happening around the country and abroad. Such services feed newsdesks with diary dates online. These can be filtered to suit the newsdesk's own choices and target audience by geography or type, so that the newsdesk is alerted to diaried events such as press conferences, government announcements and court dates in which it is interested. It can then allocate reporters to cover the story, or commission a freelance to do it for them.

Press releases

The most common source of stories, certainly on local papers and local radio stations, is the press release. These have grown in importance over the past 20 years as editorial staff on many provincial papers have been reduced and more and more organisations have become media-sensitive. A local weekly paper that, during the 1970s, had an editorial staff of ten might now struggle by with five. There are a number of reasons for this. Franklin and Murphy (1998: 9) identify seven significant factors. Whatever the reasons, newsdesks are now more likely to use press releases from local businesses, societies, sports clubs and am-dram groups than ever before. This effect has now become so pronounced that a recent study by Cardiff University for Nick Davies and his book *Flat Earth News* found that of all the domestic copy used in *The Guardian* over a two-week period (2207 pieces) '60% was wholly or mainly wire copy and/or PR material' (Davies 2008: 52). Davies's point is that if even a well respected newspaper such as *The Guardian* used so much **wire** and PR copy, what about the others? *The Times*, for instance, used as much as 69 per cent, but Davies points out these are not the worst offenders: 'They left out the tabloids, which carry far more celebrity stories dominated by PR material. They ignored the *Financial Times* and the quality finance pages where city reporting is flooded with PR' (*ibid.*: 53). Rather than admit to this use of wire and PR copy, most newspapers hide the authorship of wire copy behind the byline 'Staff Reporter' or a made-up name, and PR copy is often used without serious follow-up checks or even an opposing quote.

Reporters must remember that PR handouts are a propaganda vehicle for the sender. No-one sends a press release that shows them, their company or group in a bad light. You must read between the lines to get at the real story and you may need to ring the **contact** for further information. Some press releases, of course, are absolutely straightforward and just need to be presented in a tight, bright style. In my spare time I sometimes help out local charities with their publicity. The releases are straightforward information about local events that will interest local people and are written in an appropriate style. Not surprisingly, these are usually used in their entirety and uncut by the local papers. Only if they want more do they tend to come back to me seeking extra quotes or picture ideas. However, all too often press releases are cleverly concocted stories produced by PR companies to advertise their clients' services or to present their client in a good light. They are free advertising, and mislead readers. Nick Davies gives an excellent example of an insurance company issuing press releases that on the face of it were interesting stories, but in reality were fictitious advertising (*ibid.*: 49). Even Downing Street was obliged to close a petition back in May 2007 after it was revealed that the whole story was a hoax. A blog sent to the *Daily Express* had condemned the building of a £100 million mega-mosque, but as Downing Street explained: 'We understand from Newham Council that there is no current planning permission or application for a mosque . . . The mayor (Ken Livingstone) wishes to make it absolutely clear that these reports are entirely untrue.' (www.number10.gov.uk/Page12541). Hoaxes, self-serving and mischief abound in this world of PR and unchecked information. Using a PR handout as the starting point for a story might be OK – but putting it in unchecked and without challenge definitely is not.

Other news outlets

Other newspapers or broadcast stations are good sources of news. Competing papers and magazines and the national papers need to be read every day so that stories that may have a link to your target audience can be followed up. Radio and television need to be monitored constantly for the same reason. This is why so many media outlets all seem to zero in on the same story. One outlet carries the story and others then feel it is important enough for them to follow up.

Advertisements

Advertisements often carry good stories, particularly for regional papers and radio stations. Births, marriages and deaths (BMDs), unusual job vacancies, strange items for sale or offbeat public announcements can often lead to good stories. Public announcements from councils are also a good source of stories, as they will often signal plans for major developments or changes. Any newsdesk worth its salt will arrange with the advertising department to give them a sight of BMDs and public announcements as early as possible in the day.

Anniversaries

Anniversaries are an easy source of good stories, allowing you to relive the event using archive pictures, video or sound. Interviews with those involved a year, ten years or even 20 years on can provide good human interest features, news stories or current affairs programmes. All of us enjoy reminiscing, and these features give us the chance to say 'Is it really a year since . . .?'. Such features also allow the passage of time to add perspective to a story.

Records

Records make great stories, whether the smallest baby, the largest pig or the longest time without sleep. Some are local news standards, like the first baby born in the year in the local maternity hospital, often with the bonus of an unusual birth story. Some can be manufactured. Heavy rainfall last night? Could it have been the worst rainstorm for 20 years? Check with the local met office.

Academia

Academics and academic journals can be good sources of stories, particularly for specialist correspondents. Many academics are desperate to make their reputation and will happily talk about their latest research. While the number of academic journals available can be daunting, the internet now allows notification of when journals in which you are interested are published, and what they contain. Many journals or the articles in them are too dry by far to be of interest to a general readership, but reporters on specialist magazines or health or education correspondents do find the occasional nugget tucked away in the likes of the *British Medical Journal*, *The Lancet* or one of the science journals. The issue of climate change is often prodded along by a report of the latest research from some university or another. Medicine, too, likes to boast of its latest advances, and research papers about new drugs or treatments are another source of stories. Of course it should always be remembered that many of these are press releases and may present a distorted story. The paper that suggested the MMR vaccine given to children to protect against mumps, measles and rubella caused autism set a scientific debate raging for years until the claim was swamped by sound evidence to the contrary from a number of sources.

Official sources

Council minutes and agendas, government press releases and court lists are often sources of good stories. Careful reading of the detail (budget cuts, odd purchases or personnel changes) can often lead to good stories. Once, years ago, when reading the Social Services Committee minutes of a local authority, I realised that the figures listing the number of children taken into care each year and the number put into children's homes compared with the number sent to foster homes, meant that the vast majority of children, more than 80 per cent, were sent straight back home to live with their natural parents despite being taken into local authority care as being in danger. We were able to run the stories for weeks across the front and inside pages. Many councillors leapt on the bandwagon to make it a great story. I'd like to be able to say we completely changed the way children were dealt with, but of course we didn't. But we did force some people to treat the situation more seriously.

Parliament is also now much more accessible, with *Hansard* and all the current Bills and Acts of Parliament available on the web. Any political correspondent needs to make regular visits here. Government press releases are also available online. You can often spin a good local story from a national government press release (see www.coi.gov.uk). Every government department now has an excellent website that carries a lot of information and government reports. Of course, you can't expect to find bad news getting a good display, but it is possible to find some buried away.

Off-diary stories

Off-diary stories are more difficult to come by. These require the reporter to be more creative, thinking up ways to track down stories that are not going to be notified to the newsdesk. It means keeping your eyes and ears open for unusual happenings.

Observation

It is vital that the keen reporter keeps his or her eyes open all the time. Many stories come from spotting people behaving oddly. The gathering of crowds is always a sign that something is happening, and you need to find out what is attracting them. Sirens are another indicator. Find out where the noise is coming from and get there quickly – but try to remember that some factories still use sirens to signify knocking-off time! Changes in buildings, demolitions, site clearances, posters, planning application notifications and unusual signs can all lead to good stories.

Eavesdropping

Eavesdropping is usually condemned as rude, but a good reporter is interested in everything and sometimes can't help overhearing interesting conversations or seeing something out of the ordinary. If the overheard conversation seems to contain something that would make a good story, it seems to me that the good reporter should immediately identify him or herself to the speakers: 'Excuse me, I'm . . . a reporter with the *Bexley Bugle*. I couldn't help overhearing what you just said and I wondered if you would tell me more about it . . .'. There might, of course, be exceptions to that. If what is taking place is criminal or seriously against the public interest, then it might be important to gather the information and keep your identity secret. You would then need to make an effort to find out who the speakers were. For instance, imagine you had heard a councillor and a local builder discussing what was obviously some form of corruption. Exposing such corruption would be in the public interest, and introducing yourself would serve no purpose except to alert the speakers. You would need to find out who they are (some councils issue pictures of local councillors or you will have pictures in your library) and then track down the evidence to back up the overheard conversation.

Personal contacts

Every reporter lives by his or her contacts – they mark the difference between a good reporter and a great reporter. A great reporter knows people from all walks of life. No matter what is happening, they will know someone who can tell them all about it – or at the very least, give them the name of someone else who can tell them all about it. Radio and TV journalists often get stories from listeners and viewers who call in, building on the perceived relationship they have with this regular visitor to their front rooms. This relationship with the reporter is important. Newspapers have picked up on this, and many newspapers now use picture bylines in an attempt to build up a relationship with the reader, so that they will feel more inclined to contact the reporter. Some national papers bylines include the reporter's e-mail address so that readers can interact better with the story. National TV news bulletins regularly add their e-mail address or promote their website.

It is important that a good journalist should have as wide a range of contacts as possible at local, regional and national levels. This ensures that you can provide different levels of sourcing for any story.

Community groups

Charitable and voluntary groups are an important part of any local community. Whether a local charity, the Scouts or Guides, a church group or a social society, these are local people doing what interests them in the community, and some of it at least can be turned into news or features. Many editors like to have reporters assigned to a section of the circulation area in order to get in touch with such groups. Any such reporter needs to contact the secretaries of local community groups, the local church ministers, head teachers, post offices, libraries, publicans and others central to the life of the community. Many places, such as doctors' surgeries, libraries, post offices and shops, carry adverts and notices of the minutiae of community life, and these also need to be checked.

Social networks

Social networks are a modern phenomenon. No-one can access all the detail of any network, but they are worth watching as you use them for your own networking. They can also make great tools to access people and find out information about them. Facebook, Bebo, Twitter and the rest all have millions of people logged onto them. A short search may well throw up some details very quickly and might also give you a picture. However, they do need to be dealt with carefully. Material accessed on them may not be seen as being publicly accessible, even though it is. Many people think that what they put on a social network will be looked at only by a small circle of friends. The Press Complaints Commission has made several rulings about stories picked up from social networks, and careful consideration should be given to how the information is used. Apart from anything else, any pictures lifted from a site are certain to be copyright of someone, and that could end costing your employer a lot of money.

Calls

Calls are one of the standard jobs in any newsroom. This involves calling the police, fire service and ambulance service to see whether they have been involved in any newsworthy incidents. Daily papers tend to contact the services three or four times a day. Radio and TV keep in touch even more often. Weekly papers can make do with one contact per day. In most areas these days, the emergency services have become so bogged down with dealing with the calls that they have instituted an automated system. They record the calls for the day and local news services listen to a recorded message, only going to the press office if more information is required. This allows the press office in that emergency service to concentrate on gathering the information and answering specific questions.

Ethical considerations

There are, inevitably, some ethical considerations when tracking down stories. I've already mentioned eavesdropping, but there are other issues. Often journalists are invited into people's offices or homes to gather information. It seems to me an invasion of privacy to take the opportunity to rifle through their drawers or papers or look at documents in their computer while they've popped off to make a cup of coffee or visit the toilet. Reading someone's private papers or their mail must surely be wrong. Having said that, being able to read upside down is a useful technique – searching for material is one thing, reading it is another.

Plagiarism

Plagiarism is the offence of copying someone else's work. This is identified as unprofessional by the National Union of Journalists and is generally considered to be wrong. Apart from anything else, you cannot be sure that the tempting story that appears in the opposition paper is correct.

You might use such a story as a **tip-off**, and even contact the person named in the story to get further details, but you need to get your own version. This gives you the chance to update the information, fish around for additional information and approach other contacts for support. Of course, it is perfectly legitimate to say that such-and-such a paper or TV bulletin has reported that something has happened.

More than words

These days, it is not enough to think solely about the story and how it can be presented in words. If you are working for TV or radio, it is obvious that pictures and sound will also be required, but pictures are also important for newspapers, and the internet, whether linked to a publication or an outlet in its own right, requires pictures, audio and video.

Pictures

Good pictures can make a story. In the TV age, the ability to illustrate stories is paramount. Pictures can add emotion and authenticity. While no-one these days is foolish enough to believe the camera never lies, pictures can add a lot of detail and a sense of authenticity to a story. A picture can add context, explain what is happening, allow us to identify someone, or allow us to classify a person or group of people. It also allows us to see the non-verbal communication (NVC) in the picture and start to add our own meanings to what is happening. Lacey (1998: 11) lists facial expression, gaze, gestures, posture, body contact, and clothes and appearance as all being forms of NVC that can add strength to the story in a way words can't.

You need to think about pictures on every story you cover. For TV, this is vital and central to everything you are doing. Some photographers (or camera crews) take briefings better than others, but all of them need to know what the story is about and the ideas you have had for photographs. This could be as simple as a portrait to illustrate a news item or feature about a personality. On a more complex story you might need to explain to the photographer what it is you are hoping to achieve and how. On a major incident, such as a plane crash, you will probably need to let the photographer loose to take action pictures as they occur while you attend the press conferences and try to find out what has happened. Only later might you suggest pictures of specific people or places.

Using library pictures can be extremely useful, but there are potential problems. If you get a chance, check your library's picture file of the interviewee before you go on the interview. This means when you meet the person you can quickly tell if the photograph is recent or very dated. There is nothing worse than interviewing a 50-year-old man about the death of his granddaughter in tragic circumstances and then illustrating it with a picture of a sneering 22-year-old protester with long hair and wildly unfashionable clothes. Finding out before makes it easy to alert the picture desk, or at least gives you a chance to ask the interviewee for an up-to-date picture. On the other hand, interviewing a couple on their golden wedding and finding you have a picture of their marriage day fifty years before can add a charming memory to a feel-good story.

Asking interviewees for pictures of loved ones involved in stories is standard practice, but again try to ensure the picture is as up-to-date as possible. Only recently, a witness came forward with information in the Suzy Lamplugh case, years after Ms Lamplugh went missing. It seems that the picture the police used to seek witnesses had her pictured as a blonde, but in fact on the day of her death she was a brunette. Because of this, the witness did not put two and two together for years. Children change very quickly, and you must try to get a picture that is as up-to-date as possible. The temptation is often to use the official school photographs that are taken every year in schools for parents to buy. Even if these are a couple of years out of date, parents will often prefer you to use one of these, showing their child looking well groomed and well behaved. But often these pictures are not a very accurate reflection of the child, and are dated. The copyright also belongs to the photographer and you may have to pay him or her for its use, unless the police have negotiated an arrangement. Better to use a holiday snap, which will probably not be as good in terms of quality, but is more likely to be up-to-date and is certainly more likely to show some character.

When you borrow such a picture, you must treat it with care. This is something the family will cherish and they will want it returned. Usually they will only let you have it on the promise of returning it. Some reporters borrow the family's whole picture album in an attempt to prevent other news media getting a picture. This puts an even heavier burden on the reporter, who must make sure the pictures are returned or rob the family of precious memories – all they may have, if the child has been killed. Your best bet is to take the picture to the photographic department and get it copied or scanned into the computer system while you wait. You can then take the picture and put it into an envelope that you can keep in a safe place, and return it personally as soon as possible. The personal return ensures the picture is not accidentally lost in the post; it also ensures that if there is any follow-up story, you will have a good reason to talk to one of the family and update your information.

At news events, it may be appropriate to use your camera/phone to take pictures if events are moving quickly and a photographer has yet to arrive, or if no photographer has been allocated. While the camera will not be top quality, most camera/phones these days produce a good enough image for a website and even a newspaper. If you arrive a little after the event, don't forget to ask witnesses if they took any pictures. Camera/phones are so ubiquitous, someone is bound to have taken pictures of any event significant enough for you to get a call to go there.

Audio

Audio is as vital for radio as video is for TV, and you need to consider carefully how you add audio effects. Background sound can add authenticity to a story. Interviewing a railway spokesperson on the platform with the noise of announcements, customers and trains needs to be handled with care from a technical point of view, but says much about trains and passengers that would be difficult to get into the interview any other way. Beware of background noise or effects that detract from the story. A story about traffic congestion with the country sounds of bird calls and insect noise, rather than the growl of queuing motors, would sound peculiar. Radio likes to tell the story through the people being interviewed, and background sounds can add authenticity. Radio journalists need to consider the ethics of adding noises that were not really there. Interviewing an airport manager about traffic delays in the studio and then adding archive sounds of plane cancellation announcements might not be representing the truth, even if it sounds 'better'.

Video

TV relies heavily on visual approaches to news, and a news bulletin will select stories for their visual appeal as much as for any other reason. That means you need to be imaginative in presenting a story visually if the news editor is to be persuaded to use it. **Talking heads** and archive footage are last resorts, and you should attempt to consider unusual and active takes. You should be careful in the editing process that the impression given is what you want. The ability to strip 'snapshots' in time after each other in an order chosen by you should not be abused – the chronology of a story is an important element of the truth.

Developing the off-diary story

Today's reporter has to be able to offer a newsdesk more than just the ability to follow instructions. Reporters need to be able to think up good story ideas and develop them into follow-up stories, features or backgrounders. This is particularly important for freelances, who need to come up with good ideas in order to ensure someone pays them the following week. Being creative about story ideas and their development is crucial. It is also something you can develop in yourself after just a little thought and some practice.

What is creative thinking?

Creativity is latent in almost everyone. In creativity, the emotional and non-rational parts of our mind are as important as the logical and rational. Just as we can train our rational and logical mind to work better by educating it, so we can train our non-rational mind to be more creative by practice and education.

Creativity is often sparked by problem-solving. For the journalist, the problem is: 'How do I find stories that will excite readers or viewers, and how do I present the story in a way that will attract them to buy my newspapers/broadcasts and enjoy the experience of reading to the end?'

One of the things that often blocks our creativity is our own inhibitions. Psychologists believe we have a built-in censor that limits the information we are prepared to accept from the preconscious in order to protect ourselves from being overwhelmed by the information we contain in our brain. Filters appropriate to our situation ensure appropriate recollection. If we are in a leisure situation, leisure links are used and work recollections are unwelcome. If we are at work, we do the opposite. This could well be the reason why an idea will come to us out of context. We might have been racking our brain to consider how to extend a particular story, but as soon as we settle into a different activity, such as socialising with friends or watching TV, the idea comes to us. It seems that during the incubation phase of the idea, because we have adjusted the parameters of the censor, an association that we otherwise would not have considered will be delivered to our subconscious, and our conscious mind will suddenly recognise it as appropriate for the problem we were dealing with before.

The way we work and are trained often seems to limit creativity. We come to fear expressing the weird and unusual because of peer pressure. If we are concerned that others will laugh at our ideas, we will not put them forward, and if we never put ideas forward, we will probably stop having them at all. Creativity, imagination and good ideas are essential for success, particularly in journalism, although none of these is any good unless supported by hard work. And creative thinking is the hardest work of all, requiring intense discipline, concentration and planning.

Much of the creative thinking required of journalists is idea development. You've got a story idea but you need to develop it further – produce it as a series, perhaps, or build some background features. There are several techniques you can use.

Spider diagrams

These can be very useful for developing ideas. Write down the original idea and then spin out spider's legs to new ideas, which then themselves spin out new ideas, and so on. The disadvantage of spider diagrams is that after a few spiders have been drawn it is tempting to end the process before all the elements have been thought through, and you need to 'Beware the dangers of early commitment to an idea or strategy' (Raudsepp 1971: 114). There is an example of a spider diagram in Figure 3.1. Here I have chosen the idea of a plane crash and expanded out from there with a number of ideas, each of which has spawned new ideas. See how I've included the concept of past, present and future as these often help develop ideas. I'm limited here by the size of the page, so there is plenty of opportunity to continuing expanding the ideas to provide copy for months or years to come.

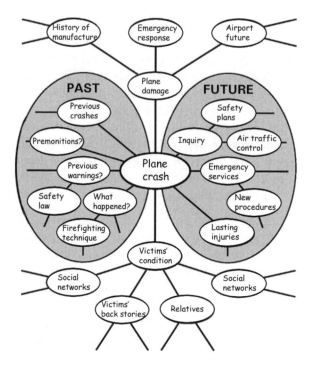

Figure 3.1 Example of a spider diagram

Brainstorming

Brainstorming was invented by Edward de Bono and given substance in his book *Lateral Thinking* (De Bono 1977). He says we should always challenge assumptions. We often say we can't do something because that is the way it has always been. But technology can change things, and what we want can change, which allows us to rethink and do the unthinkable. De Bono says we need to suspend judgement. Often we will discard an idea before we have thought it through because it sounds silly at first. Often developing the idea can change that view. Boring or clichéd ideas might be safe, but challenging, unusual and exciting ideas are what newsdesks really want – and what they are prepared to pay for.

De Bono says that: 'The four rules of brainstorming in a group are: (1) Adverse criticism is taboo; (2) freewheeling is welcomed; (3) quantity is wanted; and (4) combination and improvement are sought' (referenced in Barron 1969: 132). Despite working best as a group activity, brainstorming can work even when you are on your own – provided you take it seriously and suspend judgement. You need to note down all your ideas in a formal session. In other words, you have to say to yourself that you will think about this idea for a solid ten minutes, writing down every idea you have. Ten minutes may not seem like a long time, but to concentrate on one idea for that length of time and brainstorm other ideas is very hard work. Ten minutes can seem like an age as you struggle to write down more and more bizarre ideas. But, provided you concentrate completely for this time, you should come up with some excellent ideas based around the original spark to the story.

Following up a story

Once the initial story has been written, that's not the end of it. Some stories obviously require following up. At the start of a spell of really bad snowy weather, for instance, any reporter working on the story would be filing copy for each edition until the news editor decided otherwise, and many reporters would have to work on nothing else for days. Inevitably, though, the story would die away and the reporters would move on to something else. In all such stories it is important to note likely key dates for follow-up in the diary. The anniversary is one obvious date to pop into the diary for follow-up stories. The 'great storm' of 1988 even rated a 20-year anniversary, and even fairly modest events might be worth a ten-year anniversary. A fairly modest sprinkling of snow in February 2009 brought London to a halt for a day. It was followed up six months later for a TV programme on the 'great snow' that allowed re-use of all the footage as well as many of the pictures and video clips sent in by viewers.

The date of any deaths and funerals, any Coroner's inquiry or any other associated event should also be entered as potential follow-up stories.

Thinking about the timeline in a story is a good way of developing further story ideas. What happened in the past to lead to this story? What is likely to happen in the future – what are the consequences? In the case of a plane crash, this would lead to a series of features and news stories about the fitting (or non-fitting) of new safety devices; other plane crashes and how they link to this crash; and whether the government, the air companies and other associated authorities have done enough in the past to prevent such accidents. The future brings us stories about the inquiry; how the survivors are coping; campaigns to improve air safety; and the effect such a major disaster has had on those working for the emergency services. Just a quick glance at this list shows the wealth of good story material available after this one incident, and helps explain why you read so much about air crashes, their causes and effects despite air travel being very safe per passenger mile, with relatively few planes falling out of the sky.

It's also important to read any web comments or e-mails sent in about your story. Often readers may add extra information or sidelines that pay dividends when followed up.

4
Researching
the story

Having found your story, you now need to find out if it is something worth writing about. No good story comes to a reporter fully formed. Only boring press releases seem to contain ready-made stories – and that's only by the definition of the person who wrote it. The ubiquitous press release, indeed all story tips, should be scrutinised carefully to ensure they are not trying to disguise a story as something else. You need to discover the angle of the person selling you the story. All stories need to be checked out and sourced from elsewhere, with additional views added if needed. In order to produce good copy, reporters need to be able to trace a story back to its source. In practice, it is usually easier to have the sources and then work the story up from them. For this reason, a reporter is highly reliant on the sources that he or she cultivates. The wider the sources, the more you'll know – and the more you know, the better the stories.

The important thing to remember about any source, official or unofficial, is that they are giving you information because they want to. This might simply be because it's their job, or because they're interested to talk to a reporter, or because there's no real reason why they shouldn't; whatever the reason, we are using up their time and their goodwill, and they don't have to do it. Of course there may well be more complex reasons for them telling you things. They may have their own purpose in exposing the story they are offering you: they may want revenge on someone, to get them into trouble or expose them. They may want to win public support for a campaign. Nor can you rely on people telling you the truth, or certainly not the whole truth. Not that many people tell outright lies, in my experience, but of course the truth does get distorted because people may only hear part of an argument or only see what they want to see. You should always check with another source to verify information – until then, it is only a claim.

People

When you first start work in a newsroom or move to a new area, you will need to contact all the organisations that are the source of most stories. This means getting to know press offices for all the big local companies and public authorities – local government, police, other emergency services, the local courts, health authorities and hospitals. Many of these will already have solid links with your paper or radio station, but it is important that they develop a personal link with you. These formal sources are often a starting point for stories, and most of these people will be happy to talk to you as they need you to publicise their pet projects and promote their own agendas, just as you need their help to write your stories about their pet projects and agendas.

Your local MP is an important source and will give you a direct access to what is happening in parliament. If your MP belongs to the governing party then they are likely to support the government and its line. This may also give you some access to government ministers, who could be invited in to talk about appropriate issues. An opposition MP is more likely to be on the attack, and might be a better source of stories as he or she tries to build his or her profile. The prospective parliamentary candidate (PPC) is another good source as he or she will be trying to build a profile as the candidate who can win the next election, snatching the seat from the incumbent. In a marginal seat, which may only recently have switched sides, the pressure is likely to be high, and both the MP and the PPC will be going all out to build a high media profile to help their electoral chances.

Local councillors and council candidates also need to keep their media profile high to ensure election or re-election. Teachers, vicars, shopkeepers, publicans and activists in local voluntary organisations are all funds of local knowledge and not only should appear in your contacts book, but also should be talked to regularly to keep you in touch with the local community.

There may be one or two celebrities in your area. While these tend to be thickest on the ground in big cities or places with strong showbiz links, such as Blackpool or Brighton, even the remotest place may have a celebrity, as the *Mull of Kintyre Gazette* found when Paul McCartney moved in to make the home of several thousand sheep world-famous. Usually these celebrities are hoping for a bit of peace and quiet in their home area and you certainly can't use stories about them every day, but they should be cultivated so that the occasional low-key feature on their plans can help your readers feel they are on speaking terms with the stars.

Press officers

All government departments, local councils and moderately sized companies have press officers these days. There are now sufficient media about to make it a full-time job explaining the council's or government's policy and presenting it in a positive light. Councils and the government have long since seen the need to employ people whose particular skill is to present their employer well to the media. This is a mixed blessing to the journalist. It is certainly useful to have someone whose sole job is to tell you things, but it can be annoying that a part of their job can also be to try *not* to tell you things, or worse still, to disguise them as something else. At the end of the day, they are just people with a bit of news savvy, intent on presenting information about their employer in a good light – exactly the same as anyone else, but better at it and therefore more of a match for the journalist. Journalists can and should use press officers to their advantage. A good PR knows who to speak to in the company or council. They know how to get the information you need quickly and accurately. Don't be afraid to use them in this research role. They can often do a lot of the basic legwork for you. It is important to remember that the press officer will always follow the employer's policy line and so you will also need to build links elsewhere in the organisation. The press officer is useful for finding out basic facts and figures, but you may need to talk to someone else to find out what those facts and figures mean and how they may have been twisted or misrepresented. As always – never believe anything you are told until you've either verified it or worked out the person's motive for telling you.

Spin doctors

Spin doctors are often spoken about with either awe or loathing. They are a variant of the press officer, but are so closely linked to the centre of power that they become part of it. This means they can be particularly useful to the journalist in that they can give a unique insight into what is going on – once you get past their very careful interpretation of the facts. Spin doctors often try to pressure reporters by offering unique titbits of information in return for 'favours' at another time. A reporter who has built up a strong relationship with a spin doctor may not want to jeopardise receipt of those titbits in order to print a damaging story from another source that the spin doctor assures them is completely untrue or is at least misrepresenting the facts. It is for this reason that the relationship can be difficult. One of Britain's best known spin doctors must be Alistair Campbell, who was Communications Director in Prime Minister Tony Blair's office. Like Sir Bernard Ingham, Margaret Thatcher's spokesman, before him, Campbell was an important Downing Street player who ran the PM's press office. His job was to ensure his boss received a good press, and he did it well until he was overwhelmed by the tide of events surrounding the Kelly inquiry. There is a divide between the role of the press office in providing information about the activities of government and the role Campbell held, which was political and was about presenting Tony Blair and the Labour Party. But spin doctors are not solely the province of politics. Plenty of large corporations have them, and some of the worst are involved in sport, with many premiership clubs controlling their media image with a rod of iron. Refusing access to the ground to reporters who are deemed unwelcome is not unusual.

Experts

Experts can be called upon to add authority to a news item or feature. They are particularly useful for radio, which likes calling in local experts to add an authoritative view about a major issue of the day. Lecturers at the local college or university are OK. Top local businessmen, trade union leaders and local politicians are also standard fare. The key to a good expert is someone who clearly knows his or her subject, has an appropriate title and is able to give you a snappy, to-the-point quote quickly and easily. These people are hard to find and are worth keeping in your contacts book. Being able to get an authoritative quote on any subject from astrology to zoology quickly and without fuss is very useful. Radio and TV need to ensure such experts look and sound the part. Interviewing a farmer with an Oxford accent dressed in a three-piece suit may not carry the same conviction as one in working clothes with a soft country accent.

Ordinary people

Although journalists need to talk to the powerful, rich and famous, it is often the ordinary person who is the really useful contact. The famous will probably contact your organisation if they have a story to tell, whether you are there or not. Equally, they won't tell you anything if they don't want to, so they don't require cultivating in the way ordinary contacts do. Ordinary people get to hear a good deal of what's going on in their field, but won't necessarily tell you about it unless they know you well or you ask them.

'Ordinary' people include: committee members of local organisations and charities, trade union officials, teachers, health workers, lawyers, planning officers, police officers – the list is long because you never know who you are going to need as a contact. That's why it's so important for a reporter to socialise with as many people as possible. The official spokesperson will never tell you what they want to keep secret. The same principle applies in any organisation. The boss won't tell you anything, but if you talk to the secretary, or the person on reception, you may learn a good deal – not necessarily detailed information, but certainly an idea of trends.

If you are being kept waiting by the boss before an important interview, don't huff and puff about the damage to your pride. Charm the PA or secretary and try to find out as much as you can. Look to see who comes in and out, and ask about them. This needs to be done with subtlety, although it is impossible to be so subtle that the person will be unaware they are being quizzed. However, done properly, it can appear to be merely idle interest and therefore of little significance. Chatting to a caretaker, secretary or sales assistant can often give interesting results. They don't always know all the details, but neither have they been considered important enough to have been instructed not to talk to strangers and they can often see no harm in doing so. They can get to know a surprising amount about what's going on – after all, they do work there – and can certainly tell you things about the business or organisation you'll never hear from the boss. Everyone you meet should be cultivated because you never know when they'll ring you up with a story, or at least an idea for a story, or when a story will throw up someone you've met as the ideal contact.

Because of this, it is important to keep a note of who you know – partly so you don't look a complete fool when they ring up and you can't remember them, and partly so you can contact them if you need to. Often this sort of contact can start you on a good story by talking about a rumour they've heard. Maybe your friendly local gasman tells you (after the third pint at your local) that he's had to turn off the gas supply at a well known local restaurant – probably because they haven't paid the bill. It is but a small amount of work the next day to find out when the restaurant is due to close because of their debts. A TV programme I saw contained a story about a local restaurant whose water supply had been cut off, yet went on trading – with huge health risks. Where was the local reporter with a contact in the water company?

Reference books and archives

Although computers tend to be the first research thought of most young reporters, don't forget that there are a number of traditional reference routes that are still quick and easy. The phonebook is the easiest way of getting a local contact's address and phone number, while Who's Who does the same for the famous, Crockford's for the religious and Debrett's for the titled. There are numerous other reference books covering all the subjects one can imagine. Your own news organisation's library and archive can also be an extremely useful resource.

Freedom of information

Since the enactment of the Freedom of Information Act 2000 it has been possible for anyone, including journalists, to seek information from public bodies that was previously kept hidden. The general view of government has always been to tell the public only what government wants it to know. It would be nice to say that freedom of information (FOI) has changed all that, but we live in the real world, and old habits were formed for a purpose and die hard. However, things are slowly improving and while it is always possible to find examples of public bodies holding out on information, plenty of others are now tending to make information available when they wouldn't have before. This has been helped by the internet, which makes it easy and relatively cheap to publish information. There's not much point, for instance, in a local authority gathering information at some expense, unless it also goes to further expense to produce a nice booklet publicising the information and distributing it to people – most of whom will then throw it away. However, if the information can be gathered but then published cheaply and easily on the web for those who want it, then why not? And many do.

If the information you want about a public body is not on the web you are entitled to make an FOI application. Public bodies have information officers, but it might be quicker to contact the person concerned directly and ask for the information. Only if they refuse will you need to make an FOI application.

Applications are easy – just write to them asking for what you want. You can do this by e-mail. You must include your name and a response address. The authority is obliged to let you know if they hold the information and to tell you the information. They are entitled to charge a small fee and are obliged to respond not later than the twentieth working day following receipt (as you can see, it is not so useful for urgent stories).

An authority can refuse if it estimates it would cost more than the limit set by government (currently £600 for government, £450 for other authorities) to gather the information; it believes the complaint to be vexatious; if the information is already readily available; if the authority is intending publication at a future date; or is exempt for a variety of security reasons; or details would breach the Data Protection Act.

You can appeal about a refusal to the Information Commissioner, although this can take a long time. Some reporters, especially freelances, specialise in FOI requests, thinking up potential stories and then seeking the information to verify them. Heather Brookes and her pursuit of MPs' expenses was such a case, although there are plenty of other stories, albeit less spectacular. Questions about hygiene checks on local restaurants, health statistics from primary care trusts and refuse collection have all netted good stories based on data gathered through FOI.

Contacts book

Although your office will have a long list of potential contacts filed in an index system on the newsdesk, your own contacts book is one of your most important possessions. Your sources are the most important resource you have. If you can afford it, a digital personal assistant (such as one of the many smart phones now available) is ideal and can be synchronised to your PC, allowing you to keep information up-to-date and backed up. If you can only afford, or choose to have, paper, the best book to get is a small, loose-leaf folder of the Filofax type. These are neat and convenient to keep up-to-date. A neat book encourages you to keep this vital resource in an easily usable condition. Loose-leaf folders also allow you to add other data to the book if you want so that it becomes a complete resource.

If you can't afford this, then any smallish notebook, preferably indexed, will do, provided it is easy to fit into a pocket or handbag so that you *always* have it with you. You never know when you will meet someone whose phone number you want, or when you will want to refer to it.

Entries in your book should be made with care so that it is easy to find the name again when you need it and so you know what the name refers to when you see it again. Don't be afraid to put the name in your book two or three times under different categories.

For instance, if you were to meet Joe Bloggs at a presentation ceremony at your local working men's club, you would obviously list him under Joe Bloggs. But you might also list him under Downtown Working Men's Club (social secretary) and, after finding out that he was a railway worker and a member of the local National Union of Railwaymen committee, you might well list him under your 'Rail' entry (possibly one or two pages long) as railway station worker (NUR committee). The recent spate of rail horror stories shows how useful it could be to have a contact inside the rail system.

It is worth photocopying or duplicating your contacts book data on a regular basis. If you have a digital organiser, either synchronise it with your desktop computer on a regular basis or back it up at least weekly. If you prefer Filofax, you could also keep your contacts in a computer address book, just printing out at regular intervals into your Filofax. It would be a disaster if, after two or three years of contact building, you were to lose your contacts book.

Never leave your contacts book with anyone and never let the newsdesk or other reporters see or read it. Your contacts book is your property and should not normally be shared. It is, of course, up to you whether you share some of the information contained in the book, but it could lead to your sources being compromised. You have a duty to your contacts. It is you they know and are prepared to talk to, and they may be unhappy at being passed around the office as some sort of convenience. If you are willing to share a contact with a colleague, it may be appropriate to seek permission from the contact first.

When you enter a new name in your contacts book, you should ensure you spell the name correctly, in full, so that you know your contact entry is correct and it can be used as a reference. It is imperative that you have a home and a work number (or any other number) so that you can contact the person at any time. An address is also very useful together with a note of their occupation.

If you are really efficient, then a date of birth and some personal details (jotted down after you have left the contact) can give you a major advantage next time you ring them, as it will be an aid to your memory of them, allowing you to chat more personally and hopefully persuading them to be more chatty in return. Don't overdo this, as too much information is difficult to keep up-to-date and can end up sounding creepy. Ringing someone you've spoken to a couple of times and asking how the kids are is one thing, but ringing them and asking, 'How did little Jeremy get on, because wasn't it his first day at school last week?' and 'Did Sarah pass that important dance exam?' is creepy and likely to get you locked up for stalking.

The Data Protection Act has some sway here and is another reason to be careful about passing on details. If someone gives you their name, address and phone number, it is reasonable to interpret this, for the purposes of the Act, as permission to store that information in order to contact them again in the future. There is protection under the Data Protection Act for material gathered for the purposes of journalism, but that should not be taken as permission to publish that name and address to colleagues, or in the paper, without specifically asking permission.

While your Facebook page can be something of an extension of your contacts book, it should be seen more as a public annexe. There will be things in your contacts book that should not go on your Facebook page as you will want to keep them confidential.

Computer-assisted reporting

It's difficult to imagine reporting without a computer these days; a recent survey of teenagers found that staggering number felt they couldn't live without the internet. But 15 years ago, computers were the coming thing and anyone wanting to make something sound better and more effective added the words 'computer-assisted' in front of it. We've had computer-assisted design, computer-assisted diagnosis, and the nineties brought us computer-assisted journalism or reporting (CAJ or CAR). This buzz phrase from America was the coming thing according to turn-of-the-millennium new media conferences in the UK. Well, now it's here and we use it all the time.

There are three main types of CAR according to US writer Margaret De Fleur. The first is the collection of data and its manipulation from a range of online databases – most of them now part of the World Wide Web. The second is setting up databases to store data researched by ordinary means. This could include a straightforward list of contacts, but is likely to contain much more information, usually of facts surrounding a particular story. The third type of CAR is computer-aided investigative reporting (CAIR), which uses databases in the same way in order to investigate a story (De Fleur 1997: 73).

CAR (and CAIR) requires a stream of easily manipulated statistical data. In other words, the main use of CAR is the statistical analysis of data collected from either online databases or other sources in order to produce stories. An example I saw in a workshop I attended a few years ago included a database of hunting accidents in one of the US states. This database allowed the reporter to compare statistics for death and injury by place, time, age group, sex, type of injuries and so on. Anyone who has ever manipulated a database with a large number of fields (type of information held) and large number of records (the number of incidents) knows this can be loads of fun. You can quickly discover that more men aged 23–30 were shot in the arm on a Tuesday outside the town of Pope's Creek than anywhere else in the country. However, while this might be fun, it's not always news. As usual, all the computer-aided bit does is let you do something more easily and accurately that you used to do with paper and pencil. Just because you can manipulate data quickly to get stories doesn't always mean they will be more interesting.

An example of CAR used by Margaret De Fleur concerns an early use of the technique in the USA, when computers were still in their infancy. The director of a local government agency providing cheap mortgages for low-income families was fraudulently giving cheap mortgages to influential citizens. The evidence of this was openly contained in the records, but since searching the paper records would have been an enormous task, it seemed unlikely anyone would ever attempt it. Reporter Elliott Jaspin managed to get the electronic version of the records and ran them through the paper's computers, quickly exposing the fraud (*ibid.*: 2). The point at issue here is that Jaspin and his fellow American reporters were able to demand the public records in electronic form. In another example, reporters on *The Seattle Times* were able to build a database of information on the Green River murders by getting hold of arrest logs, police expense vouchers, budget requests, internal memos, mileage logs and case reports. This helped them produce stories about the police's inability to find the killer (*ibid.*: 81). Even now that we have a Freedom of Information Act in the UK, it does not offer access to the range of material cited above. Much of this kind of data is specifically defined by the Data Protection Act as sensitive personal data and therefore not information to be released without the data subject's consent.

Since the UK does not have such good access to statistical data as reporters in the USA, there is less use for CAR, although since the Freedom of Information Act things have improved and more and more government information is now available. Some UK government statistics are even available on the web for loading into databases, and this helps explain the growth of interest in MPs' expenses. MPs have only recently been obliged to have the range of their expenses published online, following a long campaign to gain access to the information by journalist Heather Brookes. It was the collection of this data that led to the leak of unedited data to *The Daily Telegraph*. The unedited data made analysis of their spending reasonably easy to manage, so the *Telegraph* was able to expose a number of MPs' spending habits.

However, just because we may be behind in our use of CAR, that doesn't mean we can't use computers to help us report. Things have changed hugely since DeFleur first defined CAR, in terms not just of the tools reporters use, but of our understanding of reporting. Journalists now not only want to use computers to research their stories, but also use them as part of the process itself, involved in both making, producing and disseminating the story; and also involving the audience in that story through various forms of user-generated content (UGC). John Kelly seems unhappy about the term UGC:

> There is much contained within the phrase to make journalists uneasy. Let's deconstruct it, beginning at the end. 'Content' is a word that calls to mind a commodity, something bland used to fill a hole, 'Generated' isn't much better, suggesting

as it does material that's created in some vaguely spontaneous way, untouched by human hands. It is the word 'user', however, that most illustrates how things have changed.

(Kelly 2009: 1)

Leaving aside his distaste for the words 'generated' and 'content', because content has always been generated and no high-minded optimism can alter that, he's right about the huge change this more intense involvement of the user (the reader, viewer or listener) has brought to journalism over a very short space of time. Users have always been involved in generating content: producing stories whether as contacts, readers' letters, radio phone-ins or TV guests, or providing their pictures of newsworthy events as amateur photographers and videographers. However, the new technology of the mobile phone/camera and the internet now gives easy access to the media for many people who were previously denied it. We would be wrong to think that, because of this increase in interactivity, everyone wants to become a citizen journalist, but we have to remember that everyone will be able to interact with our stories much more actively. Whether by responding to blogs, adding comments to stories, or sending in pictures or video, our readers and viewers are now even more important to the story, not just in terms of consuming it but also in being part of its production and follow-up.

Using the internet

The internet, particularly the World Wide Web, is now the sensible starting point (but only the starting point) for any research.

Whether you are finding out about a person, a place, a company, organisation, campaign, idea or leisure activity, there is likely to be loads of information on the web. Indeed, the major problem these days is not finding out information, but in narrowing down the amount you will find to a torrent you can cope with.

E-mail

E-mail can be an excellent way to get information from people who might otherwise be hard to contact. It is perfectly possible to guess e-mail addresses in order to be able to contact people who might otherwise be heavily screened. It isn't guaranteed, but it is surprising how often you can get an e-mail to someone to either ask a question or ask them to ring you. It is, of course, perfectly possible to interview by e-mail.

Most people's e-mail addresses are a mix of their name and employer's address. The employer's address will almost certainly be the web address, so to contact someone in the BBC, for instance, you might only need to type in a variant of their name and the BBC address. Since you can send an e-mail to several people at once, just work out all the name variants and make them a list. In other words, if you assume I work at the BBC, just type into the address field of your e-mail program: c.frost@bbc.co.uk, chris.frost@bbc.co.uk, c.p.frost@bbc.co.uk, chris.p. frost@bbc.co.uk, chris.frost1@bbc.co.uk. (The address that ends in 1 is included because some e-mail systems add numbers in order to differentiate between those with the same name.) In fact the BBC follows the template of forename.surname@bbc.co.uk. If you send e-mails to several addresses, of course some may go to the wrong person. That's fine unless you risk tipping someone off about a story, so this approach won't work for very confidential investigations.

It is also possible to search for e-mail addresses on several websites, although I have yet to find these to be of much use, since most rely on the person registering their address with the site. Many companies or government organisation websites will also allow you access to a search database for their staff e-mail addresses.

Travels on the World Wide Web

The web needs to be handled with care in terms of the information that it gives. Because all websites appear reasonably professional, due to the software used and the way computers present information, even the most bizarre ideas and people can look quite sensible. In the good old days, spotting those with a seriously flawed bee in their bonnet was easy because they wrote to you on lined paper torn out of an old reporter's notebook (I always worried that it *was* an old reporter's notebook – some odd people used to work in newspaper offices). The writing nearly always seemed to be in green ink and would be heavily underlined or in capitals. Now the lined paper is a sophisticated computer graphic and the subtle green type is neatly presented in Times New Roman or some other professional font of the author's choosing.

As with all material that comes into a newspaper office, websites should be treated with a good deal of cynicism. Gradually you will get to know those sites you trust and those you don't; but any new site should be treated as merely the views of that author – whoever has produced it, the material will have been edited in some form.

Sites vary from the extremely useful UK parliament site (www.parliament. uk) to sometimes entertaining but virtually useless personal home pages. The parliament.uk site offers lists of MPs' names and addresses. It gives the full text of *Hansard*, and access to the full text of all Bills and Acts of Parliament since 1997. Anything you want to know about what is happening in both houses of parliament is there, and it is a great place to collect basic information about parliamentary politics. This site is about as close to an impartial site as I can imagine. All government departments have a website, most of which are extremely useful and carry the latest developments in that field. Local government sites are useful and there is a wide range of sites, some specifically designed to help the media and others that are generally useful. For more comment in the field of politics, try the various political party sites. These give details of leading politicians, their line on various policies and, of course, suitable attacks on the opposition. A quick look through these half-dozen sites can give you good solid background on the issues facing the UK political establishment and the various party viewpoints. You can become an instant political correspondent. There is a list of useful sites at the end of this book.

Finding names, numbers and addresses

The first thing you may need to know is a person's name, whether they are the managing director of a company or a local politician. Getting names is usually easy – just ring the company or organisation and ask the switchboard. Websites can also help here, and logging onto the company's website will often allow you to find out who is in charge of what.

The obvious starting point in tracking down someone's phone number is the phone book or directory inquiries, but again the web can now be extremely useful. Some company or organisation sites allow you to search for staff names and will offer you phone numbers and e-mail addresses. BT now has all phone directories in a searchable database on the web:

log in and type in the name and location of the person you are seeking, and it will give all the alternatives.

The web can also be extremely useful for finding names and phone numbers in far-away places. Want to know who's who in some distant town? Find the town's website (they nearly always have one) and contact a local official or semi-official body. Perhaps the site lists the government offices or the local newspaper, or a local tourist information office is even better. A quick phone call or e-mail to these sites can often get you local contacts. Often a local site lists important numbers including the local hospital or police force. It can be worth seeing if the person has a personal website or is listed on another page. Type their name into a search engine and see what you get.

Another great site for tracking people is www.192.com. This allows searches for information on UK people and businesses. Basic information is free and more detailed material is available for a small fee. You can search birth records, electoral roll, phone books, business directory, company reports, credit information, maps and a lot more. You can search for people by place, and filter the searches by age, location, occupation and other classifications. You can also find out how long people have lived at an address or when they purchased property. You are charged a predetermined number of credits for each piece of information, with each credit costing 23p at the time of writing. You will also need to pay an annual archive fee to search the electoral roll. This costs £149.99 and you will still need to purchase credits to access the data.

Wikis

Wikis are web pages that can be edited by groups of people. These can be anything from Wikipedia to a small group of friends running a fan club (Lostpedia is a wiki about the TV series 'Lost'). Wikipedia is probably the best known wiki. It carries information on a huge range of subjects and can be very useful, giving basic information on almost anything, provided the usual caution about the information is taken. Several reporters have been caught out by false or mischievous information posted on Wikipedia. Wikipedia even carries a list of better known Wikis that you might find useful at some time, including Wikianswers, which compiles answers to questions, and Wikinews. Surprisingly, last time I checked, it didn't contain Wikileaks. Wikileaks accepts and publishes documents that the leakers claim the document owners (or someone else) wish to keep secret. Wikileaks.org claims to 'Help you safely get the truth out' and lists documents that are 'classified, censored or otherwise opaque to the public record' (www.wikileaks.org, accessed 12 November 2009). This is where the BNP membership list was leaked, and it also contains documents on Trafigura and the Minton Report, the Madeleine Foundation and other classified or censored documents. It's well worth a browse from time to time.

Mapping

Google Maps and Google Earth are great ways to identify local areas. You can use these to find your way to a story, of course, but they will also allow you to view an area from above in a way that's impossible unless you have your own helicopter. This can be very useful for stories about that local area. Don't forget, though, that you will need a licence to publish maps or satellite pictures in the paper or on the website.

Social networks

Social network sites have become extremely popular over the past couple of years. Many people under the age of 35 have a Facebook page or a link with one of the other popular sites. Privacy has become a big issue lately and so many people now put limits on their access, but many don't. This means if a person is involved in something newsworthy a good reporter can access their site and find out some more basic information. If, for instance, there was a plane crash, some of the victims might well have loaded material onto their Facebook page while waiting for the flight; that newly married couple going on honeymoon might well have put photos and messages on their site about the wedding. These can add a fantastic amount of colour to the story. The pictures, of course, are copyright of those who took them, but many a paper or TV station has taken the risk of using them to illustrate such stories. There are other social network sites that offer slightly different approaches, including MySpace, Bebo and Plurk.

Flickmail is another website that can be used to find story contacts, and some reporters say they've used it to great effect. If you want to access pictures, then Flickr might be appropriate.

Crowd sourcing

Crowd sourcing is a way of tracking down unusual sources who you may not know. If you are working on a story and want to get contacts, then issue a plea on your Twitter or Facebook page. You can ask people about their experiences or knowledge. Say you were doing a story about vaccinations and wanted to hear from someone who believed they had been adversely affected, this might be a good way to contact such a person. Of course, there are problems with this method of contacting. First, you would have to find a way to ensure you were not being hoaxed. Second, you would need to make sure your message wasn't picked up by someone you don't want to know about the story until publication or broadcast; your opposition or the subject of an investigation, for instance. However, this route is good for that unusual contact or for a quick vox pop, allowing you to gather comments from a wide range of people very quickly.

Another way of getting a quick response from a wide range of people is www.ask500people.com. This quick survey site allows you to ask a question and get responses that are geotagged to help you get as local as possible. Its lack of guaranteed local contact is a problem, and it could never be described as scientifically accurate, but for a quick vox pop on a straightforward question it can be useful. It also allows you to embed the poll in your website.

You can also use crowd sourcing to seek pictures or video. Putting up a plea on the website, or a caption on the broadcast, for users to send in pictures and video of an event that is either distant or difficult to get to can often provide perfectly acceptable pictures. Again the risk of hoaxing needs to be borne in mind, as do the issues of copyright and the safety of users. Journalists should not be encouraging users to go to dangerous places, nor should they be encouraging packs of would-be reporters to make life more difficult for the emergency services at train crashes, fires and other emergencies just because they cannot get there themselves.

Twitter

Twitter has several uses for the journalist. It allows you to keep up-to-date with headlines, and helps you trace people. Unlike Facebook, you don't need someone's permission to follow them and maybe find out where they are. You can also be quickly alerted to events that are happening by following a large number of twitters. The whole thing becomes a support network, something bigger than just crowd-sourcing. It is vital to get this fed through to your phone – you need to be in constant touch with your contacts to make the best of Twitter.

RSS feeds

RSS feeds brings information direct to your desktop or phone. Whatever style of journalism you are involved with, some of your contacts, local government, government departments or corporations will issue RSS feeds online. Major news outlets such as the BBC also send out RSS feeds. Feeds can be limited to particular parts of a news service. There are a number of pieces of software to help manage and filter feeds to prevent you from becoming overwhelmed by information.

Blogs

Using a blog gives you the chance to interact directly with people. This can be used as you are developing stories to find out what people are interested in, or to solicit comments. Software such as CoveritLive means you can take this a stage further, allowing you to blog live events such as trials or press conferences. It has a multi-author capability and you can easily add images and video if you want. Sports is another area where you can keep readers involved online.

Other people's blogs

Other people's blogs can give excellent insights, either into specialist subjects or about people. They need to be treated with caution as it is often difficult to identify the trustworthiness of such sources, but they often give an unusual angle to a story.

Newsgroups

Newsgroups are less popular now than they used to be, but can still be useful. There are hundreds of newsgroups and you can subscribe to as many as you want. Your browser should allow you to choose newsgroups and you can add new ones all the time. Choose the subject you are researching and you will find all sorts of people, from experts to beginners, talking about subjects of their choice, whether UFOs, crop circles, air disasters, trains or their favourite pop band. You can then either join in or quickly identify someone who will be worth speaking to by e-mail or phone.

Chat rooms

Chat rooms allow people of similar interests to get together and chat. Often these are used as dating systems, or at least a chance to meet people, and so are of limited value to the reporter, but it is important to remember they are there and can occasionally be used as a way of contacting people.

Finding a site

Search engines try to make sense out of the chaos of the internet. The internet links together networks of computers which are themselves a collection of computers, often containing thousands of pages of information posted by hundreds of users. This makes for millions of sites run by millions of users and it is impossible for the average human to cope with tracking down all that information. Since the number of computers being added to the internet and the amount of information they can access is growing exponentially, this information overload is not going to go away.

Your main access will probably be the World Wide Web, which is actually only a part (although now by far the biggest part) of the internet. Newsgroups and FTP sites make up most of the rest of the internet, but you are unlikely to use anything but the web unless you are working in a particularly specialist field.

Direct searching

Most people tend to start any search with a search engine such as Google or Yahoo!, and these are now so ubiquitous that Google has become a verb. However, it is still possible (and occasionally desirable) to search direct. A direct search is where you type the domain name of a site you want direct into your browser's 'Address' dialogue box.

A domain address is made up of several parts. The first part (http://) is the protocol that tells the computer how to read the file. There's no need to type in the http:// part of the address these days as the main browsers add that automatically. The next part of the domain name is the individual address and the final part tells you something about the address, whether it is a company or an organisation, for instance, and the country of origin.

It is much easier than it used to be to do a direct search for a site you want, because major corporations and organisations realise the importance of a good domain name. There are also more internet service providers, and companies are more likely to use their own server. This means web names are not as long and complex as they often used to be, although some can still be a little odd. When you are doing a direct search things can still be difficult, though. Would you find Marks and Spencer under MandS, M&S, MarksandSpencer, Marks&Spencer, Marks_and_Spencer, or some other variant of the famous retail giant's name? Are they perhaps part of a bigger holding company with its own name and website? You also need to decide whether the extension will be .co.uk or .com. Since Marks and Spencer is a corporation, it will be one or the other, or both.

There are a wide variety of domain extensions:

com – commercial;
org – organisations, charities, campaign groups, etc.;
edu – educational;
gov – government;
net – internet-oriented material;
mil – US Defence Department.

If the domain name is country-oriented, then it will add a two-letter country extension on the end:

uk – United Kingdom;
fr – France;
se – Sweden;
fi – Finland;

jp – Japan;
au – Australia

and so on. There are also different links for country-oriented sites:

gov – government;
ac – academic;
org – organisations, charities, campaign groups, etc.;
co – commercial.

Most big companies try to buy up all associated commercial domain options and link them all into the same site, so it is usually worth trying one or two of the obvious options. However, some companies that got into the World Wide Web a little late have found that many of the domain names they would like have been bought up. Dotcom names are at a real premium because they give international access. According to BT, all three-letter dotcom names are now registered, no matter what the combination of letters. Many site names have been registered by quick-thinking entrepreneurs hoping to be able to sell suitable names to corporations at a later date. Some are on offer for sale on the web for up to US$4 million. It costs practically nothing to register and maintain a domain name, but it is well known that getting the right name can aid searching. A domain name such as www.insurance.com could be worth a fortune to an insurance company, and it is no surprise to find that Fidelity Investment owns the site. This makes good names valuable. In order to keep track of what is out there in those millions of sites on the World Wide Web, we require directories, search systems and bookmarks.

Bookmarking

This is a basic system that you can run yourself to keep track of interesting sites that you have come across and use regularly. It is important that you keep your bookmarks as up-to-date as possible and that you go to some lengths to file them neatly and name them properly. Your browser will allow you to bookmark sites as you load them onto the browser. Your bookmarks, or Favourites as Microsoft Explorer calls them, are kept in a bookmarks file, and it is worth taking a copy of this file from time to time to ensure you don't accidentally erase it. It would be a shame to have built up a record of good sites over several years only to lose it because your hard disk crashed.

It is also possible to arrange the bookmarks into folders so that your list becomes manageable. You could have several thousand sites marked and it would be impossible to navigate this without some form of system. You can create folders in your bookmarks file so that, for instance, you can keep all the 'politics' sites together and away from all the 'journalism' sites. What folders you use are up to you, but they should help you easily to work out which folder a particular bookmark will be in. You can also rename websites in your bookmarks to make it easier for you to remember what they are or how you use them.

Search engines

Search engines allow you to look for sites about a particular subject. They allow you to type in a word, or words, and then they go off and find as many sites as they can containing that word. There are now hundreds of search engines on the web, and there are even search engines that only find other search engines. Search engines have robots that continually search the internet finding pages, sorting them and listing their entries. These cover a large number of sites but are often not well indexed. Others also use humans to look at websites and decide how to index them and whether they are worth listing. Some search sites now charge a fee for those who want to be listed. This pays for the engine to review the site and decide whether to include it. The fee does not guarantee inclusion, only a review. These search engines hope to cover only the best of sites, therefore attracting people to use their search capabilities. It is clear already that the main existing search engines are having difficulty keeping up with both checking all the new sites and deleting sites they have already listed but are no longer in operation. Choosing a site from a search engine listing only to find the site is no longer there is now a regular occurrence.

Some of the main search engines to try (in no particular order) are:

- Excite;
- Altavista;
- Yahoo!;
- Google;
- Netscape;
- MSN;
- Hotbot;

- Lycos;
- AskJeeves.

Google is by far the most popular these days, with 80% of all searches internationally being made on Google. Google is now so omnipresent in the internet world that for many people it is the only search engine, and that's a mistake – while it has a lot to offer in terms of the power of its search engine and support information, such as Google Maps/Google Earth, other search engines can sometimes come up with things that Google misses. There are also some concerns about Google's advertising policy and whether this affects its searches.

AskJeeves allows you to ask questions rather than type in words to be found. With all the other engines, you type in words that you would like to find sites containing. With AskJeeves you ask a real question – not that you always get a more sensible answer.

For instance if you wanted to find out who first used the phrase 'Journalism is the first draft of history', on most search engines you would type into the search dialogue panel 'First draft of history'. This would get the search engine to trawl through thousands of web pages seeking that phrase and it would probably come up with hundreds of potential websites, although none might tell you who wrote the phrase. Most sites would merely be using that phrase in their own context. With AskJeeves you could type 'Who first said 'journalism is the first draft of history'?'. It might not be able to find out either, but would give a different range of journalism-oriented sites that might have the answer. SearchEngineWatch.com is a good site to visit to find out more about search engines and how to search them well.

Most search engines use Boolean algebraic rules to control how you filter all the websites they have to offer. You need to imagine that each search engine is a gateway to a sea of web pages. You could put up a filter that would tell the engine to show you only those containing the word 'journalism', and the search engine will index a list of all the hundreds of sites containing that word. If you ask the engine to find sites with the words 'journalism' and 'computer', you will get only sites with both words in.

Algebra is used in slightly different ways by many of the sites, but the basic rules are listed in Table 4.1.

Table 4.1 Using search engines on the internet

What to type into your search	Search engine lists the following
A word, e.g. *journalism*	Any web page with the word *journalism* on it
Several words, e.g. *journalism, computers*	Any web page with the word *computer* or *journalism* or both
Several words added together, e.g. *journalism+computers*	Any web page with the words *journalism* and *computer* contained somewhere on the page
A phrase in quotation marks, e.g. *"computer journalism"*	Any web page with the phrase *computer journalism* but **not** pages with the words *computer* and *journalism* separated by other words
Several words added together some excluded, with e.g. *computer+journalism–internet*	Any web page with the words *computer* and *journalism* but **not** any that contain the word *internet*
Several words preceded by the word *title* (*t* in Yahoo), e.g. *title: computer journalism*	Any web page with the words *computer journalism* in the title
A domain name preceded by *domain:* e.g. *domain: Marksandspencer.co.uk*	Any web pages from that site
A host name preceded by *host:* e.g. *host: uk*	Any web page from the UK
Combine any of above: e.g. *computer+journalism+host: UK–"Computer journalism"*	Any web page from a UK host that contains the words *computer* and *journalism* but **not** the phrase *"computer journalism"*
Wild card: this is an asterisk that replaces text, e.g. *journal**	Any web page with words *journalist, journalism, journalistic, journals, journalese, journalistieke, journaliste,* etc.

After searching for pages, you will often find that while you may not find a page that gives you what you want, you will gain some idea of the terminology and language of that particular subject area, and this can help refine your search. Try using the jargon of your research subject to find other web pages.

Directories

Directories are lists of sites divided into categories provided by many search engines. These can often be easier to use than a long list of several thousand web pages. Netscape, Yahoo!, Lycos, Google and others all give directories. Type in 'business' and it will offer you a long list of subdirectories. Keep choosing subdirectories until you get to the websites of your choice. These directories rely on the people who register the websites with the search engine placing the web pages in appropriate directories, something the search engines ask site masters to do on registration.

Yahoo! Pipes

Yahoo! Pipes is a way of filtering material and combining it with material from other websites. Pipes.yahoo.com allows you to combine the output from a number of websites, filtered by subject. This means you can gather news about an event or person into the same feed and display it all in the same place, saving yourself from having to have dozens of websites open to catch the latest news.

Portal sites

These are sites maintained by special interest groups that carry some of their own information, but make a virtue out of carrying a large number of hyperlinks to other sites. Several journalism portal sites exist; a good example is Journalism UK at www.journalismuk.co.uk. This site has little direct information and is just a list of journalism sites usefully categorised. Most UK newspapers and broadcast organisations are listed, as are schools of journalism, journalism organisations such as the National Union of Journalists (NUJ), and regulatory watchdogs such as the Press Complaints Commission and Ofcom, the Office of Communications. These are good sites to list as they are easy jumping-off points for other sites

Measurability

The web allows your website to track readership and so build up a profile of what stories are interesting readers. This can influence newsdesks, who will be asking for more stories like the ones doing well in the charts. It can also add to the competitive pressure facing journalists to get the most-read story of the day. While it is useful to carry stories that are interesting to people, one problem with journalism is that the stories we perhaps ought to be covering are not necessarily the ones people want to read. If we are there to help people understand the world, should we really concentrate on celebrity?

Figures as facts

Statistics and figures are a vital part of the reporter's job these days, whether in the form of a balance sheet or a sheaf of statistics. Many reporters seem to take pride in saying, 'Oh, I'm no good at maths' as though it were a lifestyle choice, such as being vegetarian or wearing a beard. Obviously if they were a talented mathematician they would be working as an accountant or a mathematician or a statistician. They are working as a reporter because their skills lie elsewhere. But just as we would expect a statistician or accountant to be able to pull together a readable report about their statistics or balance sheets, and might sneer if they couldn't, so it is reasonable to expect an intelligent reporter to be able to understand and read a basic balance sheet and understand the basics of statistics.

So much of the reporter's work these days is based around opinion polls, government statistics, balance sheets of big companies and council budgets that not being able to sniff out when you are being fed a line means that a reporter is virtually useless. Politicians, in particular, will feed you figures that they say show one thing, when even a rudimentary glance shows that they mean something completely different.

Like all sources, figures need to be treated with caution and the motive for issuing them questioned. Why is this source giving me these figures? What do they hope to gain? Often this will tip you off to where the weakness, if there is one, lies.

Another important question to ask, according to Blastland and Dilnot, is: 'Is that a big number?' (Blastland and Dilnot 2007: 6). They give the example of a story in *The Daily Telegraph* about government plans to raise the pension age of men from 65 to 67: according to the *Telegraph*, that would mean one in five who would have survived to collect their pension would now die before collecting it. 'Hundreds of thousands would be denied by two cruel years' (*ibid.*: 6). Blastland and Dilnot point out that one in five men dying between 65 and 67 is such a catastrophically big number that someone should have picked it up before publication. With a UK population of about 60 million, half of whom (approximately) are men, one in five men is about 6 million. In fact, as Blastland and Dilnot point out, a quick glance at the National Statistics website would show that only 240,787 men of all ages died in 2007, of whom 5844 were aged 65 and 5977 were 66, totalling just 11,821 – only 3–4 per cent of 65–67-year-olds (www.statistics.gov.uk/downloads/theme_health/DR2007/DR_07_2007.PDF).

But we also need to watch out for the abuse of statistics by politicians or commercial operators, as there are some straightforward ways of fiddling with figures that can give a completely misleading effect. Say someone approached you with a poll showing that boys at a local public school had an average £10 a week pocket money compared with children at a local state school, who averaged only £3.92? First I would want to know why the public school figure is a nice round number, and then I would want to know the number sampled in the survey. If it turned out that only six pupils at the public school were prepared to answer, and one of those received £30 a week while the other five received amounts varying between £3 and £5, while the state school surveyed 60 students with amounts varying from £1.50 to £7, then the whole survey would be pointless.

Remove the one child with £30 from the survey and you then find that the averages at the two schools are remarkably similar. It shows up one of the difficulties of averages.

Averages

An average is the first tool a politician, statistician or spin doctor grabs when they want to lie to a reporter without the reporter being able to accuse them of anything. We can easily say that the average citizen of Anytown smokes 2.4 cigarettes a day. Of course, most Anytowners don't smoke at all, but those who do certainly smoke enough, so that if you divide the total number of cigarettes smoked in a day by the number of citizens, you get an average in the region of 2.4. Once you learn that only 18 per cent of Anytowners smoke, but that they average 25 cigarettes a day, then you might feel you were getting somewhere, but even here there can be wild discrepancies. Smokers could smoke anything from one to 100 cigarettes a day. There might be quite a few who smoke between one and five cigarettes a day; a fair number smoking between five and 20; a reasonable number smoking 20 to 40, but the numbers smoking more than that are likely to fall off rapidly. So these *arithmetic* averages (a *mean*) do more to confuse than to assist, and tell us little about the smoking habits of Anytown. We could have calculated the *median*, the point at which half the sample smoke more and half the sample smoke less, but this would be very close to zero because of the high number of non-smokers. The *mode* gives similar problems as it measures the most frequently met statistic. According to this, Anytown is a non-smoking town. The problem with this example is the distribution of the data. If we learnt that the height of the average man in Anytown was five feet eleven inches, we would not need to know what kind of average it was as they would all be very close to each other. All adult males in Anytown will be between five and seven feet, with the majority being close to six feet. The data distribution graph would be shaped like a bell with a few people in the low five-foot area, a few approaching seven feet, and the majority between five feet nine inches and six feet three inches. The mode, mean and median would be similar enough to differ by only decimal places. But in our smoking example, this isn't the case. The majority of people don't smoke at all, and then the distribution of smokers is very different from the bell shape of men's heights. Many smokers smoke only a few cigarettes, and only a few smoke more than 20 to 30. The only useful statistics are that 82 per cent of the citizens of Anytown are non-smokers and, of the smokers, the median (the highest point on the distribution curve, the number of cigarettes smoked by more people than any other) is 15 cigarettes a day.

Surveys

A lot of information is presented to journalists from surveys, whether produced by the government or private companies. The journalist's first concern needs to be about how the survey was produced: who was used for the sample, how many of them were there, and how representative was it?

Most government surveys use large samples; often the total number of people available, so that their samples and the way they are selected can usually be trusted. If their sample says 75 per cent of those on benefit have more than three children, it is probably an accurate figure because they have asked everybody on benefits (it is probably one of the standard questions asked on the form submitted to request benefits). Only if people have lied about the number of their children is there likely to be inaccuracy. With governments, it is changes in the way things are counted year-on-year that are likely to throw up problems. For instance, a government might change the way it defines unemployment in order to change year-on-year comparisons.

In the private sector, though, if a PR company sends you a survey claiming that 75 per cent of women found that a particular brand of wrinkle cream reduced signs of ageing after three weeks' use, then some serious questions need to be asked (such as, 'What are you doing even thinking about using such obvious advertising material?'). First you need to know how many women were sampled. If you were to find that it was ten, then the survey probably doesn't prove very much, particularly if it turned out that they all worked for the PR company. You should also start wondering how they got the figure of 75 per cent (75 per cent of ten people is 7.5).

You would also need to know the questions asked. If the question is, 'Do you think you look younger after using the cream?' then a 'yes' answer might be significant. But if the question was, 'Do you think you look older?', then it means that 25 per cent believed it actually made them look older.

At the end of the day, if you get a small enough sample, the random action of chance can appear to be statistically significant. For instance: I've just tossed a coin 21 times but only got heads seven times, or 33 per cent of the time, rather than the 50 per cent I would expect. Should I use the coin to try to win my fortune? No. What I haven't told you is that tosses 21 to 28 turned up heads every time. I just ignored the last seven throws and based my survey on the first 21 attempts.

Sample sizes are terribly important in surveys. Darrell Huff gives the example of a polio vaccination trial that vaccinated 450 children and left 680 unvaccinated. None of them later caught polio in the subsequent epidemic because the normal expectation was that only two of a sample this size would have been infected in any case. A sample 20 to 30 times larger would be required to give meaning to the trial (Huff 1954: 41).

Graphics, including graphs and charts, also need to be handled with care. Don't use any graph sent to you by an outside organisation – it has always been designed to present the information in the best light to suit that person's or organisation's case. Have the graph redrawn by your art department using different criteria if you want to use a graph at all.

Percentages

One statistical tool that often confuses reporters and readers is the use of percentages. It is usually advisable to adjust percentages into fractions both for yourself and for the reader. A press release suggesting that more than half of the people sampled preferred the client's brand of breakfast cereal while only 49 per cent preferred their rival's cereal loses its punch when you rightly suggest that half prefer one and half prefer the other. Rounding the figures of 50.54% and 49.46% to half is perfectly legitimate, particularly if we find that the sample is fewer than the total number of customers of both cereals – as it is bound to be.

Percentages should always be thought of as ratios and not as fixed numbers. A 20 per cent increase on 120 is 24, giving a new figure of 144; but 80 per cent of 144 is only 115.2. Percentages are a good way of comparing one number with another, but fractions usually do the job better and more clearly. To say a road is twice as busy, rather than that there is a 100 per cent increase in traffic, is much clearer because many people are confused about whether doubling means a 50 per cent, 100 per cent or 200 per cent increase.

Chance

The operation of chance is another problem area for journalists. Often a story will seem to arise from a small set of statistics. Maybe it is a small cluster of leukemia victims living close to a power substation. An example of this was a story concerning Manchester University. Following the fourth death from cancer of a member of the academic staff based close to the room used by Ernest Rutherford to store radium for his groundbreaking experiments, an external investigation was carried out to see if the rooms were contaminated with radiation.

Professor David Coggon, an occupational epidemiologist from Southampton University, carried out the investigation and said he was pretty confident there were only small health risks to people working in the building. 'By far the most likely explanation for the cluster is that it occurred by chance coincidence,' his report said. Quite often what seems to be a pattern is in fact merely chance, and we need to be careful we don't get tricked into chasing up such false patterns.

Statistics

You can access a wide range of statistics from UK National Statistics on www.statistics.gov.uk. For instance, you can access a document giving the causes of every death in the UK in 2007. This can make a great story when the information is fresh, and is useful background for other stories. During the swine flu epidemic, for instance, it would be useful to find out how many people normally die of flu in a typical year and their ages. A quick glance at this document would soon show that 11,253 men and 16,930 women died of influenza and pneumonia in 2007, but that the numbers per age group jump from a handful in childhood, teens and early adulthood to a couple of hundred in their 40s, 50s and 60s, and then jump again to 2000 or 3000 for those in their late 70s and early 80s, and then to more than 6000 in the early 90s, only to fall again as other causes of death take over.

There is a wide range of material available on this site covering agriculture, business, children, education, crime, economy, health and population.

Finance

I like to give an exercise to student journalists that involves them looking at a balance sheet to try to find a story. Most find this an extremely difficult exercise, and some even question whether it is right for them to do it, pointing out that they are not accountants.

Finance is an important part of everyday life these days and many stories in newspapers concern it, whether it is the budget of the local council, talk of the government's economic state, personal finance, private pension funds, the profit levels of major companies, or whether a local firm is due to go bust putting scores of local citizens out of work. Companies in the finance world are always keen to trumpet their successes, explaining when they are doing well, but are a bit less forthcoming when things go badly. The modern reporter needs to be able to understand finance and read a balance sheet. How is the government spending our money? Are people being ripped off by insurance or pension giants? What are fat cat directors of privatised companies being paid? Is the biggest employer in town financially stable? All these figures are available from press offices, on the net, or from Companies House or market analysts. The point is – can you find the story from the deliberately confusing figures?

Essentially all companies and organisations must issue accounts. For local government and public companies, this is done annually and the accounts are audited before release. Audit is a legal process that involves auditors checking the work of the accounts department that drew up the accounts to ensure they are accurate and that no fraudulent practices have been used. In reality, it would be impossible for any audit firm to go through the accounts of a large organisation such as a county council and check that every receipt matches every payment actually made to the supplier, that the payments were fair and that the goods or services they represent were used in full by the council. Nor can they check that every entry in the council's accounts is accurate. However, by using the techniques of their trade, they are able to certify that there appear to be no faults with the accounts and that all money spent was used legally and honestly. It is normal for private companies also to have their accounts audited annually.

Accounts are produced in two main sections: assets and liabilities; and income and expenditure. These must balance so that if there is more income than expenditure (a profit) there is a commensurate increase in assets or reduction in liabilities. If there was more expenditure, then there would be an increase in liabilities. This allows us to look very quickly at the asset/liability position and see whether the company is worth more or less than it was a year ago. A healthy company should be worth more, certainly not less, but just because a company's liabilities increased substantially in any particular year, that does not mean it is in trouble. Perhaps the company has paid out a lot in a streamlining exercise. It may have closed down a loss-making plant, which involved large costs in redundancy payments and demolishing the old plant. It would have borrowed money for this that would increase the company's liabilities. But now, expenditure would decrease substantially as money would not be poured needlessly into that plant and the company's expenditure for the following year would be substantially reduced, even taking into account the loan repayments. Profits should rise and the company's assets would increase. It would also be able to pay a bigger dividend to shareholders.

Private companies are usually owned by their directors. These are normally the people who started the company or their descendants. Bloggs and Sons may not still be owned by Bloggs, or by his sons (or daughters), but it may well remain in the control of the Bloggs family. Eventually, if Bloggs and Sons continues to prosper, the company will want to expand and will require more money than either the company or the individual Bloggs's can provide. They might then sell shares in the company to other people. These could either be offered privately to people they know, or offered publicly to anyone who wants to buy them.

Maybe the company is worth £3 million after being in business making Christmas decorations for 50 years. The grandson of the founder has just taken over as Managing Director and has negotiated an enormous order for decorations with a massive retail company in Germany. It will triple the company's turnover, but they do not have the capacity to make the decorations in their present factory. They need £2 million urgently to build a new factory. The bank is not prepared to lend so much, but a local Lottery winner is looking for somewhere to invest some of his winnings safely, that will give a good return but that will be reasonably secure. If he were to invest £2 million in a bank, he would receive interest payments (at 2000 rates) of maybe as much as five per cent per annum. The original *capital* sum would be safe, and he could withdraw the £2 million having made up to £100,000 per year. But by buying shares in the Christmas decoration company, investing the much-needed £2 million, he could find that the company does well and pays him a *dividend* worth six per cent of the face value of the shares at the end of the first year. The new Managing Director proves his worth and the company continues expanding. Not only does the shareholder continue to get a substantial dividend (£120,000 per year), but the value of the shares increases and, after five years, the Lottery winner finds that not only has he been receiving a total dividend of £600,000, but his shares are now worth £4 million on the open market. Of course, the shareholder would have to pay tax on the income and tax on the capital gain. Since the rates for income and capital gains will be different, this would affect any decision about where and how the investor would invest. As they say, the value of shares can go up or down. So while the bank was a safe bet, as you can remove the full value of your capital at any time, a shareholder could lose money if the company fares badly – as many who rushed to fund the new dotcom companies found to their cost.

Professional practice

There are a number of ethical issues that a good reporter needs to bear in mind while contacting and dealing with sources.

All the regulatory bodies take this very seriously and agree that journalists should treat contacts fairly. The BBC has pages of excellent advice in its Editorial Guidelines about how to behave ethically while researching a story: www.bbc.co.uk/guidelines/editorialguidelines.

Often friends and relatives of a criminal or the victim of a disaster or accident are some of the first people journalists approach to follow up a story. These people are often unwilling to take the public stage, have done nothing personally to justify it, and are being approached during a time of considerable emotional difficulty. The BBC warns: 'Reporting the facts about criminals may include detailing their family circumstances, but we should avoid causing unwarranted distress to their family. Also we should not imply guilt by association without evidence' (www.bbc.co.uk/guidelines/editorialguidelines/edguide/crime/reportingcri.shtml).

Victims of rape or sexual assault, and victims under the age of 18, are protected from being identified by law. Naming them is an offence under several different Acts of Parliament. But even victims who are not directly identified should be treated with care. Journalists need to ensure they do not join the criminal in damaging the victim.

There are other ways of gathering information that are unsavoury or unacceptable. Stealing the rubbish of a subject in order to get an idea of their lifestyle is borderline criminal and certainly unsavoury, although it is done by some journalists and private detectives. The police, of course, routinely inspect rubbish while investigating a crime because it does sometimes prove to be a useful source of information. Benjy the Binman is well known on Fleet Street for making a living going through the rubbish of the famous – or infamous – and selling the results to newspapers.

Often a newspaper will be offered papers that point to a superb story, but have been stolen. Taped recordings of phone calls or bugged conversations fall into the same category. Only undeniable public interest could justify using (or gathering) such material.

Sometimes a paper or magazine will pay a source for access to a story. While paying Posh Spice and David Beckham a huge sum to have exclusive access to cover their wedding is little more than an extension of their life as entertainers, paying witnesses for the evidence they will give in court can risk prejudicing that evidence. The Press Complaints Commission (PCC) has introduced a clause into its code to consider this:

> No payment or offer of payment to a witness – or any person who may reasonably be expected to be called as a witness – should be made in any case once proceedings are active as defined by the Contempt of Court Act 1981.
>
> This prohibition lasts until the suspect has been freed unconditionally by police without charge or bail or the proceedings are otherwise discontinued; or has entered a guilty plea to the court; or, in the event of a not guilty plea, the court has announced its verdict.
>
> (www.pcc.org.uk/cop/practice.html)

The BBC normally forbids paying witnesses before a trial. There are one or two exceptions: overwhelming public interest, or because the interviewee is an expert witness whose professional opinion is being sought.

Bribes, corruption and conflicts of interest

In my experience, bribes are not very common in the British media in the terms of a plain envelope stuffed with fivers, but threats, pressure and hidden bribes in terms of freebies are. You should always be on your guard when free trips, parties or other gifts are mentioned. The NUJ code of conduct says:

> A journalist resists threats or any other inducements to influence, distort or suppress information, and takes no unfair personal advantage of information gained in the course of her/his duties before the information is public knowledge.
>
> (www.nuj.org.uk/innerPagenuj.
> html?docid=25)

So you need to think about invitations or gifts. If you are ever threatened by anyone, whether an advertiser saying they'll remove advertising unless you publish a story or ignore a story, or someone threatening violence in order to prevent publication, you should always inform your editor.

5
Office procedures

Any journalist hoping to find stories and publish them for a particular readership has to be up-to-date with the news – otherwise it is impossible to identify what *is* news. It is vital to read newspapers, watch TV, listen to the radio and scan websites. It is also important to keep up-to-date with all the gossip within the community on which you are reporting. If you are working for a local paper, you need to know what local people are saying and who is who. If you are working as a parliamentary correspondent, you need to know all the MPs and the gossip about them. You may not use this information for stories, but you do need it for background, if only to ensure you are not publishing stories that are weeks or even months old, that will damage your reputation for providing up to the minute news.

The newsroom structure

All news providers, broadcast, print or web, have a newsroom where reporters work. Some larger newsrooms may also contain other editorial staff such as sub-editors, features staff, library, sport or photographers. District offices are usually staffed by just reporters, possibly led by a district news editor, although such offices are becoming rarer as newspapers and broadcasters cut back in order to save costs, relying entirely on a central office. The BBC now relies on regional offices and has closed many of its small district radio studios. This is partly because improvements in technology have made them redundant and partly because of staff cuts.

All newspapers and broadcast stations are structured in much the same way. The editor is in overall charge of the editorial operation, but day-to-day management of the newsroom is in the hands of the news editor. This may be an assistant editor (news), a news content manager, or on a small paper it may even be the editor – but whatever the title, their role will be to supervise reporters, to ensure the stories they want covered are covered, and to ensure the editor is kept in touch with what's going on.

They may also commission freelances, organise **stringers** and liaise with sub-editors, photographers, advertising and other departments in the organisation. In a big office, the news editor may have several deputies and assistants. This is particularly true of a daily paper or a radio or TV station, where the news operation is six or seven days a week. Even news editors need time off.

A big newsroom may have some reporters working as correspondents, specialising in some aspect of news work: education, local government, crime or health, for instance. Some may have correspondents for aspects of work that are particularly important locally. Maybe it is a rural area and a farming correspondent is needed, or a seaside resort requires a tourism correspondent. There would then be a pool of general reporters covering the everyday work. A chief reporter is sometimes appointed. He or she might help run the diary, or it might be a courtesy title for a well respected reporter taken off diary to work on his or her own initiative. In addition, stories are often produced by freelances and stringers.

Freelances are self-employed journalists who often prefer working for themselves, as it allows them to pick and choose the work they do. This can suit those with a specialist interest or those who want to work unusual hours or part-time to fit in with family commitments. For instance, it may be that a local freelance specialises in finance and normally sends copy to the financial papers. He or she may send copy to the local paper only if a story of local interest is found.

Stringers are local people who write a few hundred words every week about their community, social group or sports club. They are amateurs, although they may be paid 'lineage' – a small fee depending on the length of the copy. The growth of ultra-local websites produced by some newspapers and the demand for user-generated content, particularly pictures and video, has seen a growth in the number of stringers and the work they produce. These amateur reports or pictures are usually rewritten or edited by sub-editors, or may be strong enough stories to require extra work from a reporter. A local journalist can also work as a stringer for a national.

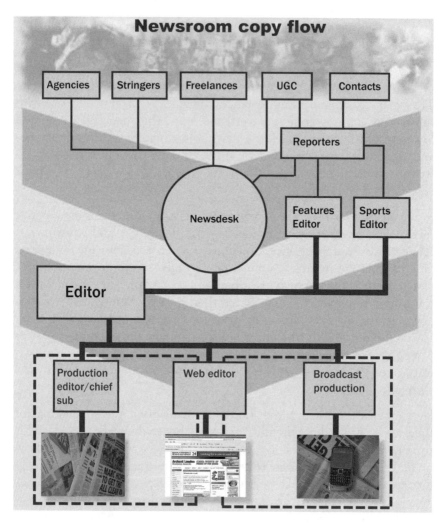

Figure 5.1 Newsroom copy flow

The news conference

Just as you need to keep up-to-date, so does the news editor, so that he or she can make decisions about the news. The news editor will also notify photographers if pictures are needed and will keep the editor and the chief sub-editor in touch with the progress of the more important stories. It is vital that you keep your news editor in touch with what's happening: the key issues that are likely to bubble up and affect the future of a story.

The news editor needs to know what stories are available and when they will be ready for publication. These stories will then be discussed in a news conference – a gathering of all the editorial executives. On a daily paper, TV or radio station, there will be at least one conference a day and possibly more. A conference early in the day will discuss the latest news to go on the live news pages for that issue of the paper or to use in the next bulletin. Conference will then discuss forward planning – stories for later bulletins or to go on feature pages. There will also be some discussion about what will be used on the website and how that might be developed. The conference gives all the executives a chance to detail the stories or pictures they have and explain how they envisage using them. This gives executives the chance to liaise and cooperate, so that the editorial team produces the best product possible.

The news briefing

When a news editor asks you to do a story, he or she will provide you with a briefing about the story and its potential, together with any paperwork to support the story – council minutes, a report or a press release. There may, of course, be no briefing at all apart from, 'Get to such and such by this time and see what's going on'. Make sure you understand what it is the news editor is after. He or she should tell you the kind of story hoped for, how much space (or time) may be available, and where it's likely to go in the paper or bulletin. Instructions such as: 'I'm looking for this to lead an inside page', or 'I'm looking for twenty to thirty seconds from this', should give you some idea of what's expected. This does not mean you need to stick rigidly to the brief. If the circumstances have changed radically when you arrive, plans may need to be rethought. You should alert the newsdesk so that they can reconsider what they want to do. It's no good dashing back into the office two minutes before deadline to tell the news editor that everything's changed and the story's now worth the front page or five minutes at the top of the bulletin. It may well be too late to make those changes. But if you warn the news editor as soon as you can, then he or she can have made arrangements to change the running order so that things are all ready if you come back with the goods. On radio, the reporter should also brief the news editor on the type of treatment the story can offer, such as a live two-way discussion between the reporter and the presenter, an interview or a package.

If you are working on a story of your own, tell the news editor about the story and its strength in an e-mail, phone call or chat, depending on the urgency of the story. If you are out and about, and see a news event such as a major house fire or a road accident, then a phone call is clearly the way to contact the news editor so that they can arrange coverage. Remember – don't just ignore the job you had been going to unless the news editor says so.

Office diaries

The office diary is kept by the newsdesk and contains all the notes on newsworthy events in the area, along with a note of who is to cover them. The news editor will mark up the diary every day based on events notified to him or her by e-mail or through the post, over the phone or from editorial staff. Many of the events will be notified by press release. The news editor will put the item in the diary and store the press release electronically or physically if it's been sent by post. Many newsdesks now e-mail the job to the reporter, whether the diary is electronic or paper. A copy with the reporter's initials alongside the event will be marked up in the newsdesk diary. If the newsdesk is sticking to the traditional paper diary, then all reporters should check it at least twice a day: once in the morning, after the news editor has checked the post; and once in the evening before going home, to see if there are any new evening jobs or early calls. Checking more often is a good idea. Most workplaces now use some sort of electronic system, either a calendar-based system or an organisational system such as the Electronic News Production System (ENPS) used by the BBC and others. ENPS and other organisational systems allow reporters to access information about a story and insert notes for the newsdesk, for example what video or audio is available and how soon it would be ready to air. Newspapers are less likely to use an organisational system and are more likely to use an electronic calendar or a traditional diary.

Whatever system your newsroom uses, the chances are the news editor will let you know of a job by e-mail or by shouting across the office (or both). When you get the e-mail, check all the details are there and that you understand it. Also check if there is an attached document (there may be a press release, for instance). Occasionally events require tickets or passes and you will need to collect these from the newsdesk.

On-diary/off-diary working

Working to the instruction of the newsdesk, covering stories in the diary, is called on-diary working (see Chapter 3). This is the staple of most newsrooms and all new reporters start here. On-diary stories are those notified to the newsdesk in advance by others. This would include court and council, public events, press launches, sports events, community meetings and other pre-arranged events. These stories are the bread and butter of daily coverage, but are often a little routine. As you become more experienced, the news editor may give you more opportunities to work on your own initiative. This is called off-diary working and is much more exciting, either because you have initiated the story or it is a fast-breaking news drama. The best way to persuade the newsdesk to let you work on your own initiative is to show the news editor you've got some. Start bringing in stories of your own. Then you can start asking the news editor to let you have time to follow up ideas that you've had. You'll need to brief the news editor on the idea, so be sure you know enough about the story to give him or her some idea of what it's about and what you hope to get out of it in copy terms. The story doesn't have to be the next Watergate, but it does need to be something you've managed to find out about from personal contacts. A good time to approach the news editor about this kind of story is when things are quiet. If the diary is already crammed and the newsdesk is rapidly running out of reporters, it is unlikely you will be let loose on your pet project. But if things are quiet, the news editor may well be prepared to give you a chance. Once you've proved that you can come back with good stories that you have found and developed yourself, you are more likely to be allowed to do it again.

Story support material

Press releases, reports or minutes are often provided to help you write a story. While these can be a great help in producing the story, it is unwise to rely on them too heavily. Names can be misspelt or facts used incorrectly. As always, you need to check. The same is true of your own organisation's archive or library. Just because you've carried a story before, that doesn't mean the facts in it are correct, and you should be very careful about using old cuttings, recordings or library records.

The Press Complaints Commission (PCC) carried a warning in its March 1992 bulletin: 'Cuttings are an essential part of newspaper research but too many journalists now seem to act in the belief that to copy from 10 old stories is better than to write a new one with confirmation by proper fresh enquiry' (PCC 1992 Report no. 7: 2). The PCC went on to give two examples. In the first, a newspaper strung together information from several other newspapers to produce what they presented as a first-person interview. In the second example, a magazine put together a number of reports and invented dialogue in the magazine's style to produce 'an article which contained serious inaccuracies and was to a degree fictitious' (PCC 1992 Report no. 7: 2).

Embargoes

Press releases often carry **embargoes**. These say that the story can be used only after a certain date or time. A good example of an embargo comes from the Central Office of Information when they send out details of the New Year's Honours list. This is embargoed until the end of December so that the secrecy of who is getting what award is not breached. However, they realise that it would be impossible for any news organisation to then get in touch with the people on the list in order to interview and photograph them, so the list is sent to newsdesks earlier so they can arrange for interviews and pictures. This means the newspaper can have pages all set up for distributing from midnight onwards and broadcast outlets can also produce bulletins from midnight onwards with archive footage, new pictures and interviews.

As embargoes can be useful to journalists, it is often in their interest to adhere to them. But they are not legally binding (although there may be copyright implications) and, if abused by the organisation citing them, can be ignored, although the PCC or Ofcom, the broadcast regulator, may well have views on your decision.

Faced with an embargo, you should alert the newsdesk. If you think the embargo is unreasonable, then explain this to the newsdesk, but it will be up to the editor to decide.

Names and addresses

Publishing names and addresses can be problematic, and there may be times when this is not appropriate.

Members of the police force or the armed forces, for instance, are often concerned about revenge or terrorist attacks, so it is regular practice for the police and armed services to refuse to name serving officers. Publishing their names is usually not the problem, but publishing addresses could put them at risk, so most media limit an address to a town.

The PCC published guidance about addresses in its August 1992 report. It advises regional newspapers to publish only the street name and not to identify a particular house by name or number, partly to protect the news source and partly to reduce 'the possibility of error: if you do not publish the number, you cannot get it wrong' (PCC 1992 Report no. 12: 5). This would be normal practice for broadcasters as well. While a national broadcast station would rarely give more than the town, even local broadcasters would not normally use the house name or number.

The PCC warns journalists not to encourage the harassment of individuals named in their stories by publishing telephone numbers or addresses:

> It is true that in the case of prominent people addresses are readily available but the press is not under an obligation to make it easy for cranks and criminals by saving them the bother of researching telephone books and directories.
>
> (PCC 1992 Report no. 12: 5)

The PCC upheld a complaint against a newspaper which, after giving the address of a prominent individual's weekend home in Wales, suggested: 'He had better not tell the Welsh nationalists or they will come and burn it down' (PCC 1992 Report no. 12: 5).

You should also be careful with addresses in stories that make it clear a house is likely to be empty for a period. Many a newly married couple or recently bereaved person has returned home to find they've been burgled because the newspaper published their address. Ofcom also gives advice on giving addresses in reports, and on filming properties.

Groups of people you should be particularly careful of publishing addresses for are:

- police officers;
- prison officers;

- members of the armed forces;
- people (especially women) who the story indicates are living alone;
- children;
- celebrities;
- judges;
- magistrates;
- those accused of very serious crimes;
- relatives of those accused of very serious crimes;
- AIDS victims and their care workers;
- domestic violence and abuse shelters;
- Lottery and other prize winners.

PCC (1995 Report no. 29: 32) gives specific guidance.

Journalists should be particularly careful to refrain from publishing the addresses of refuges and shelters for those who have been the victims of domestic violence and abuse. This would put the people seeking refuge and the workers in the refuges in danger. 'The very purpose of the refuges is invalidated if addresses are made public' (Frost 2000: 87).

Library

All newsrooms will have a library, even if it is only a filing cabinet with pictures and details of leading local citizens and a file of back-copies of the newspaper. Details of local events and people are stored here for back-reference. In a well run library, file copies of stories – probably in digital form these days – are stored for future reference, whether for the annual look back at the past year, details for an obituary, or a 20-year review of the local festival. It is worth putting effort into ensuring the library is up-to-date and it is vital that any false information is tagged in the archive so that future reporters or researchers are not misled. If someone rings up to complain their name is spelt wrongly, for instance, make sure not only that an apology is published, but also that the archive is tagged to ensure the mistake is not repeated.

6
On the road

Although the phone and the internet have become much more important as a way of contacting sources, many reporters still spend a lot of time on the road. This is particularly true of broadcast reporters, who still need to speak to people to get that all-important sound interview or video footage, but newspaper and magazine reporters also prefer to sit face-to-face with their interviewee whenever possible. Sometimes you will be travelling with a camera crew, sometimes alone, and sometimes with a pack of other reporters. During all this travelling you need to ensure you make the best use of what is available to gain the maximum advantage in getting the story, especially if there are competitors. For the best stories you will often be working alone, trying to build an exclusive. But this may mean tracing sources who don't want to be traced, or tracking people who would prefer not to talk to you. Other big stories might not be exclusive, and being able to get to the source first can be vital. Learning how to find people quickly and work well out on the road can make the difference between always being first with the story and just being one of the pack.

Looking good

All reporters need to be appropriately dressed and reasonably well presented when they go out to meet the public. You never know at the start of the day who you may be speaking to. You may wish to dress like a goth in the evening, resplendent in black leather and silver buckles, but this is unlikely to help your interview with a local politician. Your hair, make-up and possible body piercings also affect how people view you. Knapp and Hall point out that 'The length of a person's hair can drastically affect perceptions and human interaction' (Knapp and Hall

1997: 223). One often hears people, especially teenagers and young adults, saying that the way they dress, wear their hair or adorn their body should not affect the way they are perceived. In an ideal world they may be right, but in such an ideal world these youngsters would probably cease to wear such extreme fashion items to express individuality, peer identity and rebellion because such fashions would cease to be perceived badly by those in authority (*ibid.*: 1997: 230). This all suggests that the way you look plays an important part in how you are received. If you want to rebel by looking like an extra from *Conan the Barbarian*, you are probably better doing it at night with your friends; your aim while out working is to ensure people will talk to you and give you information and, if you are seeking to film and interview, that they will talk to you on camera.

While at work for a mainstream news outfit, you can't go wrong with a suit and a raincoat, as this will fit you in with most people and circumstances. There will be some occasions when you might be a bit over-dressed, but these are often occasions when it might be better to stand apart from the crowd. There is a risk that you end up looking like a cheap imitation of one of the leads from the *X-Files*, but then FBI agents probably dress this way for the same reasons. A suit or sober jacket and matching trousers are safest, and you need a coat that protects you from the wind and rain on the doorstep, but that doesn't leave you baking when you are stuck wearing it in a hot, stuffy magistrate's court. (Your speed of exit in order to file the copy at the end of the case may not leave you time to pick up scattered belongings.) This mode of dress (as the *X-Files* proves) applies to both sexes. If you are working for TV, then that uniform is even more important. You are being pictured in thousands of people's homes. Better to look smart than scruffy, and this includes hair as well as clothes. Of course, there may be times when you are able to dress down a little. Covering climate change camps or farming stories might call for more rural dress. If you are a broadcaster, check your clothes won't look odd on TV and that they don't rustle or make noises that will be picked up by the microphone. Jewellery that might jingle should be avoided for the same reason.

General grooming and personal hygiene is important if you are to be taken seriously and gain the full concentration of your interviewee, particularly for radio work, where you might have to stand very close to someone holding the microphone. Visible body piercings for either sex should probably be left out during work time, particularly for TV. Your interview with the Prime Minister is not likely to be taken as seriously if your eyebrows and nose are chained together.

If you are working for a specialist publication, serving an audience where the dress code is specific, then it is possible to dress in that way. You will soon get to know your audience and the type of people you regularly interview and what they wear. Reporters for GQ or *Vogue* would be expected to be dressed in the latest designer labels, while reporting for *Kerrang* or *Clubbing Magazine* would allow a reporter to wear much more casual clothes than those suggested above. But even here, it's probably better to be the best dressed (or at least the coolest dressed) person in the room.

Locating the story

Often, for an on-diary story, you'll be given the address of a press conference or can quickly find the address from the phone book or online. Just punch it into the satnav or grab a cab and you are there.

However, occasionally you will have to track someone down from scratch (see Chapter 4). The most obvious place to start searching is the phone book, either online or on paper. If that fails, then move on to a web search, starting with Google. If you know more detail about the person than their name, include that in the search. Facebook or another social network site might be able to help locate them. Even if you can't get a home address you should be able to get a picture and their business address, which means you can approach them as they leave.

When you are dealing with some stories, planning or land development for instance, you need to get an impression of the local geography. Google satellite is excellent for this, giving you an aircraft view of an area. Publishing the pictures requires a commercial arrangement with Google.

Communication

Keeping in touch with the office is vital. Your news editor needs to know how the story is shaping up, what you have found out, and when he or she can expect you to file. Modern mobile phones with the ability to choose voice, text or e-mail make this relatively easy, but even the best behaved mobile can run out of battery or leave you in a communications black spot, so being able to use more traditional methods can still be important. Should your phone let you down, ring the newsdesk (memorise the number or make sure it's in your contacts book and not just in your now-useless phone), and let them know; then ring in regularly so that they know what's happening. Keep your eyes open for telephone boxes, although these are becoming rarer. *In extremis*, it might be worth considering buying a cheap mobile from a supermarket.

Travelling

If you end up in a job that requires long-distance travelling, you must learn to find your way around strange towns. Although satnavs are great for getting you to your destination, they don't give you any real feel for a strange town, and understanding what sort of town it is or where its various parts are (the shopping, the industrial sector, the dormitory areas, for instance). Getting to grips with the shape of a town is fairly easy. Seaside towns are easiest – just head for the seafront and everything will be close at hand. Inland towns can be more complex, with perhaps a traditional city centre, possibly based around the railway station, but also with a more modern centre based around a shopping mall. Aim for the railway station as it will be signposted and gives a good idea of the shape of the town. The town may be big enough to have a tourist information office, or there may be a local council office that carries out the same function if you need more detailed local information.

If you need a map, you can probably buy one from a newsagent near the station, or service stations carry a wide range of goods and will often stock maps. The person at the till may well know more details and may be willing to help once you've bought a map. If you have time, look the town up on the internet before leaving your home or office, or on your laptop if you have broadband access. Google maps will quickly find you an address, while satellite view on Google maps lets you view the local area.

If you don't have a full address for the person you want, then accessing the electoral role will get one for you. Use www.192.com if you can't find them direct through BT (see Chapter 4). If you know approximately where the person lives, then good old-fashioned inquiries at the local post office, newsagent or perhaps the video shop may well find the address for you.

Your on-the-road experiences will tend to vary with the type of paper or broadcast station you are working for. A weekly newspaper or local radio station is unlikely to ask you to do more than hop in your car for the fifteen-minute trip to the outskirts of town. A national broadcast station or newspaper could have you living in your car for days on end. Either way, it needs to be in good condition. Below is a checklist of items it's worth keeping in your car:

- a couple of bottles or cans of drink;
- snack bars or similar long-life foodstuffs;
- heavyweight anorak or coat with a hood or hat;
- waterproof hat or umbrella;
- wellington boots for trekking across fields or building sites;
- satnav or street maps and atlas;
- spare notebook, pens, batteries, tapes or digital disks;
- mobile phone;
- in-car charger for your mobile phone;
- cash – keep a £20 note to buy food and drink where there are no cash machines;
- change – keep £10 worth of assorted change for carparks;
- basic personal grooming items.

Public transport

Travelling on trains, buses or taxis may be necessary occasionally. Make sure you keep receipts so that you can reclaim your expenses. Expenses should be done at least every week to ensure you don't forget where you've been.

Equipment

If you need to take camera or sound equipment with you, check first how the story is to be transmitted. Are you able to return to base to edit, or are you going to need to plan where you will feed the output? Before you leave the office, check the equipment is working and if it is unfamiliar or new, try it out or read the instruction manual. There's nothing more likely to damage an interviewee's confidence than watching a reporter struggling to activate a camera. If the equipment requires batteries (and almost everything does), check they are fully charged and ready to go. If you are going abroad, get the appropriate international power adaptor. Whether you are using tape, hard-disk recorders or memory cards, check that they have plenty of space on them. Running out of recording space is every bit as bad as running out of battery.

Travelling abroad

Only the lucky few travel regularly by plane for stories abroad. Always try to book plane tickets through the company's agent in advance unless the job is a rush one. Scheduled flights can be heavily booked, especially just before weekends and public holidays. If you are in the kind of post that's likely to see you jetting off at a moment's notice, then it's worth trying to persuade the newsdesk to issue you with a company credit card to allow you to buy tickets rather than using your own card. Give the agent approximate travel times and don't be too fussy about which airline you use. This only becomes significant on really long-haul flights.

Check whether you need a visa – plenty of countries will not allow you access without one. The Foreign and Commonwealth Office will give advice. Its website provides a wealth of useful information and has specific pages of advice on every country you are ever likely to travel to. Visit www.fco.gov.uk/travel where there is a country list you can choose from. It will give you details of visa needs, trouble spots and local customs. You don't need a visa to travel in EU countries, but some of the former East European countries might require one. America requires you to apply for an 'I' visa if you are working as a journalist to media at home. If you are working for US-based media then you need a different visa. Many countries requiring a visa will sell you one on arrival in the country (e.g. Turkey). Many require you to get the visa first, but can arrange it on the same day from their embassy or consulate. For instance, you can get a visa to travel to India on the same day from India House in London. Some visas take longer and you cannot travel until you get one. Get a visa for as long as possible – after all, you might have to go back.

Most companies insist that you travel economy. While this is acceptable for short-haul flights around Europe, I think it's asking a bit much to expect someone to leap straight into a difficult job at the end of a 12-hour flight in economy – push for the company to pay for business, there are a number of good deals about these days if they shop around. Business class means more space and much better seating, which can be reclined properly in order to get some sleep. It also means slightly better meals. The facility to use business lounges in airports is the major advantage. While the business lounge in European or American airports is a pleasurable improvement, in some developing countries' airports it's a necessity. You may have to wait hours before your flight, and business lounges ensure access to working phones, fax machines, the internet, and good quality food and drink. Attempting to find this in some of the world's airports might be quaint, even amusing, while backpacking around the world, but it is an additional unwanted pressure if you've been working on a story for 14 hours and are now trying to catch a plane overnight to another continent, where the time difference means you've got to be in a press conference 40 minutes after landing and filing copy an hour after that. Check-in and check-out are also easier when travelling business, as there is usually an express facility that means you can leave it much later before arriving at the airport and still get through much more quickly.

Always aim to sit in an aisle seat. Watching the view soon palls, while easy access to the lavatories, and being able to flag down stewards for extra food or drink, or move to a more congenial seat easily, are major benefits. You will also be able to leave the aircraft more quickly. If you travel lightly enough, you should be able to get your luggage in the cabin with you. You can take a surprisingly large bag as hand luggage and I have often travelled with my small shoulder bag, laptop and a decent-sized grip (large enough for a week or so away) inside the plane. They are likely to be even more lenient if you are travelling business class.

All except the very shortest scheduled flights offer meals. The longer the flight, the more substantial they are, so there is no need to get to the airport early in order to eat.

If you travel in this country or abroad fairly often, keep a bag permanently packed with basic kit such as your washbag, including any medications you need. It should be heavy-duty woven nylon about $60 \times 25 \times 35$ cm (small enough to take as hand luggage) with hand grips and shoulder strap, and at least two outside pockets. I always keep a couple of tee-shirts packed as they can double up for warmth, nightwear or just for a clean change. An international power adaptor, a bottle of water, a pack of biscuits and a paperback for those long waits are also useful additions.

Just add clothes and you are ready to go. If you don't carry your driving licence and passport with you all the time, keep them in this bag. Move them to a safe place on your person once you are on the move.

You should have a full passport – if you do not possess one, get one soon. Often the best trips are announced at short notice and require your passport. One reporter made his career because, shortly after starting with a national paper, he was the only reporter in the office with his passport on him the day a big story blew up. His news editor despatched him direct to the airport and he made the most of his opportunity.

If you can afford it, keep a US$100 note in the bag (or more). Hard currencies can usually be exchanged anywhere. It's getting easier to get by with just a credit card, but there are still places in the world where finding an ATM and using it safely is not easy. If you don't have local cash, change some when going through the airport, either departing or on arrival. Having enough cash to get a taxi to your hotel or meeting when you arrive can make a big difference to getting the story. If you are going to a disaster area, take a large cash float as it may not be possible to get cash once you are there. Airports are international communities and you have to travel a fair way to find one that won't accept sterling, but once you are outside, you are on your own.

If there is any chance of you travelling to the Far East or Africa, then it is worth purchasing sterile hypodermic needles in case you happen to need medical treatment. The risk of AIDS from infected needles in these areas is very much higher than in Europe or America. Boots and other chemists sell medical packs for travellers that contain these sorts of supplies and it's worth investing in one if you travel a lot. It's also worth keeping your jabs up-to-date. This is partly so you can leave at short notice, and partly to ensure you don't have to have about ten at once in order to travel somewhere at a week's notice.

Never pack more than six days' worth of clothes. Use laundries or buy cheap clothes abroad and leave them there. You don't want to be cluttered with loads of bags – you'll have enough to carry with important things such as your notebook and computer.

Many airports are well served by train systems and these are often the fastest, and certainly the cheapest, way to get into the nearest city. Ticket sellers at most train stations, certainly in Europe, nearly always speak serviceable English provided you are talking trains.

It's well worth learning a foreign language as even a few words can make a big difference to people's decision to speak to you. Likely languages to learn include Arabic, French, Spanish and Chinese.

Accommodation

If you are staying away from home overnight, you will need a hotel room. Ask your newsdesk secretary to book the hotel before you leave – this will ensure a reasonable hotel with the bill sent direct to the company. If they can't arrange to pay direct, make sure you know that. You don't want to end up paying twice.

Most hotels in Britain are now far better than they used to be. Any hotel or guest accommodation with two stars or better will ensure a clean room with a comfortable bed, *en suite* bathroom, telephone, TV and coffee-making facilities. Usually there will be a bar in the hotel as well. Minibars always seem undersupplied and overexpensive to me, so either carry your own choice of alcohol, use the hotel's bar on a cash basis, or don't drink. One colleague of mine allowed his room to be used for a bar once and woke in the morning with a splitting headache to find two strangers sharing his room and a bar bill of £400.

Some private guest houses or one-star hotels can offer excellent accommodation, so if you are on a fixed claim rate, it can make sense to look at some of these. Check out the lobby and public rooms. Are they clean and well maintained? If so, the rooms should be as well. Ask to see a room before booking in. A reputable hotel will not object. If the room is up to scratch, leave your bags there and go down to check in. This ensures you get the room you've checked.

Check on the power points. You may have a laptop, cameras and recorders, and you'll certainly have a mobile. Most power supplies for these are intelligent and will be able to deal with any difference in voltage. However, you will probably have to get an adapter for the plug. Check the instructions on the power supply before you use it. Some may require you to alter a control before plugging in to a different voltage supply. If all else fails, find a local electrical shop and buy a new power cord or charger suitable for the local power supply. When you check out of a hotel, you may want to stay in the town for some time before catching your plane. Ask the hotel if they'll look after your bags. Don't forget that many foreign countries still have left-luggage lockers at airports or train stations. This will allow you to leave your luggage there for a few pounds while you carry on working

Personal safety and security

Your personal safety is important when you are out and about. The Suzy Lamplugh Trust is a charity that works to improve everyone's personal safety and reduce the risks of personal violence and aggression. The charity points out that public transport and other forms of travel in the UK are incredibly safe, and that crime against passengers is very rare. They offer good advice as well as safety training and safety products (www.suzylamplugh.org). Most of the charity's advice is fairly obvious, but one of the surprises about obvious advice is how often people refuse to take it. They also offer or advise on a number of products that you might want to buy, especially if you are particularly nervous. Attack alarms have been around for ages, but more modern devices, such as GPS trackers, are now available. These devices will tell a central system your location at the press of a button. Pressing a further button will send a panic alert that can be forwarded to whoever you wish. These devices are linked in to your ordinary mobile phone.

Just some very simple everyday precautions can ensure that your journey, whether by car or public transport, is as safe as possible. You should make sure you lock your car if you leave it and also lock it if you are inside it at night. Having remote central locking on your car is essential, as you will find should you ever need to make a snappy get-away, particularly if you are sharing the car with a colleague. An attack alarm or a dog deterrent is invaluable at the right moment, although not if they are at the bottom of the glove compartment or a handbag. An attack alarm can be just enough to put off a would-be attacker who you've managed to upset, at least for long enough for you to get in the car and away. You need to ensure they have working batteries.

Letting your office know where you are and ringing them before you go in to interview anyone is a wise precaution. You should always make sure you have plenty of fuel in your car and never let the tank go lower than quarter-full. Membership of one of the motoring breakdown services is also essential to ensure that, should you break down, you'll be moving again as soon as possible.

It's worth checking whether your insurance company offers you a special deal. Several offer hefty discounts with RAC or AA membership as part of their comprehensive package.

Safety in the UK

Safety is usually a matter of common sense, but often a reporter's desire to get a great story can get him or her into trouble. Covering events such as large-scale demonstrations that may become riots can be dangerous, and you should take care.

When covering potentially dangerous events, you should choose your clothing carefully so that you don't look like either a police officer or a rioter. Some reporters wear their press card on a chain or clipped to their clothing. This might help in some situations, but it could antagonise in others. It certainly might prevent casual conversations with people at the event, which are often useful. You should avoid antagonising anyone. Arguing with a demonstrator could quickly attract a crowd who might turn ugly.

Avoid getting caught in the middle. Talk to people at the edge first so that you have enough material to do a basic story yet can slip away easily. Always keep your eye on an escape route to a safe area and ensure it remains clear. You should bear in mind any police instructions, and ignore them only if you think you will be safe doing so.

You should always take care with expensive equipment – not only is it a potential theft risk, but it may present dangers to innocent bystanders. Runs of cable, lights, cameras and tripods can all cause injuries and you need to ensure you do all you can to minimise that. If you are using a small, hand-held video camera or a stills camera or radio recorder, keep the equipment hidden away where possible and certainly try not to be obvious with it.

If you are arrested, don't resist. The police might well use 'reasonable force' and worry about the potential bad press later. Try to get receipts for any equipment that is confiscated by the police. Make sure you know the PIN number for your press card. All press cards issued under the national press card scheme have a PIN number to allow the police to identify that you are holding the card legally. Show the card and give the PIN number when requested by a uniformed officer. If you are a member of the National Union of Journalists, there is an emergency number you can ring for immediate legal help, and you should memorise that number or have it somewhere you can find it easily (in your mobile's memory, for instance – but remember, that will be confiscated if you are arrested or may already have been stolen).

Safety abroad

Scores of journalists are killed each year around the world, and many are hurt or arrested. Working abroad raises a number of safety issues – if you are going anywhere off the beaten track, to a war zone or anywhere with a poor record for journalistic safety, persuade your newsdesk to send you on a safety course. Many places run these for journalists, government officials and business people. They are not cheap, but they are better than being killed or ending up as the next terrorist kidnap victim. The International Federation of Journalists (IFJ) has an excellent little booklet with much advice, and the Committee to Protect Journalists and Reporters Sans Frontières are among several organisations that also offer advice.

No story is worth getting killed for – if the situation gets dangerous, get out. Often it may be bureaucracy or obdurate officials that pose a problem. Always be polite and cooperate. The last thing you should be is obstructive. Remember, you may not have the same protections as you have at home. It is always easy to arrest journalists on trumped-up spying charges, and it may be days or weeks before you even get to see someone from your embassy. Be prepared for it all to take a long time, particularly if you don't understand the language. Keep asking for a phone call to a lawyer or the embassy but, above all, stay patient. The Foreign and Commonwealth Office offers advice on English-speaking lawyers abroad on its website. It might be worth checking there before you travel. It's always worth learning enough of the local language to seek medical help, ask for food and water, get to see the person in charge and ask for a telephone.

The IFJ advises that you should always carry your papers with you when you travel, along with plenty of cash – you may be able to buy your way out of trouble. Watch what you wear. If you are with a lot of military personnel, you might wish to be easy to differentiate. But if you are in a lonely part of the country, you might want to blend in. As one journalist pointed out:

Earlier this year I was near the Afghan front line snapping teenage soldiers. Alan Pearce, the BBC correspondent, calmly suggested that the bright orange fleece I was wearing – Marks and Spencers, much admired – was not quite the right thing in the circumstances.

(Jenny Matthews, quoted in the
Journalist, January 1997)

You might also want to consider a flak jacket if you are travelling in areas where snipers, mines or shelling are a risk. The BBC and other major news outlets normally offer these as a matter of course.

The bottom line, as always, is to do your homework, think about the risks and plan for them where you can. One can never remove risk entirely, and life might be less exciting (but possibly longer) if one could, but you can minimise it to maximise your safety.

7
Making contact

People are nearly always the key to a good story. They are the reason why a story is interesting, they are why people want to read it, and they provide the best support for a story – good witness statements or quotes – that explain how the people involved feel about the issue. A personal account not only adds to the strength of a story, but it is usually the best part.

You need to plan carefully who you intend to speak to in order to get the facts of the story (the who, what, where and when), and who you need to interview in order to give it depth and drama (the why and how). You need to interview a sufficient breadth of contacts to ensure you are getting to the truth, not just a small part of it.

Take the example of a road accident. You might talk to the police and the other emergency services first. They will tell you in fairly professional and unemotive language what happened, as far as they know, and when and where it happened. This flat, dispassionate telling of the drama of a road accident in which people were injured or even killed is fine for official reports, but we really need to get at the human drama behind what has happened.

This can be done in several ways. The first is to talk to people about those injured or killed in the crash. Perhaps there was something special about their life, or even their death, that makes them particularly interesting. Maybe one was a well loved school teacher and her class of six-year-olds is to hold a special service in the next day's school assembly. Perhaps one victim was a local politician, a national celebrity or a notorious criminal. The Princess of Wales's death, for instance, is just a small, boring road crash in Paris of no interest at all to UK readers until you add the extra ingredient of a royal celebrity passenger. Then it's a story worth millions of words.

There could be something special about the crash itself. This could be anything from the make of vehicles involved, to the site of the crash. An accident involving two steam rollers (and I mean a steam roller, not road roller) would be of more interest than two modern family saloons; an accident at a notorious blackspot already responsible for six deaths that year is also destined to be a bigger story. An accident caused by a driver having a heart attack or being momentarily blinded by a hooligan with a laser also adds a twist that makes the story more interesting. It is these extras that give stories what some editors call the 'pub factor' – that is, when a drinker in a pub turns to their companion and says, 'Did you see that story in . . .?'.

So who do you speak to when you've found out the basic facts? If you are following up a story about a local hero or celebrity, you need to talk to family and friends. In the example of the teacher, you would talk to colleagues, friends and family. You would also talk (after getting permission from teachers or parents) to the children. Don't forget pictures. Is there one of the teacher with the schoolchildren? Can you get a photographer to the special service? Pictures of children clutching handkerchiefs or little posies of flowers say more about the reality of the relationship between the teacher and pupil than you possibly could, no matter how much space you were given to write it.

If the people involved were of no particular interest but the circumstances were, then you would need to talk to a different set of people. If it was mechanical failure, then maybe you would need to talk to the garage that last serviced the car (they often put little stickers in the window of the car to remind the driver of the date of the next service – have a look and see if you can see anything like that). If it is a regular fault with that type of car, then talk to the press office of the car manufacturer. If the accident is caused at a blackspot, then local politicians and action groups would probably be delighted to speak to you, and then you can get an official comment from the local authority.

Never forget to talk to the 'little people'. It is often tempting to speak only to the police officer in charge of the situation, or the politician complaining about the accident blackspot, or somebody's press officer. But often the people who witnessed the accident, or who are only peripherally involved, can give you an angle on the story that others can't. Theirs is a vital voice in telling the story, whether as quotes in print or direct in a broadcast.

This is particularly true of stories that are not so cut-and-dried as a road accident. Talking to the managing director about whether his or her company is going bust will only give you the official line. Talking to the workers who are going to lose their jobs will give you a much clearer idea of the truth. It may not all be material you can use, but it will help you decide whether to continue with the story.

Building trust

Talking to people requires you to be able to deal with individuals and quickly build their trust. Observations such as 'Things seem a bit quiet around here', dropped casually into the conversation, are not easy to make unless the subject has already fallen easily into conversation with you. Developing with a stranger a conversation that you want to go on to become an interview is a difficult art to master. If you are meeting someone who is expecting you, or someone in a position of authority, you will want to introduce yourself as a reporter straightaway by giving your name and the name of your employer. However, if the contact is more casual – someone in a crowd at public occasion, for instance – you may not want to start by introducing yourself as a reporter, as they may instantly refuse to talk to you; however, not identifying yourself would be to attempt to get information by subterfuge, and that is unethical. The best approach in such a situation is to use the loosening of social inhibitions that such events allow to start a conversation. If it becomes clear that the person knows something, or witnessed events, then introduce yourself as a reporter and ask them if you can talk to them about the event. Hopefully, they will have spoken to you long enough to be willing to carry on talking. Then is a good time to produce your notebook and get their details. Of course, sometimes people will then refuse to comment, but I'm afraid that has to be accepted. Thank them and then move on to seek other sources.

No matter who the contact is, we need to build a relationship. People in official positions often will give only the bare facts of a story unless you get them to warm to you a little, so that they relax and allow their more human side to show. Witnesses or those involved may often be nervous of giving information or talking to journalists. For them, this is a new and perhaps unwelcome experience. There are two ways in which you can start to gain people's trust: by your appearance, and by your conduct. As soon as we open our mouth, we are judged. Instant assumptions are made about us by others. Assumptions about our intelligence, our background, class, race, education, abilities and, ultimately, our power. We have to give them a message that says, 'I'm interested in you. Talk to me. Trust me.'

Fight self-consciousness and show that you are confident and in control. Take charge of the situation – the subject will usually be happy to submit, after all, this is often a new experience for them and they may be happy to rely on you to guide them through it. While you are talking informally, listen carefully for any free information and be ready to respond. For example, if you ask how they are, they may tell you they have just returned from holiday in France. Do not let it pass without asking, 'Did you have a good time?' You need to be interested in people for themselves, not just for what they can tell you. They need to be convinced this is more of a conversation than an interrogation. You'll need to ask questions in order to get the information you seek, but don't be in too much of a rush to lead them in any particular direction. Let them tell the story and avoid interrupting unless there is a detail you need to confirm, such as a name or place.

Body language is important if people are going to trust you. You need to stand close enough so that they feel you are interested, but not so close that they feel uncomfortable. Eye contact and smiling are vital. Do not fold your arms or put your hand up to your mouth. These are 'stay away' signals! If the person is an important contact, offer to meet them for a drink after work. Politicians and police officers have particular pubs or clubs where they go to relax with their friends. If you meet them socially, you are likely to meet other people, who may turn out to be valuable contacts in the future.

Cultural expectations and problems

Reporters are used to dealing with people from all sorts of different backgrounds, but for many people, dealing with strangers is a new and difficult experience. Psychologists suggest that when we meet someone new from our own culture we are usually guided by norms and rules of behaviour that allow us to predict or explain their behaviour (Gudykunst 1994: 18). But when we meet someone from a different culture, these guides may not apply. From a psychologist's viewpoint, a different culture

could mean someone from a different class, background, gender or race
– never mind from a different national culture or religious background
– so this applies to many people we meet.

In addition, journalists often meet people who are under particular stress
or pressure, even if it is only the knowledge that their words will be
printed for all to see in the newspaper, and this can lead them to behave
in a way that is unusual for them.

Gudykunst says there are two main elements of uncertainty that people
try to reduce on meeting a stranger. The first is when we are unable or
unsure about predicting how the stranger will behave (*ibid*.: 19). The
anxiety often felt by people on being accosted by a drunk in the street
is this type of uncertainty. The normal rules of behaviour are not being
applied by the drunk and we are unable to predict how the drunk will
behave. This makes most people feel uncomfortable, and they will break
off the contact as soon as possible and leave. The second type of
uncertainty arises when we are not able to explain a stranger's behaviour.

One of the major problems a journalist often faces on first contact
interview is described by Habermas as *pseudocommunication* (Henley and
Kramarae 1991: 34). This happens when people who

> share a common language and many common experiences,
> are likely to mistakenly assume that a consensus exists among
> them concerning the meaning of communicative behaviours.
> This mistaken assumption 'produces a system of reciprocal
> misunderstandings which are not recognised as such' or
> pseudocommunication.
>
> (Henley and Kramarae 1991: 34)

If someone assumes, for instance because of a reporter's polite inquiry
about their activities, that the reporter is actively sympathetic, they may
say more than they would normally intend, working on the assumption
that the reporter will protect them from themselves because of their
sympathetic approach. When this later turns out to have been a mistake,
the interviewee will often blame the reporter for betraying the trust that
was only ever a one-way thing. This sort of behaviour can usually be
detected by the reporter in the closeness of the responses and also in
the use of language that indicates the interviewee's belief in a common
bond. This might include specialist language, or contacts named or
gossiped about as though they were common friends. Whether the reporter

wants to use these indications as a sign that he or she should attempt to put some distance between them by cooling down the contact, risking persuading the source to shut up all together, or whether the reporter risks being accused later of betraying the contact's trust, is a decision that can only be taken on a case-by-case basis.

When a reporter sets up a relationship with a contact, they are trying to find out a lot about them very quickly. Reporters need to break down the usual social barriers to uncover intimate details that the contact would never normally share with a stranger. In major incidents, this is often not a problem. Psychologists tell us that people talk much more freely when disaster threatens, hoping to gain information and to pass it on (Shibutani 1966).

However, when the story is a normal, everyday occurrence, we have to work harder at building a relationship with the person. For this to be a real relationship on the contact's part – which is what the reporter wants – there has to be warmth and trust. This puts the contact in a very vulnerable position. The reporter learns a lot about them because of this position of trust. This artificial relationship-building is often seen as highly cynical behaviour and is certainly part of the reason why reporters are often portrayed as cynical, shallow and manipulative. However, it need not be so. Just because the relationship has been manufactured for a specific purpose, and there may be little expectation of continuing it in many cases, it does not mean that the reporter has to completely betray that person. They are hoping for a fair and accurate account of their side of the story, and it should be within the reporter's gift to give them that. If there is a feeling of betrayal and the reporter has done his or her best to be fair and accurate, then it should be relatively easy to use that relationship to explain.

According to Argyle, all cultures have greeting rituals but these can vary widely (Argyle 1988: 62). While working in your home country, these rituals will be well known to you and should be followed, but if you are working abroad, try to adapt to the local rituals and, if you are meeting people from abroad, please try to be considerate to their rituals. This will make you less alien and ease the process of relationship-building.

Once conversations are under way, try to be aware of what is cultural difference and what is just the person's personality. Argyle (1988) identifies six elements of potential cultural difference.

- *Proximity, touch and gaze* vary extensively. Britons often feel uncomfortable talking to those of Arab or Indian descent because they stand closer than the British are used to while talking. This can make them seem over-familiar and threatening, and Britons must work hard to prevent that feeling souring their discussion. Conversely, Chinese and Japanese people prefer to stand a little further away than Europeans, and this can make them feel a little distant and aloof to the European.

- *Expressiveness* varies from race to race, from the so-called inscrutable Japanese to highly expressive Africans. The levels of facial, hand and body gestures vary widely around the world, and can affect how a person is perceived.

- *Gestures* and the use of certain words can also vary, with a gesture or word being acceptable in some cultures but not others.

- *Accompaniments of speech.* These are the responses we give when being spoken to, and are cultural. Argyle tells us that 'black Americans often annoy white interviewers or supervisors by their apparent lack of response while listening' (*ibid.*: 69).

- *Symbolic self-presentation.* While some badges and symbols can seem obscure, their meaning can be very important. I visited China in the 1970s, and all soldiers were supposed to wear the same uniform so that rank was not detectable. But in fact it was easy to tell the officers by the number of pens they carried in their breast pocket. Choice of clothes and designer labels can make very clear statements about what kind of person we are.

- *Rituals.* Argyle warns that it is easy to cause offence by ignoring the rules of local etiquette. 'Pike (1967) reports the case of a missionary who got into difficulties with a cannibal chief because she tried to throw him to the floor (shake hands) and laughed at him (smiled)' (*ibid.*: 69).

There may be a limit to how far you need to go in adhering to local customs and rituals. While a white, western woman reporter would be well advised to wear concealing clothing when reporting from Muslim countries, she would have to ignore many of the local customs with regard to women in order to get the job done. In any case, there are now very few places around the world that have not seen Hollywood movies or western TV programmes, so there is much more awareness of different cultures.

Just as there can be difficulties in the initial meeting, so the conversation or actions of a stranger can be misinterpreted, particularly if that stranger is from a different background. 'When we are communicating with strangers and base our interpretations on our symbolic systems, ineffective communication often occurs' (Gudykunst 1994: 27). Gudykunst goes on to point out that we often don't realise these misinterpretations have actually happened. There are several reasons for such a misinterpretation, including the obvious unfamiliarity of language on at least one side, but it is also possible that one participant does not have the cultural background to understand what the other means (*ibid.*). Once, when in India, my host was in awe of a public building he was showing me. It was an important building, but not particularly imposing. I finally realised that he was incredibly impressed by the wood panelling throughout the building, something I discovered was rare in India. Wood, I was told, was rarely used because it was very expensive, but it might also have been that its upkeep in the hot, damp climate of India would also have been difficult and expensive. Coming from a country where wood is often used to decorate even relatively modest buildings, I had not appreciated its full significance.

Gudykunst gives another example of misinterpretation with the example of a white, middle-class teacher in the USA interacting with an African–American student raised in a lower-class subculture. 'The teacher asks the student a question. In answering the question, the student does not look the teacher in the eye' (*ibid*: 27). He goes on to describe how the teacher would in all probability interpret this as being disrespectful or showing that the student was hiding something, because that is the behavioural norm in middle-class, white America. For a lower-class African–American, however, lowering the eyes would be seen as a mark of respect. This misunderstanding could lead to ineffective communication.

As well as problems with different national cultures, journalists need to be aware that the differences in indigenous culture can be as great. There are huge differences in approach to conversation between different classes, races and genders in the UK. Henley and Kramarae identify a number of different theories of male/female miscommunication (1991: 20) saying the two most influential are: 'Female Deficit' theory, which 'identifies it [women's language] as inferior to "neutral" or men's language and as contributing to women's inferior status' (*ibid.*: 21); and the 'Two Cultures' theory, which suggests that 'Men and women come from different sociolinguistic sub-cultures, which have different conceptions of friendly conversation, different rules for engaging in it and different rules for interpreting it' (*ibid*.: 24). Whatever the cause, both male and female reporters need to be aware of the differences in approach and interpretation that may be needed when talking to someone of the opposite sex, or from a different subculture.

Several areas are identified by psychologists as being the most likely for miscommunication.

Minimal response. The minimal response (the uh-huhs or mm-hmms of conversation) are important for the reporter as they are an encouragement to the interviewee to continue telling the story. But we rely on them in all conversations, and Maltz and Borker say that the positive minimal response (PMR) is used by women to confirm that the speaker can still hold the floor and that the listener is listening. Men use it to confirm support for what is being said. These differences help explain why women often complain that men aren't listening, and why men complain women are always changing their mind. Women saying something of which men disapprove will not get the PMR they require, while men take the PMR to express approval when that is not what the woman meant (*ibid*.: 25). Phrases like 'Oh, I see' are more neutral and can ensure that is the most likely message taken from your PMR.

The use of questions is another area of difference. Women use them to maintain conversation, while men use them to request information. This means that a reporter using questions is more likely to get strict answers from a man but might get more of a conversation from a woman, particularly if the interviewer is a woman. Interviewers of both sexes need to be aware that disguising questions when talking to men might get more of a conversation going, which might get broader and more interesting responses.

The use of names can also tell us a lot about the reporter's approach to the contact. Whether the reporter uses 'Mr Jones' or 'Bill' can say a lot about the class and relative position of the interviewer and interviewee. It is wise to always use the full surname and title with strangers unless invited to do otherwise. The risk is that otherwise some subjects will feel dominated if addressed by their forename. 'Now tell me, Mary, how did it happen?' reduces the status of the elderly person, shop assistant or home carer to whom it was addressed in a way that 'Now tell me, Mrs Jones . . .' does not. The only probable exception is children under

16 years of age. It sounds impossibly formal to address a 12-year-old as Master Smith – better to use a forename.

Ethics

There are a number of ethical issues journalists need to consider when dealing with people. A reporter's dealings with children (or those who are chronologically adults, but are not in any other sense of the word) need to be carried out with the permission of responsible adults and usually with an adult present. This could be a teacher or a parent, but might be a medical worker or some other agent. Even with adults, reporters need to consider carefully the questions they are going to ask and the effect this will have on interviewees.

Intrusion into grief

The Press Complaints Commission (PCC), BBC Editorial Guidelines, Ofcom's code of practice and the National Union of Journalists (NUJ) Code of Conduct all warn against intruding into people's lives while they are grieving. The death of someone close affects us all in slightly different ways, and the reporter should be particularly sensitive when dealing with people in this situation.

The **death knock**, as it is known, is a situation that few reporters relish. There has to be considerable public interest in a story before a reporter should approach a grieving relative. Having said that, relatives are often very keen to talk about their loved one. People in the UK find handling death difficult and consequently tend to ignore people who often want to talk through their loss. They have lost someone close, often suddenly and under tragic circumstances, and want to talk about them. They want to explain to the world what a wonderful person their loved one was, why it is such a disaster that the person died and why they miss them so much. These can be difficult interviews. People talk in clichés, because they are too distraught to think in any other way. The reporter must also be much quieter than normal, allowing people to say what they want in their own way. It is an interview that may take much more time than normal – you can't rush away when you have what you want. Disengagement can take time and tact. You should never do such an interview by phone or e-mail.

Often newsdesks will ask you to get photographs. Always ask permission to borrow photographs and ensure they are returned. Remember that official school photographs may well be copyright of the photographer, so make sure you take some home-produced snaps in case there is a problem later. You won't want to go back again. Accessing their Facebook page is the best way around this problem as you will be able to get a photo that can be easily used on a website, paper or broadcast and that does not require you to return it (although it is still their copyright). If you are unable to access their Facebook page because of the privacy settings, ask a member of the family to e-mail you a picture either from a Facebook page or direct from their photo album.

Door-stepping and harassment

Often when journalists are pursuing major stories, they need to **doorstep** people who are deeply involved in a story but refuse to speak to the media. This can be particularly difficult if many reporters (a press pack) besiege the person's home or workplace. Even someone who is willing to talk can feel intimidated by a pack of 50 or 60 reporters, photographers and film crew all yelling questions, pointing bright TV lights and setting off flash guns. More reprehensible examples cited by The MediaWise Trust, a charity dedicated to supporting the victims of such incidents, have seen scores of reporters walking around a person's garden, looking through windows, yelling through letterboxes and keeping the phone ringing off the hook while the person they are seeking cowers upstairs, scared even to come down. This can be a difficult problem to deal with from both sides. The press want to speak to this person, and the person has the right to refuse.

These days, the police often act as facilitators. The local force press office may arrange a press conference for the person at the centre of attention. Or they may interview and photograph the person themselves, providing a transcript and pictures to the media. While this is bound to raise accusations of the police attempting to control the media, it can also ensure the media at least get something. Inevitably, these solutions are not ideal. All reporters would like to have a one-to-one with the subject of the story. They would also be concerned when they have only the same information as everyone else. But at least it provides everyone with a story in a reasonably civilised manner.

Other options can mean the potential interviewee never talking to anyone, and the press appearing to behave in a manner that is becoming increasingly unacceptable to ordinary people.

Reporters and photographers need to be careful about invading people's private property, something both the PCC and the BBC warn against. The PCC code of practice says that 'It is unacceptable to photograph individuals in private places without their consent.' (www.pcc.org.uk/cop/practice.html). It identifies a private place as somewhere 'where there is a reasonable expectation of privacy' (*ibid.*). This is particularly true of hospitals, according to the PCC Code, but would also obviously apply to homes, hotel rooms and the homes of friends.

Misrepresentation

All UK ethical codes of practice also warn against reporters pretending to be someone else and misrepresenting themselves, unless there is a real public interest. Pretending to be a police officer is specifically illegal, but borrowing a white coat and stethoscope to pretend to be a doctor, for instance, is just as bad, ethically. The same is true of using hidden cameras or microphones. The PCC Code specifically bans the use of 'clandestine listening devices' (*ibid.*) or phone-tapping. The BBC has a long passage in its editorial guidelines about the use of hidden cameras or microphones without consent. The story would have to have a strong public interest defence for it to go ahead.

Protection of sources

When we promise a source that we will not reveal their identity, this is a promise we are obliged to keep. A source may be telling us information that could lose them their job, or even their life. But, of course, you don't have to promise to keep a source's identity confidential if you don't want to, provided you understand that the source may well then refuse to talk to you. This may be acceptable because a story without the name of the source may not be of much use. The only reason for promising confidentiality is because it is the only way you will find out about the story. You will then have to worry about how to source it properly, later on. It is possible that a court in the UK might try to force you to reveal a confidential source, and several British journalists have been punished by the courts for this type of contempt in the past.

The BBC, NUJ and PCC codes of conduct all remind journalists of their obligation to keep confidential sources of information confidential.

In practice, it is extremely rare for a journalist to promise confidentiality to a source because you will need to use their material in the story and will want to name them. If their position is so sensitive that secrecy is imperative, you will need to agree this from the beginning. You will need to be certain that the story is worth it, and for that you will need to get some idea about the story from the contact. Having decided the story is important enough to risk proceeding with a promise to keep the source's identity secret, it is important that you are very careful about collecting documents from the source, or anything that might identify the source. The courts could insist on you handing over this evidence and it would be an offence to destroy or dispose of it.

Notes or evidence from a confidential source should be kept separate from general material so that this information can either be destroyed as soon as the story is published or sent somewhere for safekeeping where you no longer have control over its availability.

Protecting notes, pictures and sources

Just because you haven't promised confidentiality to a source, however, that doesn't mean you don't want to protect information, people or contacts you did not name in the published story. It is possible that the police or others will try to get you to show them notes, pictures or contact names that were not published. You have a duty to the source, not of confidentiality (unless you promised that), but certainly of privacy. If you did not need the information for the story, and therefore did not publish it, you should keep it private. If the police seek to force you to reveal the information, this could compromise your future activities. If people get the idea that journalists freely allow the police to trawl through unpublished material, photographers and reporters may find their safety, and occasionally their lives, put at risk. If every protester or rioter knows the police will be shown unpublished pictures or video, journalists may well find they are not safe to cover such events as they will be seen as police informers. Suzanne Breen, for instance, a reporter in Northern Ireland, was approached by the police seeking mobile phones, computers and other information. She refused to give the information, saying it would have put her life in danger from the Real IRA, who the police were attempting to track and believed had been in contact with Ms Breen. The courts eventually agreed that handing over the material could risk breaching her right to life and security (as identified in the Human Rights Act). Each case is different, and journalists have an obligation – just like all other citizens – to help the police, but you should always think very carefully about your approach if contacted by the police for information. The BBC insists that a court order is obtained before such material will be shown to the police, and others have followed suit. Journalists are not there to act as an investigation unit of the police (although they may do that job on occasion, after exposing wrongdoing).

Security

Some places that you will go to for stories require particular security measures. Coverage of royal visits, for instance, is limited to reporters who are on the royal rota. This system limits the number of reporters and photographers and obliges those given a pass to share their copy and pictures at specified rates. Rota passes for newspapers are arranged through the Newspaper Society (www.newspapersoc.org.uk/Default.aspx?page=1190), and your news editor should have done this if he or she wants you to cover a royal visit. Party conferences and many other big governmental conferences also require you to apply for a press pass some time in advance. For everyday identification, you may already have a press card issued by the UK Press Card Authority. If not, you can apply for one through one of several organisations. The NUJ is one of the scheme's 'gatekeepers' and authorises several thousand cards a year to members, staff and freelance. The Newspaper Society and the Newspaper Proprietors Association also authorise cards to journalists, staff or freelance, working in the newsrooms of their members. It is usually worth ringing the press office of any organisation that is running a conference or meeting, big sporting event or major entertainment event to check whether you need a pass and whether you can have one.

Photographs

No matter what medium you work for, you'll often be required to take photographs or a small video clip for the website, or to support the story in a more traditional format. Modern technology has made it easy for anyone to be able to take a picture – although not necessarily to be a good photographer. However, pointing and shooting to get a picture of a scene or a person shouldn't be beyond most people's capabilities, whether with a mobile phone or a point-and-shoot-style digital camera.

Taking pictures in public can lead to problems, with some people being concerned about their pictures ending up on the news. TV viewers of a recent demonstration will have seen protesters surrounded by much larger crowds of photographers, mostly mobile camera/phone wannabes, all hoping something exciting will happen. So where do they all stand with regard to permissions? Can they use any of the pictures, either for sale or personal use, or do they need permission from everyone involved?

The first thing to check is whether you are taking pictures on public or private ground. If where you are standing is public ground, then you have reasonable freedom to take the pictures. Second, is the subject on public or private land? If public, then no problem, but if the subject is on private land – their home, a hotel or restaurant – they may have a reasonable expectation of privacy and the PCC, Ofcom, the BBC or the courts might well support such a complainant.

Taking pictures of children is not in itself illegal, although there are ethical issues. The PCC, Ofcom or the BBC will prefer you to have parental or school permission, or a very good public interest defence, if a particular child is featured. Taking pictures of adults is fine so long as you are not harassing them by following them or thrusting a lens in their face. Of course, it may well be sensible to move on or stop taking pictures if asked to do so, particularly if such requests are accompanied by threats. However, if you are intending to sell such pictures to an agency, you must remember that their use will be limited to the UK because the law is different elsewhere and may well require signed permission. If you want to sell such pictures to a potential international audience, then get the subjects to sign a model release form. Of course, they may well seek a fee for this.

There is also a risk that using such pictures will be subject to the Data Protection Act, as it could be conceived as processing personal data, although no such case has yet been brought before the courts. While this is unlikely for news use, it does explain why Google's Street View pictures automatically pixelate people's faces. If you are taking a picture for a feature, or intend to keep it on file to use again, you should bear that in mind.

Security and terrorism are probably the biggest problem facing the photographer today. First, there is a long list of places where it is prohibited to take pictures that might be of use to an enemy: defence establishments, airports and munitions stores are top of the list. What sort of picture is of use to an enemy? It's difficult to say and would be up to the courts to decide, but an accusation from a police officer and confiscation of equipment, followed weeks later by an apologetic letter withdrawing charges and offering the return of your gear, can be just as damaging to your livelihood as a court case.

The Terrorism Act 2000 and the Counter-Terrorism Act 2008 are now perhaps the most widely used legislation to attempt to prevent photographers from taking pictures. The Terrorism Act section 43 allows police to stop and search people they suspect of terrorist activity. This could include taking photographs of targets, but the law does not specifically allow the confiscation of equipment unless the officer believes it to be evidence of an offence. Section 44 of the same Act allows police to stop and search anyone without cause provided there is an authorisation from a senior officer. Following complaints about limitations on photographers, Home Office junior minister Shahid Malik told parliament in 2009: 'I would like to make it clear that section 44 does not prohibit the taking of photographs . . . The police may stop and search someone who is taking photographs in an authorised area, just as they may stop and search any member of the public, but the powers should not be targeted on photographers.' After several papers started blanking out pictures of police officers, the Home Office issued new guidance to police pointing out that although the Counter-Terrorism Act 2008 made it an offence to elicit and publish information about a police constable, newspapers should be more relaxed: as Mr Malik stated, 'A photograph of a police officer may fall within the scope of the offence, but would do so in only limited circumstances. The important thing is that the photographs would have to be of a kind likely to provide practical assistance to terrorists, and the person taking or providing the photograph would have to have no reasonable excuse, such as responsible journalism, for taking it. I want to be clear about this: the offence does not capture an innocent tourist taking a photograph of a police officer, or a journalist photographing police officers as part of his or her job.'

Otherwise, taking pictures of street scenes or incidents is reasonably straightforward.

Filming road accidents or other incidents involving injuries or death for broadcast or publication may bring yet more limitations. Both the PCC and Ofcom have upheld complaints where someone injured in a road accident was identifiable as they were loaded into an ambulance for treatment. Although coverage of such incidents was identified as being in the public interest, the identification of the victims was said to be an intrusion into their privacy. Matters of health are identified as sensitive personal data by the Data Protection Act, and while this has not yet been upheld by the courts, there seems to be a growing view among the public that their identity should not be revealed automatically.

If you borrow pictures or video, make sure you get a copyright release form. Anyone who takes a picture or video owns the copyright to those pictures, and it is as well to get written permission to use them or you could face a hefty bill. Most newsrooms carry such forms, and you should always have one or two in the car or tucked in your notebook.

8
Getting the story

You've identified your story, you've decided where to go and who to see in order to get the information – now you're all ready to get out there and nail that exclusive.

Taking notes

It's not much good doing a brilliant interview if you can't remember a word of it once you step outside the door. Some form of system is required to ensure you are able to remember what was said, in order to write the story, and also to be able to prove what was said in case of later dispute. A court hearing a defamation action, for instance, might require evidence that the interviewee said what you claimed. More routinely, your editor might also require such evidence. If the interview is for broadcast, then there will be some sort of tape, whether audio or video, and this may be sufficient for both the court and your editor, but good notes are still important and a full shorthand note is even better. Make sure original tapes, of contentious interviews at least, are kept for a minimum of a year. Broadcasters are obliged to keep tapes of transmissions, but not for long enough to protect against a defamation action.

Because recording is so easy these days, it is often tempting for a reporter to record any interview. While small handheld recorders can be useful for a one-to-one, in-depth interview, they are of much less use for short interviews with a number of people. A reporter's shorthand notebook is still the best and most efficient way of taking notes for research.

Recorders are prone to run out of batteries at the vital moment, or run out of space. They often fail to pick up the sound of the interviewee unless you use a proper tie-clip microphone. I once interviewed the

Swedish Press Ombudsman in Stockholm using a tape recorder. We were alone in a quiet room and I anticipated no trouble, although fortunately I stuck with my habit of using a notebook as well. On leaving the office, I stopped at a café for a coffee and checked the tape. All her softly spoken words were merely a dull, barely audible fluttering. I could not make out a single word. My notes were just about good enough to give me what I wanted, fortunately, because it was not possible to repeat the interview.

Often you will not be allowed to use a recorder while on a story; they are illegal in UK courts and many other public bodies ban their use. In any case, they are rarely any good at big meetings because of the noise. If you must use one at press conferences, put it in front of the PA speakers, not the actual person speaking. The final nail in the coffin of recorders as far as I am concerned is transcription. In order to write your copy, you need to listen to the whole tape – often stopping and starting it in order to transcribe choice quotes. If the interview or press conference you attended lasted 30 minutes, you can guarantee it will take at least 45 minutes to write the story. Using a notebook, the whole story could be written within ten minutes of finishing the interview. A notebook is easy to use, doesn't run out of batteries, is cheap and is unlikely to be stolen. Even if you lose it, it's probably not a disaster (unless you've got unwritten stories in it). Even if it is lost, it's likely still to be where you lost it – who would take a notebook?

Using a notebook is simple. Write the date and the names of the people at the meeting at the top of a clean page together with a note of the story, and then start writing notes to remind you of what is happening. Try to take verbatim notes of what people are saying. Most reporters develop some form of speed writing or learn shorthand.

Teeline shorthand is very popular as it is relatively easy to learn and can allow a proficient reporter to write at up to 150–160 words a minute. Most trainee reporters are expected to reach 100 words a minute: this is the speed the National Council for the Training of Journalists insists on for its exams, and is the speed most editors require from new staff. Most university or further education courses that claim to prepare students for a career as a newspaper reporter will teach shorthand in some form.

The broadcast industry is less insistent on shorthand than the newspaper industry, and most training courses for broadcast journalists no longer include it on the curriculum. Most broadcast interviews are recorded, and broadcasters tend to produce only short reports of courts, council and parliament. Even a major court case is likely to be no more than a five-minute package on the main news bulletin – something a good reporter can easily cope with using their own speed writing, particularly as interviews are videoed or recorded and so do not need to be noted.

Shorthand is particularly useful for a new reporter, who is still not certain what will be used in the report, or for a reporter covering court, council and other stories that are likely to require lengthy reports and a guarantee that you can recall what was said, months or even years later. Notes can be taken during debates or throughout the interview or press conference, then during the boring bits, or in breaks, the reporter can quickly read through the notes and mark the interesting passages. This early editing of what has been said can really speed up the writing process. Many reporters draw a vertical line down the page, writing only on the right-hand side, leaving the left-hand column to make annotations. New reporters and students find note-taking difficult and so often abandon it to concentrate on conducting the interview. This is a waste of time because, of course, they cannot remember the interview afterwards because they have become so flustered. Don't be afraid to take your time and write down the notes you need. On the other hand, be careful not to take the opposite approach and concentrate so hard on note-taking that you forget to listen to the answers given to your questions. Many editors complain that newly recruited students concentrate too hard on their shorthand, to the detriment of the story.

It is important to remember to ask the interviewee before starting the interview if it is OK to take notes or to record what they are saying. In legal terms, what the interviewee says is their copyright and we can only note or record it with their permission on the understanding that it will be used in a news item or feature. Should you accidentally record someone who had not given permission, but there was a public interest reason to use the material, you might get away with its use. 'This defence is not set out in the CPDA [Copyright, Designs and Patents Act] 1988 but the courts have shown a willingness, in exceptional cases, to allow a defendant to avail himself of it' (Carey 1999: 106). John Major, while he was Prime Minister, famously referred to some of his Cabinet colleagues as 'bastards' while waiting in a TV studio for an interview to start. While the interview had not started, recording was continuing from a previous interview. This story was clearly in the public interest and was widely published.

Good note-taking is vital to ensure the accuracy of your stories, in terms of both using accurate quotes and noting down names, addresses and any figures accurately. Always double-check names and figures with the person concerned.

Actually taking notes during an interview is not easy. A notebook can be intimidating for an interviewee not used to talking to the media. Slamming your notebook down on the desk and leaning over it while you scribble down everything they say is going to make them far more cautious. Sit back in your seat and rest your pad discreetly on your lap. Crossing your legs can allow you to slant the notebook towards your hand and away from the interviewee, so that you can make full notes without being too obvious about it, allowing the interviewee to relax.

The same applies to recorders, whether for note-taking or broadcast. Always ask if you can use the equipment and discuss with the interviewee where to put it. Cameras require the same courtesy, although since it is much more obvious what you are doing, it's easier to ask permission.

The news theatres

Courts, councils, inquests, press conferences and parliament are all routine theatres of news and each offers its own particular challenge. It is likely that, if you are working on a local paper or radio station in the UK, you will regularly attend court or council and the occasional inquest, although many commentators claim that newspapers are covering courts and council much less than in the past (Davis 2008; Banks and Hanna 2009).

Court

There are two main types of criminal court that you are likely to end up covering: magistrates' courts and Crown court. Magistrates' courts are presided over by three Justices of the Peace (JPs) – lay persons appointed by the Lord Chancellor. There are about 25,000 JPs in the country working part-time (usually two days a week) in about 1000 courts (Crone 1995: 78), usually situated in larger towns. Because these JPs are not lawyers, they are assisted and advised by the court clerk, who is a qualified solicitor or barrister. He or she sits immediately in front of the JPs and ensures the smooth running of the court. Some larger magistrates' courts in big metropolitan areas are staffed by full-time stipendiary magistrates. These are qualified lawyers and generally sit alone, while lay magistrates sit as a committee of three. The magistrates' courts deal with summary offences, such as careless driving, speeding or common assault, or what are known as either-way offences. These are cases that can be tried in either a Magistrates' court or a Crown court. Normally the choice will be that of the accused, who may wish to be tried by judge and jury. Sometimes the magistrates' court may transfer a case to Crown court because a Crown court can give harsher sentences. A magistrates' court is limited to imposing a fine of £5000 or a jail sentence of six months for a single offence (*ibid.*: 79).

The magistrates' court also deals with bail applications and transfers to Crown court. When a person is charged with a serious offence, this must be heard in the Crown court. The magistrates' court usually hears the transfer procedure in private, and the only way a reporter can hear about it is by reading the order of transfer on the court notice board.

If the defendant is charged with a serious offence, the police may want to remand the suspect in custody. They must bring the person before the next available magistrates' court, where an application for bail can be made. A magistrates' court can refuse to allow bail, holding the person on remand, if there are substantial grounds for believing the accused will:

- fail to appear at court in answer to bail; or
- commit further offences while on bail; or
- interfere with witnesses or obstruct the course of justice.

(Carey 1999: 27)

Most cases before magistrates are the minor day-to-day iniquities of modern urban living – motoring offences, drunkenness, small-time violence and petty theft.

Only if the offence is indictable does it go before the Crown court. There are three types of judge on each Crown court circuit. High Court judges, who should be addressed as 'Mr Justice Jones' or 'Mrs Justice Jones'; circuit judges, who are addressed in reports as 'Judge John Jones' or 'Judge Joan Jones'; and recorders or assistant recorders, who must be barristers or solicitors of at least ten years' experience, and who are called 'the Recorder', 'Mr John Smith' or 'Mrs Joan Smith'. Barristers are usually the only people with right of audience in the Crown court, and all cases are heard before a jury of 12 people.

The High Court judges sit in the more important centres and must hear the most serious cases, such as murders. They may also try cases of rape, unlawful killing and other serious crimes. Their wigs and robes, recently brought a little more up-to-date, are still very traditional and can be a little intimidating. They are designed to represent the full majesty and authority of the crown, not something to be done in jeans and a tee-shirt, so that the court and its business are treated with respect.

If you are covering a case in the magistrates' court, you will first need to find out in which court your case is being heard. Most court buildings contain several courtrooms and you will have to choose which to attend. In days past, newspapers might have had several reporters at court, but it is more likely these days that you will have to go to court to get the court list (unless your local court is kind enough to post it on each week) and study it to see which, if any, cases you want to report. Most cases are listed in advance, but of course some involve incidents that happened overnight. If there has been a major incident, then you might need to turn up at court, otherwise a sympathetic worker in the court clerk's office might ring you, provided you have kept up close contact.

The government has agreed that it is important for the media to have access to justice, and so Her Majesty's Courts Services (HMCS) has developed a protocol for sharing magistrates' court lists with local newspapers. This says that court registers should be provided by e-mail without charge. If e-mail is impossible, the newspaper can collect a list or pay the cost of postage, but not be charged for copies. These lists should include defendant's name, age, alleged offence and address. It should also include details of any reporting restrictions. Newspapers should destroy the lists after six months and be responsible about their use and not pass the lists to third parties.

Crown court lists are available over the internet from CourtServe (www.courtserve.net). This is subscriber-based, but the fees are modest (£75 a year for the main service at time of writing).

It can be tempting to try to cover courts without actually attending, but the law requires that, if you cover a court case, you do so in a fair and balanced way, and this is difficult to do with a bare-bones report of the charge, verdict and sentence. Fewer newspapers use news reports from magistrates' courts these days, and radio reporters are rarely there. However, an interesting-sounding case will come up occasionally. Most magistrates' courts have a press bench and you should find out where it is if you don't already know. It is permissible to come and go during a trial, but it is polite to wait for a suitable occasion – a gap in proceedings or the end of a case. Sitting at the press bench offers no direct benefits, but it does allow the court to know the press is there, and if the clerk decides to offer you some papers or copies of material the court has seen, it is easier for them to do so.

Once in court, you should identify who is sitting on the bench. Once the case starts, the name of the defendant and the charges will be read out. You should confirm these against your court list. The prosecution will then outline its case, calling witnesses as required. Once finished, the defence can either claim no case has been made out, or, more usually, present its case, again calling such witnesses as required. Both sides then wind up and the magistrates decide on their verdict. If it is 'guilty', they will then need to decide on a sentence. They may then ask the defence to make a plea on sentence and a further short speech will be made, perhaps supported by witnesses such as a social worker, priest or teacher to give a character reference. The sentence will then usually be passed.

Occasionally, after a court case, someone such as the defendant or a relative of the defendant might ask you not to cover a case. Some of these pleas can be heart-rending, but all you can do is say you will pass the information on to the editor. The same is true if you are threatened. In both instances you must inform the editor that you were approached, and tell him or her what was said. It is the editor's decision whether to use copy or not.

If it is the magistrates who ask you not to cover the case, that is different. Magistrates can instruct the media not to identify participants under the age of 18, but any other attempt to postpone reports or exclude the press can normally be made only if there is a risk of prejudicing the trial. If you are excluded, ask for the section of the Act being applied and tell your editor immediately.

Once the trial is over, you will need to write up your story. In order to qualify for privilege – the system that allows you to report what was said in courts or council provided your report is fair, accurate and contemporaneous – you must publish as soon as possible. If the court case goes on for several days, you must ensure you continue to cover it, in order to report it fairly. Reporting the first day, when the prosecution case is put, missing the next two days and then reporting the prosecution winding up and verdict would make for an unfair report and put you at risk of contempt proceedings.

There is no law preventing you from interviewing participants in trials once they are over and only the normal rules of sensitivity apply.

Interviewing jurors at Crown court can be more delicate. It is illegal to ask them about their deliberations and what took place in the jury room while they were making their decision. To report one juror saying that another said, 'I knew he were a wrong'un from the start – his eyes were too close together' would be an offence, while reporting on whether the juror enjoyed the experience of deciding a fellow human's fate might not be. Some lawyers believe that naming a juror could put a reporter at risk of contempt of court, as it could put a juror at risk of intimidation or attack (Welsh et al. 2007: 74). There have been no prosecutions that I am aware of, but on the other hand, such interviews are rare.

The Crown court is altogether more daunting than the magistrates' court. Trials go on much longer, for a start, requiring careful concentration. It may be that you will have to pop out several times to transmit material to your newsdesk, especially if you are working to a busy broadcast newsdesk where you are providing regular updates for bulletins. Working closely with your producer in these circumstances, to ensure nothing of importance is missed while you do a live report, is vital.

Again you should use the press bench in order to get a good seat, but one where constant comings and goings can be more easily masked. Remember that you should be respectful in court and avoid attracting the attention of the judge. Turn off your mobile phone or switch it to vibrate-only mode. Make sure it is set to divert calls to your voicemail so that you can pick up the message at a more convenient time. Some of the big trials see so much media interest these days that the courts sometimes set up special rooms. The Harold Shipman trial (in 2000) was held at Preston Crown court, as was the trial of Jon Venables and Robert Thompson for the murder of James Bulger (1993). Both saw hundreds of reporters in town. Special press rooms were set up so that media reporters could watch the trial on closed-circuit TV and had suitable places for reporters to write up copy, record audio or produce pieces to camera. It can sometimes be advantageous to work from here rather than in the court. Keeping contact with newsdesk is easier, you can use your laptop and you may still be able to carry on blogging or twittering throughout the case if you need to – something you can't do within the court itself.

It is illegal to take pictures or use tape machines inside the court – anyway, even if you could tape-record the proceedings, it is unlikely that the quality would be good enough to use. You must rely on your notebook and shorthand. Working in the precincts of any court with a still or video camera is against the law. Taking pictures or filming needs to be done away from the court. You might get away with doing it on the opposite side of the street with the court in the background, but it is probably better to try to find another building close by that is similar in design to the court, and to film outside there.

Contempt

Any attempt to interfere with the courts and the administration of justice in the UK is called *contempt of court*. This is taken very seriously by the courts and offenders face large fines or even prison. The law in the UK takes the view that the accused is innocent until proven guilty, and that a fair trial requires that the courts and jury have not previously been prejudiced against the defendant. This is reinforced by the Human Rights Act, which says that people have the right to be presumed innocent, have a fair trial, and not be punished except by the law. All signatories to the European Convention of Human Rights or the UN Declaration on Human Rights support the right of a fair trial under the law. However, this is interpreted in different ways in different countries. Some see media coverage as unfair and an additional punishment, and it's certainly true that it's something of a lottery as to whether your case is covered in the media or not. In the UK, however, and other countries with similar traditions, it is viewed as important that justice is seen to be done. We should know who has been arrested, what they have been arrested for, and what happened to them in court. We need to know these details without risking prejudicing their trial by presenting information that would suggest they were either guilty or not guilty. It has been agreed over the years that the easiest way to do this is to prevent the media from publishing anything other than standard details about alleged offenders, such as the fact of the arrest, the suspect's name, their general background, and broad details of the charge. You must not mention whether the accused has a criminal record; any facts linking the suspect to the crime; any facts that will be used in evidence; or whether the accused has a criminal record, background or criminal contacts.

There are now two offences of contempt: in the UK:

- strict liability – as defined by the Contempt of Court Act 1981;
- the old common law offence of contempt.

Strict liability is defined by the Contempt of Court Act. It means that the prosecution no longer needs to prove that the defendant intended to prejudice the trial, as would be the case under common law contempt. The prosecutor only needs to prove that there was a substantial risk of prejudice in 'active' proceedings. In the Harold Shipman trial, for instance, a radio DJ broadcasting in the Preston area, where the trial was being held, said on air during the trial that Shipman was 'as guilty as sin' and should own up in order to save the cost of the trial. He was obliged to face the court and was given a strict dressing-down by the judge. Fortunately, no members of the jury had heard the radio programme, otherwise punishment might have been much more severe. Proceedings are normally considered to be active once someone has been arrested or a warrant for arrest has been issued (see *Press Gazette* 4/2/00: 1). A recent change in practice means that reporters can now attend some family courts that decide such matters as custody of children and adoption. At the time of writing, this was a very new change and it was still not clear what limitations would be put on coverage. Generally the child's identity should be protected and the courts will seek to protect their privacy. However, the courts have said that celebrity will not by itself guarantee anonymity.

Reporting restrictions

There are a range of other restrictions on reporting crime and the courts, all aimed at ensuring defendants receive a fair trial and that juries are not unduly influenced. In addition, there are a number of laws designed to protect minors and other vulnerable groups in society, as well as a significant number of laws designed to support the state in the fight against terrorism, which offer protection to witnesses and law officers. The Judicial Studies Board in cooperation with the Newspaper Society and the Society of Editors has recently produced an updated guide to reporting restrictions, and it is well worth getting hold of a copy of this (www.jsboard.co.uk/downloads/crown_court_reporting_restrictions_021009. pdf) as it gives up-to-date guidance on hearings from which the public are excluded, automatic reporting restrictions, discretionary reporting restrictions and additional matters relating to court reporting.

Council

Council meetings are also set-piece situations. There are several types of council meeting in England and Wales, and you may attend all of them at some time in your career. Scotland and Wales have their own assemblies and so much of the local government system is structured differently.

County councils control the English counties. There are also district councils that control parts of counties, unitary authorities (they have the powers of counties and districts) and London borough councils. There is also the Common Council of the City of London and the Council of the Isles of Scilly. In Wales there are county councils or county borough councils.

County councils are traditionally responsible for services such as transport, education, social services and the fire brigade. The police come under the auspices of their own Police Authority, a mix of local authority representatives and independent people appointed on the authority of the Home Office. District or borough councils traditionally control such activities as housing, planning, roads, street lighting, waste collection, parks and gardens, and leisure activities. The National Health Service and hospitals are administered by health trusts. Parish councils (or community councils in Wales) are the smallest councils, and control small amounts of spending on local activities.

According to the Local Government Act 2000, all councils have the power to do anything they think will promote or improve the economic, social or environmental wellbeing of their area. Every local authority is obliged to prepare a 'community strategy' that explains how they intend to do this.

Local authorities are made up of councillors – local people elected by local people to run the business of the council. They are elected every four years and are usually members of one of the main political parties. Occasionally some councillors are independent or belong to a local 'ratepayers' party. There are three election methods. In one, all the councillors retire every four years and new elections are held. In the next, half the councillors retire every two years and new elections are held; in the third, elections are held every year other than the third year and one-third of the councillors retire each year.

The Local Government Act 2000 introduced a number of changes in the way local government works. Rather than have committees and sub-committees overseeing the council's work with regular council meetings to review it, the local council changed in 2003 to a cabinet style of operation with a 'local authority executive'. This means that there is either:

- a directly elected mayor who will appoint an executive of two or more councillors;
- a council leader elected from and by the elected councillors with an executive of two or more councillors appointed either by the leader or by the local authority;
- a directly elected mayor and a council manager appointed by the local authority; or
- an executive elected directly by the electors to either specific or non-specific executive posts.

If a local authority chooses any style of executive other than a council leader, then a referendum is required of local electors. No executive will be allowed to have more than ten members, including the mayor or leader.

The executive will then have its decisions overseen by an overview and scrutiny committee. This will have the power to recommend either that the unimplemented decision be reconsidered by the person who made it, or that the decision should be reviewed by the local authority. Neither the overview committee nor the executive is required to apply section 15 of the Local Government and Housing Act 1989, which makes it a duty to allocate seats to political parties in a balanced way.

In practice, this is likely to mean that the council's policies and actions will be controlled by the mayor, the executive, a member of the executive or a committee of the executive, or by an officer of the authority. The executive can decide which of its meetings to hold in private subject to regulations issued by the Secretary of State.

Whichever of these options the local authority opts for, the councillors will then meet about four times a year to oversee and scrutinise the work of the mayor or council leader and his or her cabinet. The meetings are chaired by the local authority chairman or vice-chairman, neither of whom is allowed to be in the executive.

Each local authority is obliged to draw up a code of conduct and have a standards committee that promotes and maintains high standards of conduct. There is also a Standards Board for England and Commission for Local Administration in Wales, which monitors and advises on standards of conduct in their areas. They have ethical standards officers to investigate complaints and monitor local authority conduct.

Each local authority has to keep a register of members' interests, and this is available for scrutiny by any member of the public. Any local government reporter is going to need to visit this register for a serious session.

Councils are also obliged by the Audit Commission Act (England) 1998 and the Public Audit Act (Wales) 2000 to allow local people, including journalists, access to their books every year (usually in August). This allows them to examine invoices, private finance initiative (PFI) agreements, bills and receipts. The council must give 14 days' notice of when the accounts are open to scrutiny, and is not allowed merely to provide spreadsheets or lists, but must give full access. Journalists and the public can copy such documents, although the council may apply a reasonable charge for this. It is a criminal offence for a council employee to obstruct anyone exercising this right. A list of councils and when their books are on display can be found at www.orchardnews.com/accounts.htm.

Elections

Elections make for good stories. More and more people are becoming cynical about politics, and local elections are not taken very seriously, despite the fact that local councils deal with millions of pounds of taxpayers' money. Nevertheless, reporting on elections, whether local or general, is still important. Newspapers have a pretty free hand about the way they cover elections provided they don't print false statements. They can be partisan and decide to support any party they choose. They are not obliged to give equal coverage to the various parties, although many local papers choose to do so as a matter of policy.

Broadcasters do have to be fair (Representation of the People Act 1983). The law says that they should give balanced coverage to the various candidates over the period of the election. This also applies to their websites, but not to the websites of newspapers, which are regulated by the Press Complaints Commission (PCC) rather than Ofcom, the broadcast regulator.

Election coverage can be fun. You will need to keep in touch with the various candidates, and in a parliamentary general election there are likely to be daily briefings by the parties at national and local level. Each party will try to lead the agenda – to control what is published or broadcast – but it is important that you try to ensure the candidates are obliged to keep to the issues you think are important. This is particularly true of local reporting, where the big issue for your constituency may be very different from the line the main parties are attempting to follow nationally.

The actual election count will usually be held on the night of the election. Most polling ends at 10 pm, and the ballot boxes are swiftly whisked off to a central point in the constituency to be counted. This may be the hall of a local school or a community hall of some kind. The introduction of proportional representation and party list seats for Northern Ireland, Scotland and Wales makes some of our elections a little more complicated, but most are straightforward, first-past-the-post elections in which each elector gets one vote and has to choose one candidate. First, ballot papers are sorted by candidate, and any in which the voter's intentions are not clear are removed – there are usually only a few of these 'spoilt' papers. Then they are sorted by choice of candidate and bundled together in hundreds. It is then relatively easy to count the bundles and declare a winner. If the election is a one-horse race, that is often obvious from the start as the bundles are in plain view.

If the votes are very close, a recount might be called. Initially this would just mean counting the bundles, but could eventually mean checking each bundle to ensure there are no wrong votes and that each bundle is complete. No matter how close the vote, it is unlikely that a compact urban parliamentary seat will take longer than three or four hours to count and recount, and many parliamentary seats vie with each other to be the first to announce their result at a general election, with several declaring around 11 pm. These results are pounced upon by the statisticians and fed into computers to try to determine the likely national position.

Each parliamentary seat announces its votes straight after the count. The acting returning officer (usually the council chief executive or a similar senior local government officer) will announce the result in the hall or on the town hall balcony (should they have such a luxury). The results are then pinned up at key points around the town.

Commercial organisations

Business reporting is important at local and national levels. People need jobs, and business is the heart of the economy. As the credit crunch has shown, it is business that provides many of the wealth-creating jobs on which we all depend, and so the health of a particular business can be paramount to a local or national community. The mergers of many banks, the slowdown of car-building and the closure of numerous small businesses over the past couple of years have been big news and received headline coverage in newspapers and on TV. A story involving a major international company and potential financial hardship for thousands, possibly for years, shows the importance of keeping in touch with the business world.

Each business is owned by shareholders and run by a board of directors, chosen by the shareholders at the annual meeting. A director is normally a person with considerable business experience, who is seen by the shareholders as the right person to decide company policy and strategy. A director may well be on the board of several companies.

Shareholders own the company by buying shares. These may be publicly quoted and are then bought and sold on the Stock Exchange. The price of shares will rise and fall depending on the performance of the company and the general estimate of future profitability. Companies that are seen to have a bright future, even if they are not presently profitable, may have a high value. The dotcom companies of the late 1990s fitted this pattern. Of course, the reverse can be true, and that is what happened in the credit crunch. Banks that were highly profitable, through selling mortgages to people who would not normally be offered them for fear they could not repay, found their profits falling as their new clients defaulted on the loans. These 'toxic debts', as they were described, had been bundled with other loans and sold in packages as bonds to the worldwide banking market. Eventually banks were afraid to lend to each other for fear that the borrower would go bust because of the amount of debt it was owed that would not be repaid. Fears for their future profitability saw share prices plunge at the same time as lending froze, preventing normal business from taking place.

Company directors are paid a fee for their services. Some directors are described as non-executive. These are directors who do not work full-time for the company. They attend board meetings and give the company the benefit of their experience and contacts. Many a former Minister of the Crown has become a director of several companies after leaving office because companies welcome the chance to have a director so much in the know. Parliament's standards committee has strict rules about how soon ministers may join the board of a company they have dealt with while in office in order to minimise corruption, but following the expenses scandal there is to be a further review and a likely tightening of the rules.

Other directors are employed full-time by the company. These include the managing director, and there may be other directors such as the sales director, finance director or marketing director. The board is led by the chairman, who can be either executive or non-executive. Most large and even medium-sized companies these days have a press office, or at least a communications department, and they are often the best starting point for enquiries. It is their job to know who to contact in the company to get the best quality information, and they are often able to do a lot of your basic research for you. As always, you need to remember they are only telling you what is good for (or at least not damaging to) their company. These are not the only people to approach, and there is nothing to stop you contacting anyone in a company who can give you what you need. Individuals are not obliged to talk to you, and might refer you to the press office, but it may well be worth trying them first.

Companies are obliged by law to lodge details of their financial dealings and their directors on an annual basis with Companies House. These records can be searched by anyone to gather basic details of the company's financial situation, what it owns and who its directors are. Directors must also give their private address. Companies House is on the web (www.companieshouse.gov.uk) and you can access very basic details there as well as a list of disqualified directors who are forbidden by law to hold any future directorships.

Companies that have failed are often insolvent – they have gone bust. These insolvencies are also listed on the web, and this site can be worth checking from time to time: www.insolvency.gov.uk.

Companies hold annual shareholders' meetings to report on how business is going and to elect or re-elect directors. Normally these are dull affairs, but occasionally, if the company is going through a difficult patch, they may be worth attending. The company is not obliged to let you in, but you can still doorstep the meeting in order to try to talk to disaffected shareholders.

The company also issues an annual report and you should be able to get hold of a copy of this. It will contain the annual accounts as well as reports from the chairman of the board and the managing director.

Quangos and NGOs

Quasi-autonomous, non-governmental organisations (quangos) or non-departmental public bodies (NDPBs) are independent agencies set up by the government to deal with a range of matters, from regulation to the arts. They have committees of lay people appointed by government departments, and many are paid a fee for their work. There are several types of quango, including executive bodies such as the Arts Council and the Environment Agency; advisory bodies such as the Advisory Committee on Historic Wreck Sites; and tribunals. As a system, NDPBs are politically sensitive and are often accused of being wasteful or being a 'gravy train' for faithful supporters. There were 790 NDPBs with more than 92,695 staff in 2008 (www.civilservice.gov.uk/Assets/PublicBodies2008_tcm6-6429.pdf).

These quangos range from the Advertising Standards Authority, to the Hearing Aid Council, to the Zoos Forum. Many are involved with health or education. Many of the roles that used to be carried out by local authorities are now dealt with by quangos. These include the police authorities, health boards and various regulatory bodies that oversee transport, water, electricity and gas. There are far too many quangos to list here, but there is a full list in the *Public Bodies 2008* report referred to above; this and reports for other years are held at www.civilservice.gov.uk/about/work/codes/ndpbs.aspx.

Whatever story you are working on, there may well be a quango with some official involvement, whether it's health, water or fuel, all with potential contacts to comment on the story. Usually those serving on quangos are particularly knowledgeable about the subject and so, although they may not be directly involved, they can be useful sources.

Non-governmental organisations (NGOs) include charities, campaign groups and trade unions. Again, they are worth keeping in contact with as they have special knowledge and information, and are also very useful for quotes about matters within their particular interest.

Charitable and voluntary organisations

When people are not at work, they are often carrying out some sort of charitable or voluntary work. This could cover anything from a fund-raising dinner for a local school to a meeting of the local train-spotters' club; or from the London Marathon to an amateur dramatics club. All are potential story sources – leisure activities play an important part in community life. Most charities and voluntary organisations are run by a committee of enthusiasts with a chairman, a secretary, a treasurer and other such officers as are felt necessary. A football club might have a fixtures secretary, for instance, while a photographic society might well have a competitions officer. The committee, usually of six to ten people, is elected at the annual meeting (often called the Annual General Meeting or AGM) by those members of the organisation who bother to turn up. Most annual meetings are dull affairs and it is usually sufficient to ask the secretary to send you a list of the officers elected after the meeting and details of any business.

There are several ways of generating contact with such groups. If you do not already have a record, you can find the names of the secretaries of many local voluntary groups and charities by visiting the local library. Noticeboards and the voluntary register can often provide the vital contact. The Citizens Advice Bureau sometimes has names as well. Some charities and voluntary groups can be tracked down through their website. Although these are usually national, if you are after a local contact they offer a useful starting point.

Trade unions

Trade unions are national collectives of workers in the same trade or profession, working together to protect and advance their working conditions and rates of pay. Only by combining together can most workers gather sufficient bargaining power to convince an employer that they should have better working conditions or wages. Journalists belong to the National Union of Journalists (NUJ).

Although most unions are nationally based, for many people their main contact is with the workplace collective. This may be a local branch or shop (for members of the NUJ this is called, rather quaintly, a chapel). These are led by a shop steward or branch committee. An NUJ chapel is led by a father or mother of chapel (F/MoC). Workplace collectives are often gathered into branches, although if the employer is big enough, that workplace might also be a branch. This means that most unions have a three-tier structure: local (led by a shop steward and works committee); regional or district branch (led by a branch secretary, chair and committee); and national (led by the president, general secretary and national executive committee).

A considerable number of Acts of Parliament have been produced over the past 150 years to restrain trade unions or offer them privileges. The law lays down labyrinthine conditions on how unions should control their activities: who can be president or general secretary, the conditions that apply to this, how many people can picket outside a workplace, and so on.

But the main rights are: the right to belong to a trade union; the right for that union to seek recognition and bargaining rights with the employer; and the right of people to withdraw their labour (go on strike) in pursuit of a grievance over working conditions or pay. Essentially, at present, if trade union members in an identifiable workplace vote by a majority in a secret ballot to go on strike, that strike is legal and the employer is not allowed to sack anyone who fails to turn up to work.

Most trade unions are much more media-savvy these days than used to be the case, and their national office will have a website and a press office. Some of the bigger unions will also have large regional offices, particularly in areas where many of their members work.

Often the local union officers in a workplace are volunteers: activists who work in the factory or office and are members of the local committee. These are the people you really need to know, but they tend to change regularly, moving to other jobs or different activities. If there is a regional office, it is more likely that this will be staffed by full-time officers, employed and paid by the union as experts in trade union organisation to support the lay activists. These change less often and so should also be in your contact book. The national office of a union with a particular influence may also be a regular contact. If you work at a major seaport, for instance, you may want to keep in touch with the press office of the National Union of Rail, Maritime and Transport Workers.

Press conferences

Press conferences are called by a number of organisations: a local council wanting to announce its new anti-litter policy; a company launching a new product; or a campaign group launching a crusade. Some press conferences are regular briefings, such as 10 Downing Street's daily briefings. Some are called just for a specific event – a product launch or a policy announcement. Attendance at press conferences is not obligatory and it is up to your news editor to decide if you should cover a particular press conference. If your news editor does send you, then it is important to make the best use of the conference to try to get your questions answered.

Making promises

Occasionally a contact will ask you to do something for them. If it is just a question of sending a copy of the paper, then you can either agree or make an excuse. If you promise something to a contact, though, you *must* carry it out. How can you expect them to trust you over something important, such as protecting a source, if you can't even be trusted to keep a promise to send them a paper?

Other requests may not be so simple. Missing out people's names from stories, not carrying stories, or erasing quotes given and taken in good faith are all things that you may be asked to do. Never promise to do what is asked. Say you will raise it with the editor and that is up to him or her. Editors are there to take some of the flack. If you are propositioned in such a way, report it immediately to your news editor or editor and then follow their instructions.

Occasionally you may be asked to provide a copy of what you have written for the interviewee's perusal before publication. While reading someone's quotes over the phone to them may on occasion be justifiable, providing a copy of what is to appear in the paper is never right. Apart from anything else, no-one can ever resist the chance to treat it as proof copy and to ask for alterations. Again, you should refer such requests to the editor, pointing out to whoever asked you for the copy that it is not policy and could get you the sack. It is becoming the norm these days for celebrities to demand copy approval before granting an interview. Again, this is a decision your editor will need to take: is the publication going to act as a PR arm for the celebrity or risk losing the interview? The biggest magazines, newspapers and TV can afford to refuse, but many of the smaller ones often feel obliged to accept.

Pictures

It is also important that a good reporter thinks of picture ideas. When working with photographers, it is important to brief them fully about the story on which you are working. Photographers are the experts when it comes to pictures, but they can only be as good as the brief they receive. It also does no harm to suggest ideas to the photographer, so it is important that you think of picture ideas while you are working on the story. Not only can you then see if the photographer agrees with your idea, but you can also pass on other picture ideas to the newsdesk so that library or archive pictures can be included in the final package. It is also becoming normal practice for reporters to take their own pictures with digital cameras, or video with small digital camcorders. A good reporter also remembers that most witnesses these days carry a mobile phone, and often they take pictures or video. Any witnesses should be persuaded to send you their pictures, together with an agreement for them to be used on air, or on the website. (See Chapter 3 for more on sourcing pictures.)

Avoiding disaster

Filing copy gives you your last chance to check that it is right. The modern newsroom is shedding sub-editors, and the emphasis is more and more on reporters getting it right first time – so your watchword must be to check, and check again. There are obvious things, such as names and addresses, that can be got right with only a modicum of care, but you also need to remember to check the rest of your facts.

Watch out for obvious slip-ups, like using a name after you have promised that person anonymity. Have you also used the name of the victim, or an innocent relative or friend of a criminal? Sometimes it is unavoidable but you must be certain you are using the name in the public interest. The BBC covers this at length in its Editorial Guidelines, and the PCC also talks about it in its Code of Practice:

(i) Journalists must identify themselves and obtain permission from a responsible executive before entering non-public areas of hospitals or similar institutions to pursue enquiries.

(ii)   The restrictions on intruding into privacy are particularly relevant to enquiries about individuals in hospitals or similar institutions.

(www.pcc.org.uk/cop/practice.html)

After Harold Shipman had been found guilty of killing more than a dozen of his patients, his wife Primrose was pictured by some of the press, but use of the pictures was much lower-key than in many stories about wives and husbands used in the past. Her name, and that of her son, were used, but the stories were commenting more about how her life had been destroyed and how the family had stood behind the doctor until the end. We have to consider the extent to which it was in the public interest to discuss how a woman could be taken in by a husband who, it turned out, was guilty of many murders.

The PCC and the BBC Editorial Guidelines also advise that reporters should be careful about publishing names and addresses (see Chapter 5).

Defamation

Defamation is a complex subject, which I intend to mention only in the broadest terms, but getting it wrong could cost you and your editor a lot of money. You should always warn the news editor if you think what you have written may be defamatory.

The law takes the view that everyone is entitled to maintain a good reputation and enjoy the respect of their fellow citizens. If you damage the reputation of a person by writing something that 'tends to lower him in the estimation of right-thinking members of society generally or tends to make them shun and avoid him' (Carey 1999: 39) then they can sue you, seeking an apology and/or damages. There are two types of defamation: libel and slander. Since defamation in a permanent form is libel, it is usually an action for libel that journalists face. The Broadcasting Act 1990 made it clear that broadcast material would be subject to an action for libel. For a libel to be actionable, defamatory material about the plaintiff must be communicated to a third party. The plaintiff must be able to prove that any reasonable person would be able to recognise who he or she was from the defamatory article, so just because you didn't use a name or a title doesn't mean it can't be libel, although it is not possible to defame a class or group of persons unless a specific individual can be identified.

There are several defences against an action for defamation. They are:

'justification (or truth);
fair comment on a matter of public interest;
privilege – absolute or qualified;
innocent dissemination;
offer of amends; and
apology.'

(Carey 1999: 45)

The first three tend to be the main defences used by journalists. The first involves the journalist proving that the defamatory material is true. The burden of proof is on the journalist and the court will assume that the material is not true unless there is sound evidence to the contrary.

Fair comment is used to allow comment on matters of public interest. This includes everything from criticism of a football team or the production of a new play to the political career of a politician. Fair comment is not always an easy defence. First you have to prove that the comment is one of opinion, not fact. The opinion must be based on true facts. It might be fine to comment that somebody's performance of Hamlet lacked power because he had not rehearsed enough as he was always in the pub, if you could prove he was always in the pub. Otherwise it might be better to content yourself with the view that his performance seemed to lack power.

In order to use fair comment as a defence it must be proved that:

- 'the words complained of were a comment or opinion, not a statement of fact;
- the words were about a matter of public interest;
- any facts on which the comment was based on are true, or subject to privilege; and
- the comment was made without malice, which in this context essentially means that it was made honestly.'

(Quinn 2009: 216)

Another important defence against defamation is privilege. Proceedings of parliament and judicial proceedings attract absolute privilege. In other words, no matter what is said, the person saying it cannot be sued. Unfortunately, our reporting of what was said attracts only qualified privilege. The main difference is that those with absolute privilege can be motivated by malice and still not be sued, while qualified privilege does not apply if malice is proved. Privilege provides the media with protection from libel proceedings provided a fair and accurate report is given, and provided a letter or statement of explanation from the plaintiff was published by the defendant if requested.

Privilege covers meetings, reports and decisions of parliament, the courts, local authorities, public meetings, sporting associations, associations of art, science, religion or learning, public inquiries, tribunals and public registers. In a decision by the House of Lords in November 2000, qualified privilege was extended to press releases from such meetings.

The Defamation Act 1996 also introduced the idea of an offer of amends. An offer of amends allows a publisher to make a suitable correction of the statement complained of. By combining this with an apology and agreed compensation, the defendant could save him or herself from an expensive libel action. This offer of amends is not available if the publisher knew the article to be untrue and defamatory. An apology can be made that might persuade a litigant against action and certainly might limit any further damages.

Copyright

Copyright is your rights in the material you have written. Intellectual property rights and moral rights allow authors to control their property and determine who has the right to exploit it. It also prevents others infringing those rights.

The Copyright, Designs and Patents Act 1988 gave authors three moral rights:

- the right to be identified as the author;
- the right of the author to ensure work is not subjected to derogatory treatment;
- the right not to have work falsely attributed to one.

The intellectual property rights ensure that the copyright-holder (usually the author, but not always) has the right to control how the work is used, and to be paid for its use. The right for authors to be associated with their work and to prevent alterations or misuse needs to be asserted by the author (my moral rights over this book should be asserted on the frontispiece). However, if the work is produced by someone in the course of his or her employment, then copyright will be owned by the employer, unless you have agreed otherwise. This does not apply to freelances who may have a contract for services, but only to employees, whether full- or part-time, who have a contract of employment (Quinn, 2009: 316). Thus freelances are free to retain rights over any piece they have written, even after a paper uses it, unless they specifically agree to extend the publisher's rights. However, the first two rights (to be associated and to prevent derogatory treatment) do not apply to the reporting of current events.

The Act can give journalists rights over material they have produced unless it was in the course of their staff employment. This is a tricky area of law, but the reporter's contract of employment should make it clear where the dividing line is. So if, for instance, a reporter on *The Times* were to write a whodunnit, then his contract of employment would not normally cover that, so while Times Newspapers would own all his copyrights in articles written for *The Times*, if the book turned out to be a best-seller, it is the reporter who would own the valuable copyright.

Copyright protects a wide range of creative endeavours: writing, plays, films, speeches, photographs, pictures and sculptures, to name a few. The media cannot just copy a photograph or a picture, a speech or an article without gaining permission from the copyright-holder.

There can be no copyright on facts, news, ideas and information – only their presentation. Copyright can be sold like any other property and so the ownership of it can be important. If you borrow a wedding picture from a woman whose husband has gone missing in newsworthy circumstances, you may need permission from the copyright-holder to publish it. If that is the woman, then her loan implies approval. But if the picture were a professional portrait, then the copyright might not be hers.

There are some protections journalists can use for what would otherwise be breaches of copyright.

- Incidental inclusion: if, for instance, an artist was filmed being interviewed in a gallery, and a picture by another artist could be seen in the background, the production company might be able to claim its inclusion was incidental.

- Fair dealing: this is the defence journalists are most likely to depend on. In order to report the news, reporters consistently use small excerpts from speeches and other copyright work, such as reports and statements. Provided the speaker has not prohibited its use (something you can take as read in a public meeting), you can reproduce sections of a speech with impunity provided it is a fair and accurate report. The same applies to criticism. If you wish to criticise a film, book, play or anything else, then provided the copyright-holder is credited, and the amount of the work shown is fair, it is allowed to use someone else's copyright work. The courts have also shown themselves willing to consider a defence of public interest, even though it is not included in the Act.

Data Protection Act

The Data Protection Act 1984 was designed to protect people from computer invasions of privacy. It was introduced at the start of the computer revolution at the end of the 1970s. Computers had been a part of our lives for a decade or more, but they were still enormous and fantastically expensive mainframes that could only be afforded by banks and large institutions. Personal computers (PCs) were introduced in the very early 1980s and caught on quickly. It became clear that, in order to protect the privacy of people whose personal details were being gathered on computers, an Act of Parliament was required. The Data Protection Act 1984 and then 1998 brought considerable protection from 'Big Brother'. The Act is built around eight data protection principles that require the data to have been obtained lawfully, used only for the purpose it was gathered, not kept longer than necessary and kept reasonably secure from unauthorised access. The data also have to be accurate and up-to-date, and the subject of the data has the right to check such data and ask for its erasure.

The 1998 Act widens the meaning of data beyond the old 1984 Act. The whole Act only came into effect in 2007, and now also covers paper records. Any accessible record system or filing system is covered by the Act, and the information can be required by the subject. The Act introduced the concept of *sensitive personal data*. This is described by the Act as information about:

- racial origin
- political opinions
- religious beliefs
- trade union membership
- physical or mental health

- sexual life
- commission or alleged commission of an offence
- any proceedings for an offence or alleged offence.

This section has considerable impact on the work of a reporter. The morning calls, for instance, may tell of a major road crash. Neither the police nor the hospital is now able to give information about any living victims. If the victims don't give permission to release information, then it is up to a senior police officer to agree to release information if there is a good public interest reason. A senior officer may well decide that an accident involving the local MP, who was on his way home from making a speech about safe driving, is a story in the public interest, but he or she may not. Since the reporter does not know who is involved, he or she can't argue there is public interest. Nor is the hospital likely to give a condition report for the same reason. While this may well be a reasonable protection of people's privacy (did we always need to know that burglars stole a TV set from the home of Mr John Smith of . . .?) it is also a limitation of the ability of the media to bring people the news.

The Act allows for special purposes that offer some exemption from the need to inform data subjects:

- journalism
- artistic purposes
- literary purposes.

Confidential information

Breach of confidence is being used more often these days to protect the secrets of corporations and rich individuals. Any leak of confidential information could be a breach of confidence, and Lord Denning has already ruled that one should not take advantage of information disclosed in confidence. While this rarely applies directly to journalists about stories they wish to publish, it may well apply to the source. Someone who believes his or her confidence is being breached can apply for an injunction to prevent publication. The Blairs did this when *The Mail on Sunday* first attempted to publish the memoirs of the former nanny to the Blair children. Any such injunction is enforced by the court, and breach of it would be contempt. Once an injunction is in force with one newspaper, it applies to all the media.

There are three tests under the law to determine whether something breaches confidence:

- the matter must bear the appropriate quality of confidence;
- the circumstances must impose an obligation of confidence;
- an unauthorised breach must be detrimental.

The quality of confidence is tested by the court by asking if a reasonable man in the position of the defendant would have realised the information in his possession was confidential. An obligation of confidence can be found in a number of relationships such as employer/employee, doctor/patient or student/teacher, so someone who was seeking to reveal information about his or her employer could be breaching confidence, as in the Blair case mentioned above. Although there is now legal protection for those who want to expose malpractice in their workplace or elsewhere, that protection does not apply if they tell their story to the media.

If you are covering a story that requires a breach of confidence – maybe an employee is giving you a good story on their employer – you should make the person aware that they risk an action if their name is revealed, and you may need to promise them confidentiality if you think the story is worth it.

Protection from Harassment Act

The Protection from Harassment Act 1997 was designed to protect people from stalkers, but it could be used against a particularly persistent journalist. The law says that a person must not pursue a course of conduct which amounts to, or which he knows or ought to know amounts to, harassment of another. There is a public interest defence when investigating crime, but it is doubtful that that is intended to protect journalists.

9
Interviewing

Interviewing is one of the most important skills of the reporter – this is the tool you use to persuade witnesses to give their impressions and evidence. Any reporter who hopes to do a good job should be able to talk to an interviewee, quickly making them feel comfortable and willing to talk. If the interviewee does not trust the interviewer to deal with them fairly, they will not talk as freely as they would otherwise, so it is vital to build a relationship of trust as quickly as possible, even if the interview is little more than a grabbed couple of questions from a fleeing figure out on a rainy street.

What the public expects

The public's view of reporters often seems to be coloured by the reporters of fiction. This impression comes from films and TV, where reporters are portrayed as unpleasant characters in order to build the moral uprightness of the hero. Even when the reporter is one of the main characters, there is often more drama in making them unsympathetic. This almost always means that the reporter is seen as someone who is either self-obsessed or rude and overbearing. Michael Elphick, for instance, starred in the TV series *Harry* as the eponymous freelance reporter who seems to have no redeeming features at all. John Gordon Sinclair starred as Nelson in *Nelson's Column* – playing a reporter whose selfishness and ambition were the keys to the comedy, while reporters in *Drop the Dead Donkey* and *Hot Metal* were all deeply flawed human beings. As Keeble points out, on their first contact with the media the interviewee may also feel intimidated by this 'awesome and seemingly powerful institution, the press, so capable of destroying reputations' (Keeble, 1998: 69) – but they are often pleasantly surprised. Nearly all reporters are (or can be) polite, even charming, human beings – at least for the length of the interview. The best reporters quickly relax their subjects and soon make them feel able to confide their secrets.

Types of interview

There are two main types of interview:

- as research for a news story;
- as a performance – part of the story in its own right.

It is important not to confuse the research interview for a news story with the performance interview for a TV or radio bulletin or web video. An adversarial interview by Jeremy Paxman for *Newsnight* is completely different from the interview you might carry out with the same politician for the same story, but off-camera or microphone. Many young and inexperienced reporters fall into the trap of believing that a research interview is the same as the performance interview, and that a hectoring, intrusive manner is required. This is likely to lose you the interviewee very quickly, and will certainly not encourage them to tell you anything useful. Even as a performance it is not always productive, and several top-notch professionals, including Sir Robin Day, have had interviewees walk out on them (although of course this can be a good result in terms of TV drama).

There are several different types of research interview used by reporters.

- *The formal, arranged press-conference interview.* This allows many reporters to interview one or more persons at once. It has the advantage of being efficient for the interviewee, but is limiting for the reporter as all media get the same material.

- *The one-to-one short interview.* Short conversations with police officers, emergency workers and plant operatives. None of these are long (the interviewees are too busy for long conversations) and they are focused on specifics, but they can still be useful for pointing up issues, confirming details or adding background colour. They can involve speaking to a number of people. These types of interview are most likely to be done face-to-face, but are also often done on the phone, or possibly by e-mail.

- *The one-to-one interview*. This is the reporter speaking to one of the key people involved in a story. This could be a senior police officer or the most senior representative of a company. These are often difficult to arrange on a big story, as this is what all the reporters want and these people are busy. It can be done by phone or e-mail, as well as face-to-face. It's also a widely used technique for longer articles such as celebrity interviews, or when you are seeking to learn about a new project, development or organisation.

- *The vox pop*. This involves speaking to a number of people and asking their opinion about an issue. Vox pops (derived from Latin meaning 'voice of the people') are great for providing variety for website video, TV or radio, but they are less popular in newspapers than they used to be. People are asked their opinion on a burning question of the day such as, 'Should we join the euro?' The short **soundbites** are then used to add colour to, or often to introduce, a discussion around a major debate that might otherwise be heavy going and full of quotes from dull but worthy politicians and economists.

- *The profile interview*. This is an in-depth, face-to-face interview that is likely to take time: an hour or more. Most likely to be used to research a feature or personal profile, it is used to get under the skin of the interviewee. It is almost impossible to do well over the phone, because of the inability to see all the non-verbal communication. An e-mail interview of this type would take even longer than a face-to-face interview, but might conceivably be useful for someone geographically remote. Of course, the possibility of such a person using a PR to write their responses, or at least advise on them, makes this type of interview technique for a profile practically useless, but it might offer some basic information for an in-depth feature or news interview about a project or event.

Your approach to the interview

The interview starts outside the door. You need to be clear why you are there, what you are going to ask and what you want to know. You must be on time and you need to be appropriately dressed with the tools of your trade – notebooks, recorders or cameras discreetly out of sight. You should not be smoking, chewing gum or doing anything else that is likely to spark an adverse reaction. The trite, old phrase, 'There's never a second chance to make a first impression' is annoying only because it's true.

Interviewing allows you to find out the who, what, when, where, why and how of the story and retell it in the words of those who know about it with conviction, credibility and authority. It is all very well for us to say that a chief constable has supported the decriminalisation of soft drugs, but we much prefer to hear it from the man's lips. A video interview or blocks of quotes with a picture in the paper add credibility and authority. They also bring the story to life and add interest. Without good solid quotes to support what you write, your story will be thin and unbelievable, and will certainly not carry conviction either to the reader or to the High Court judge who may be called upon to set a level of damages if your story is inadequate enough to end up in the courts.

The first thing to do for a good one-to-one interview is to carry out a little research. Google the subject; read *Who's Who*; go to your news library and get out the cuttings. Having some details of the subject at your fingertips is both flattering to them and important for you, if only on a basic level: your interview is not going to go well if your first question is, 'Well, Prime Minister, what party do you represent?' It does not raise your standing in the eyes of the interviewee and is likely to lead to them cutting you short. But knowing that a politician once held directorships in certain companies might well give you the insight into a good story, allowing you to link that knowledge with a remark made by the interviewee that might otherwise be inconsequential.

Having done your research on the subject (assuming you have the time), it is also often worth researching the venue for the interview. If, for instance, a Cabinet Minister is visiting and you are able to grab him for a few minutes for a private interview, it will make you look more efficient, and give you the chance to cut out the opposition, if you are able to say, 'If we just go over here minister, there is a quiet office where we can talk.' This is where a local journalist can often outwit the nationals – provided you do your research first. This knowledge is vital if you need to make audio or video recordings, as most reporters would prefer a bit of space in a quiet, controlled environment to make the most of the interview. As in all things, preparation is the key to success. You have researched the subject and the venue, now you need to be sure you are clear about what you want to know. It is no good blindly asking questions in the hope that you will strike it lucky and get a good story. You need to know what you are after.

If you are talking to the Minister for Industry, it's not much use talking about the health service, unless you are working in local media and the minister happens to also be your local MP. Instead, you need to know as much as possible about industry, particularly local industry, and be aware of any controversial issues. Put yourself in the place of the reader: what would they want to know if the minister dropped into their house for a chat?

Try to prepare questions that get to the heart of the issue. You are not there specifically to embarrass the minister or to show how clever you are – although if they put their foot in it, you can certainly make the most of it! You are trying to find out about the person, the policies and the plans. Your aim should be to give the reader a clear picture of what is happening that might affect their life.

Asking questions

Having done your preparation, you are ready for the interview.

Start by being polite. Remember, people do not have to be interviewed – they can easily give you the brush-off or even just tell you to push off. Only courtesy and charm are likely to change their minds, so you need to practise these. The only person who can improve on this is you. Practise being charming to people (it's a skill, after all), even if it is just your friends, parents or partner/boyfriend/girlfriend. Watch guests on TV chat shows and copy the mannerisms of those you thought charming and witty. It's perfectly possible to pick this up as an act until it becomes automatic, everyday behaviour.

The first rule of civilised behaviour and courtesy is not to be late. Turning up late implies that you think yourself more important than the interviewee and that they are not deserving of respect, which is not likely to improve your chances of a good story. The interviewee may no longer have time to talk to you, and is unlikely to be as cooperative as if you had turned up on time. If they are late then, of course, you have no option but to take it in good part and accept their apologies.

I have already mentioned that it is a good idea to dress appropriately. Whatever we like to think, appearances are important. People are inclined to make snap judgements, and someone with dirty hair, two days' stubble, smudged make-up, torn jeans or a grubby green sweater is not going to get as good an interview as someone clean, neat and well groomed and dressed in a smart suit. Personal hygiene is vital – no-one likes talking to someone who smells as though they died three days before. Avoid eating garlic or spicy food for lunch, and if you smoke or drink then breath mints are a must.

It's also important to turn off your mobile phone before you start. Having your mobile ring during an interview can only be worsened by you answering it and effectively putting the interviewee on hold in his or her own home or office. Turn it off (remembering to turn it straight back on afterwards) or put it on silent profile so you know that you have received a call. Most phones these days have systems to let you know if you missed a call or have a message.

Start the interview off as you mean to go on by greeting all those present in a friendly but business-like manner: smile, nod, handshake and greeting, including your name. If everyone from the receptionist to the second in command finds you approachable and friendly, you will not find it so hard to get to see the great man or woman next time you call. This obviously applies to the interviewee as well, whether protected by a staff of thousands, or just by a spouse answering the door.

Once you meet the interviewee, introduce yourself fully. 'My name is . . . from the *Anytime Reporter*, thank you for sparing the time to see me, I'm sorry to bother you like this', accompanied by a handshake, ensures direct contact with the interviewee.

It is important to offer to shake hands with the interviewee. Touching is an important part of an initial contact because it has an enormous affect on the interviewee's perception of you. In one experiment, psychologists found that students evaluated librarians who touched them briefly while handing back the library card much more favourably than clerks who did not touch (Knapp and Hall 1997: 297). It seems that touch can be 'functionally influential' (*ibid.*: 298). Too much touching too early can, of course, be counter-productive and will be seen as over-familiar. Unless you know the contact well, just a straightforward handshake with your greeting is enough. You can use the handshake to weigh the person up. Markham identifies eight different types of personality who give themselves away in their handshake, from the *cold fish* to the *finger-shake* (Markham 1993: 81). These early indications of personality type can help you quickly to work out what makes this person tick, and allow you to decide more quickly how to handle the interview.

Once in with the interviewee, you should remember that you are on their territory. Unless you are meeting on neutral ground, such as a hotel or public building, you should assume that the office, room or home you are meeting in is theirs. Humans are very territorial animals and although you have been invited in, this does not give you *carte blanche* to do what you like.

Psychologists identify three types of territory: '*primary territories* are clearly the exclusive domain of the owner . . . they are guarded carefully against uninvited intruders . . . *secondary territories*, that are not as central to the daily life of the owner . . . *public territories* are available to almost anyone for temporary ownership' (Knapp and Hall 1997: 155). Even a temporary invasion of someone's primary territory will still be seen as a *violation*. Moving furniture or using items without permission on primary territory, such as someone's home or office, is likely to be perceived as an attempted *invasion* invoking a strong antipathetic reaction. Imagine how you would feel if you invited someone into your home or office and they started moving the furniture.

You should wait to be invited to sit down. It is probably OK to take off your coat, but it also doesn't hurt to ask the interviewee if he or she minds you removing your coat. Don't move the furniture around without at least asking. If the only other chair in the office is across the other side of the room, ask if you can move it: 'Is it OK if I bring that chair over here and sit down?' I have a modest office but I can accommodate up to three or even four visitors. I lock it when I leave it, and I expect people to announce themselves when they enter, with a knock or a greeting. There are four guest chairs in the office strategically placed for visitors to sit and talk. I am always amazed at the number of visitors who, having come to see me, move the chair, despite the fact that there is not really anywhere to move it to. I am also amazed at how much it upsets me. Why don't they ask? Why do they need to move it? I know it's silly, but they'd find me much more cooperative if only they'd leave my chairs alone.

You also need to ask permission to take notes or tape an interview. This is, in part at least, a realisation that what people say in interviews is their copyright and to record it needs their specific permission.

From that permission flows the understanding that you can use their answers in a news report. If you are going to record a radio or TV interview then this is the time to mention it and explain that you will interview them on camera or recorder as soon as you've talked to them about the story.

Handling the interview

While no interviewee, in the UK and western tradition at least, wants to spend ages setting the scene, a little ice-breaking in all but the most urgent of situations is an essential aid to good communication: a sort of throat-clearing that allows interviewer and interviewee to gather their thoughts and concentrate wholeheartedly on the business at hand. Offers of coffee, getting notebooks and papers out, assessing character and situation, arranging the scene, queries about the weather, etc., can all be got out of the way in this period, leaving you clear to get on with the interview.

I find one of the easiest ways to get people into the interview is to ask their name, address, occupation and phone number. This has two purposes: it guarantees you have that basic information should something happen – a fire alarm or whatever; it also eases the interviewee's nerves. Just as the TV quiz show *Who Wants To Be a Millionaire?* helps the contestant settle in by asking laughably easy questions up to the first £1000, so your early questions should do the same. If their name is unusual, ask them to spell it out or even write it themselves in your notebook in capital letters. Trying to write Takitheodopoulos when spelt out by a man with a strong and unfamiliar accent can lead to inaccuracy.

You must always be polite and sympathetic. It doesn't matter how probing or unwelcome your questions are, if they are asked with enough politeness and sympathy and with a smile in your voice, the person will often answer, particularly if you make it clear you are waiting politely for their sparkling response. People are so highly conditioned to respond to questions that, no matter how much they may not want to answer, they often feel compelled to do so, unless we interrupt them. When an interviewee is holding something back, you can just sit there looking expectant. Often they will fill the vacuum that quickly forms by expanding on their answer. Although this rarely fools the experienced or well trained, who will merely say something they want to say, rather than something you want them to say, it is amazing how often people will say a little more than they intended. Eddie Mair on Radio 4 is the perfect example of the polite and charming interviewer who is not afraid to ask probing and incisive questions. He does it with constant courtesy and a smile in his voice that brings excellent results in terms of information for the listener.

Whether for TV, radio or newspapers, your job is to persuade the person to talk in the hope that they will eventually say something worth hearing. It is your job to sift through half an hour of drivel to find the few seconds of gold that explains your story. This is why a shorthand notebook is of more value than a tape recorder. If you are working for print, you will then include that quote in the story. If you are going to record or video an interview you will try to get them to say it again for the broadcast.

Try to build up a relationship with the person. They have to be confident that you are going to treat what they tell you sympathetically; they have to feel comfortable talking to you. While they must dominate the conversation with you prodding them in the right direction with questions from time to time, you can often get someone to open up further if you can relate a brief anecdote that shows a shared experience. The fellow-feeling that this induces can often bring the best out of an interviewee. Most people feel most comfortable when the conversational load between two people is about 50/50. Take the balance too far one way and the person will feel that the other isn't interested, or conversely that they are being marginalised. An interview is different in that the interviewee expects to talk more, but you should still aim to talk about 30 per cent of the time, not just quizzing them with question after question, but talking to them and, above all, listening to what they are saying. You don't want the interview to feel like an inquisition. Some interviewers are so keen to show how good they are, that they are asking the next question before the interviewee has finished answering the last one. Not only is this irritating, but it can confuse and fluster an interviewee. A major press conference when scores of reporters are yelling out questions rarely persuades the interviewee to open up – it's too easy just to ignore the barrage of questions and speak to the pre-prepared text. Some reporters' rapid-fire approach often has a similar effect.

A good interviewer is someone people trust, and to whom they feel comfortable talking. Everyone likes a good listener. Small encouragements of the 'How exciting', 'Did it really?', 'Now, I've never heard of that happening before' variety can persuade the interviewee of how interested you are. Our questions and conversational gambits need to prove that we are listening to what they are saying and that it interests us. Body language and eye contact can be extremely important in this dialogue. 'Nonverbal communication comprises 65 per cent of all communication' (Webbink 1986: 9). Some researchers put the figure even higher (Markham 1993: 68). While a lot of this non-verbal communication supports and contextualises verbal communication, it is also a useful tool to hold up your end of the conversation without speaking. Nods of the head, hand movements, gestures and facial expressions can all show encouragement and interest, and these are vital for a broadcast interview where verbal encouragement is not possible. Nods, smiles and head movements must replace the short affirmative comment. It's important to be aware of trying to do this while still remaining natural about it. Having built up a relationship in the research interview, this should carry over into the broadcast interview.

The temptation for the rookie reporter at an interview is to concentrate on note-taking, which means looking down into your lap. But this can give the interviewee the impression you are not interested. You also need to be looking at the interviewee in order to pick up the non-verbal cues they are offering you: 'nods or sweeps of the head, eye blinks, brow movements, and hand or finger movements occur in association with points of linguistic emphasis (Argyle and Kendon 1967, cited by Webbink 1986: 11). Establishing reasonable eye contact allows you to pick up the non-verbal cues and to offer some of your own to prove your interest. Some communications trainers, particularly those training sales people, favour a technique called 'mirroring', where the salesperson mirrors the body posture of the potential customer in order to appear to be on the same wavelength. This picks up on the widely observed phenomenon that people who get on well mirror each other's body posture. While it is important to listen and try to exude sympathy, mirroring can seem too artificial. As Markham warns: 'you would have to be extremely skilled to get away with it. If the other person were suddenly to become aware of what you were doing, he might think you were making fun of him and refuse to have anything more to do with you' (Markham 1993: 81).

Try to structure the interview so that your questions allow you to build a picture of the story, although there may be considerable detail that you will need to go back to. It is often best to let the interviewee tell you the story in their own words, unless they are one of those people who are easily distracted by their own thought processes. If you know that you have contentious questions to ask, these may be best left until the end. Get basic details first and then move on to the contentious issues. That way you won't come away empty-handed should the interviewee terminate the interview.

The vital thing to remember about interviews is that you must *listen* to what the person is saying. The whole point of the interview is to find out what the person thinks. If you don't listen during the interview, the interviewee may open up a whole new line of information and you will miss it. If you were listening, then you would be able to follow up this new line and perhaps get an even better story. It is for this reason that note-taking must be a secondary occupation to listening, and you must get into the habit of taking notes on autopilot, rewriting startling bits of information. Jot notes as the words come to your ears, while you concentrate on watching the interviewee and listening carefully to what they say. This is much easier if your shorthand is well practised. If what they say is brilliant, don't be afraid to say, 'Sorry, just a minute', and then write it down and rephrase any question you had. Markham talks about active listening that involves concentrating 'on what is being said' offering 'feedback by paraphrasing or asking questions that indicate that you understand what is being said' (*ibid.*: 77). She warns that people with low self-esteem or the very shy often do not listen because they are too busy worrying about what to say next, in case they make themselves look foolish or in case people are looking at them (*ibid.*: 82). Offering feedback persuades the interviewee you are listening and have understood his or her point of view; it also allows you to give the interview a more conversational style. You can also use it to check you've got important facts right and have understood their significance: 'So you're saying that your company's profits have risen by three percent – that's very good at a time when most companies are struggling, isn't it?' will ensure that your interviewee gave you the right figures, you've got them right, and your analysis is correct. It might also give the bonus of getting them to open up about why, or about their competitors.

If you are also watching them properly, so that you can take account of their body language and verbal style, you will often be able to tell when they feel uncomfortable or under pressure. In some instances this might mean that you would ease off, in others that you would press harder to give you the opportunity to probe further, depending on whether they are hiding something you think should be exposed, or are protecting personal information that they have a right to keep private.

Never be afraid to ask for further information, particularly if you did not understand their answer. 'I'm sorry, I'm not quite sure I follow that, could you go over it again?' or 'Let me see if I've got that right. You're saying . . .' are perfectly acceptable ways of double-checking information, particularly if it is something new and possibly contentious. In my experience the apparently silly question rarely is. Either the person has taken for granted that you know more than you do, or they have failed to explain properly.

Drawing the interview to an end should be relatively easy if you have remained in control. Often it is worth asking a general question along the lines of, 'Is there anything you'd like to add . . .?' or 'I think I've got the full picture now unless there's anything you think I've missed?'. Often people will add a piece of information that you were completely unaware of. Once the interview is over, it's time to go. Again, politeness should be the rule. Thank them for their time and shake hands again. It's worth remembering that the interview isn't over until you've gone. Often the interviewee will relax as you start to terminate the session. They may well politely escort you from the premises and will continue talking. It is perfectly all right to continue interviewing. This is, after all, a continuation of your previous conversation.

Rules of engagement

There are a few rules of interviewing that journalists adhere to, and that are generally recognised by politicians, PRs and others who regularly mix with the media.

Reporters talk about an interview being *on the record*. Anything said in such an interview can be used and the person can be quoted. Unless someone says anything to the contrary before the interview, you can assume any interview, where you have told the interviewee who you are, is on the record. Although it might be wise to ask the interviewee to sign a release if you are going to tape the interview for later broadcast, particularly for documentaries and longer current affairs material, you can assume consent provided they knew who you were.

Off the record means that none of the material can be used directly in a story, although it could be used as background – as narrative in a story, or for forcing attribution from elsewhere. Nor can you quote the source of the story. This tends to make the information of very limited use.

There's not much point in being told the local mayor is on the take if you can't use a source to say so. Don't feel forced to accept an off-the-record briefing if you don't want to. Asking for an off-the-record briefing is sometimes used as a way of tying a reporter's hands, limiting the ability to publish the story. If you decide that you would rather seek another source than risk tying your hands with an off-the-record pledge, you can legitimately refuse to accept information off the record. This may mean, of course, that your interview is over.

Non-attributable interviews are agreed to only in certain circumstances. In this kind of interview, the quotes and information can be used, but not the interviewee's name. This leads to the use of phrases such as, 'A source close to Number 10', 'a well informed source', and others. Unless the interviewee specifies beforehand that the interview is non-attributable or off the record, then it is on the record. It's no good someone being indiscreet and then trying to drag the indiscretion back. They must have your agreement that off the record is OK before proceeding. On the other hand, it might be wise to alert someone that your chat is on the record, especially if you know them fairly well.

Sometimes people will ask you for money to be interviewed. Unless you have a specific budget for this, just say you have no money and if they still refuse to talk, then try to find someone else. If they are the only contact, then seek advice from your news editor.

Telephone interviews

Telephone interviews are one of the standard ways of interviewing these days. It's so easy to be able to get in touch with someone quickly by phone. It's time-efficient, in that even if they live a long way away, you can conduct a 20-minute interview and have the copy written within half an hour. No long journeys, no trying to find the venue, but also no face-to-face contact and no real chance to measure what the person is thinking. It's still better to interview face-to-face when you can, but these days it's often difficult to justify the time, especially if all you want from that person is a specific piece of information or a confirmation. Radio, and to a lesser extent TV, find telephone interviews an acceptable alternative to the real thing. If you are unable to go out to interview the person and can't persuade them to come to the studio, the telephone is now widely used.

Using the phone can be a useful way of finding out who to speak to. If you are after a particular person then you will need to ask for them by name, but often you want to speak to the person responsible for a particular job and then the telephone can come into its own as the switchboard for the company or organisation you are contacting will usually be able to tell you who that is. You may not get directly to the person you are after. A switchboard operator and then a personal assistant might try to field your call. Always be polite but firm. If you are just seeking the answer to a question and the assistant can help, then that's fine, but if you need a quote from the boss then hold out for that. Whoever you speak to, make sure you get their name and job title. If what they said was contentious and they rang you, it might be advisable to find a number other than the one they gave you and check that they were who they claimed to be.

Using a phone gives you one major advantage. Hopper calls it *caller hegemony* (Hopper 1992: 199). You make the call and the answerer takes a chance, because he or she doesn't know who is there and is obliged to interrupt other, possibly more important, activities in order to answer. How often have you halted something really important because the phone was ringing, only to find out that it was someone trying to sell you double glazing or something else way down your list of priorities? You need to apologise to the person you are calling so that they realise you consider them as important as you and that they are not just someone you can interrupt with impunity. If the caller is busy or if your call has taken them by surprise, then provided deadlines permit, it may be worth quickly sketching out what you want to know and offering to call them back or let them call you so they have a chance to think through their answers before speaking to you. This will increase their trust. However, it may also give them a chance to run away, so it is up to you to decide if it would better speaking to them straight away.

When using the phone, you are not in a position to use body language, contact or gesture to help put over the message, so you have to rely entirely on the pitch of the voice and your use of language. You need to be able to get your tone of voice to add all the body language you can no longer include. Don't be afraid to make your voice sound smiley. If you laugh, do it in a way that ensures the other person realises either that you were making a joke or that you understood what they said was a joke.

Always say clearly who you are in a friendly but firm way. Once you get to the person you want to interview, repeat who you are and ask if it's OK to talk to them for a story you are working on. If you want to record the conversation, then ask them if they mind. It is certainly bad practice, and arguably against the law, to record someone's conversation without their permission. On the phone it is even more important to leave the most difficult questions towards the end – it is too easy for someone to hang up.

If you use the phone for an interview, it would be unethical to give the reader or viewer the impression that the interview was done face-to-face. The Press Complaints Commission (PCC) warned in 1992 that such practices could give rise to complaints of publishing inaccurate and misleading material.

> In one article the reporter said of the interviewee: 'Watching her, sitting up in bed . . .' when in fact the reporter had never visited the house. This led the reader to understand that the reporter had been invited into the person's home when in fact what had really happened was that a short, and somewhat reluctant, telephone interview had been given.
> (PCC report No 7 March 1992: 3)

Ringing back

If they have rung you back, then don't forget to thank them for taking the trouble to do that. If they promise to ring back, then don't rely on it. Often these promises are made by colleagues or assistants, and the person you are seeking may not have the time or inclination to carry out a promise made by someone else. Leave it for a suitable period and then ring them again. Usually it's best to ask when the person you are trying to contact is expected, so that you can ring them then. You don't want to keep ringing, wasting both your time and that of the person who has to answer your call, if the person you want to speak to will not be there.

E-mail interviews

E-mail interviews are becoming more widely used for finding information and can be very useful if you want to interview someone abroad or in a different time zone. The huge advantage of e-mail is that you can send someone a message and they will respond when they are able, saving you the trouble of having to track them down or wake them up. But many people have e-mail addresses they look at only every few days, and some people don't answer their e-mails for weeks. If you don't hear from someone after a few hours, it might be worth ringing them.

E-mails are also useful in that you can cut and paste the answer into your story, ensuring that you don't accidentally distort what the person said. E-mails are great for contacting experts who you have discovered on websites. Perhaps you are doing a story about swine flu and its possible effects on human health. You are bound to find a website with the names of a number of experts at hospitals or universities. You can then e-mail them all and hopefully get some very usable quotes. Tracking down half a dozen university professors from all around the world by phone would take ages, but a group e-mail to addresses found on a website is the work of a few minutes and can reap great results. Don't forget to make it clear you intend to use the results for publication. This is one time when you really have to be specific so that you are sure the interviewee understands how you intend to use their answer.

Always ask all your questions in your initial e-mail. This saves a ping-pong approach that can become long-winded by e-mail. Remember that these people are often busy and have no obligation to respond to you. If you keep your questions specific, they are more likely to send a short, highly quotable answer.

E-mail interviews are of less use for the 'How do you feel now that it's all over?' type question than for the technically based question about how something works. If you want to interview the victim of a rail crash, go and visit them. If you want to ask a professor of engineering about metal fatigue in rails, then e-mail may be the easiest and fastest method. Certainly e-mail is at its worst for the profile interview. That requires a face-to-face approach; it's the only way to ensure you are interviewing who you think you are interviewing; after all, it could be anybody on the other end, from a public relations expert to a hoaxer.

Interviewing difficult people

There may be people that you want to interview who simply don't want to speak to you, or behave in a difficult manner if they do agree.

If, after speaking to a person, they don't want to talk to you, then there is no point in trying to bully them into it. You can certainly try to persuade them that it might be in their best interests to put their side of the story, but at the end of the day people have as much right to keep quiet as they have to tell their story. Your major problem will normally be the news editor back at the office, who is up against a tight deadline and wants the best story. Persuading him or her that you have done all you can to try to convince the person to speak without success is never easy. One way to get around this is to find a substitute. Who else can give the information you were looking for? Even if the substitute is not quite as good as the original, being able to ring the news editor and say that while your first choice refused to speak, you have managed to get material from a reasonable substitute will usually get you off the hook. The news editor wants reasonable copy and if you've got it, he or she will be less worried about whether you are using precisely the contacts you promised. If the person you are after is the only person who can comment on that story, then it might be worth pointing out to them that 'no comment' can often be very damaging and that some comment, no matter how anodyne, might be better.

Sometimes you meet people who are rude or abusive. There is no point in being rude back. Reporters often meet people who are under heavy stress. They are, perhaps, being accused of wrong-doing, their lives may be falling apart and it should be no surprise if the media are often blamed for this. Just console yourself with the thought that at least they can't chop off your head like messengers of yesteryear. Take a few deep breaths and respond as calmly as you can that you understand how they feel, but that it is your job to convey their views and feelings to others. Is this rage and abuse really how they want to be portrayed? This unaggressive but assertive approach often helps them reconsider how they should handle you. Violence can be a problem on occasion, particularly if there is a press pack about. Being confronted by scores of reporters and photographers outside a building you are trying to leave in a hurry after a highly emotional confrontation can often lead to the person you want to speak to turning violent, or at least uncaring, in their efforts to push through the crowd. Large crowds can be very threatening and in this kind of scenario it is hardly surprising if the person uses violence to try to escape. If it is possible to follow them without it turning into a hunt with scores of journalists pursuing a single car, then you might be able to approach the person later on when they have got over their panic.

Occasionally people will try to bully you into writing what they want written. While it is OK for an interviewee to control what they are reported as saying – it's their words, after all – it is up to you who else you speak to and what is written. It is important that you do not make promises you will be unable to keep, such as saying you will not speak to a particular person, but otherwise it's worth trying to placate this sort of person by trying to appear to agree with them without committing yourself.

Sometimes an interviewee will try to find out what you know and will end up quizzing you. You must not allow that to happen, and should turn the question back on them. Ask them how they feel about it or what they know about it. Flatter them: 'You're the one in the know – what do *you* think about it?'

Ethical matters

We need to remember that our contact with interviewees does mean that we have a duty to treat them fairly. Journalists should not normally use subterfuge or deception unless these are the *only* ways of getting a story that is in the public interest. If you wanted to interview someone about how they dealt in drugs, for instance, you might want to talk to them without revealing you are a reporter. This does not give you the right to buy drugs from them or pretend that you will – both would be offences and risk putting you in the same position as them.

A journalist should normally be both fair and honest with interviewees. It would be an abuse of trust to trick an interviewee into revelations they had not intended – unless the story is important and in the public interest.

While, as noted above, it is good sense to let the interviewee know who you are, it is also the ethical thing to do. When it comes to a broadcast performance interview, this is even more important. A good professional should do all he or she can to put the interviewee at ease. The interviewee should feel able to put their case as they want, and while it is fine for the interviewer to test that case and point out the criticisms that others may have made of it, it would not be treating the interviewee fairly to use the interviewer's skill and experience to pressure the interviewee.

I've often been an interviewee on radio in the UK over the years, talking about journalistic ethics. Some interviewers have attempted to make it look as though they are giving me a hard ride; others have been fair and straightforward, but have tested the case I have put forward by putting the other side of the story in a straightforward manner. Those seeking to show how clever they were, were always easy to trip up and provide weak and unconvincing radio. Those who were fair, but testing, usually built intelligent, useful discussions that helped me to explain myself more clearly and thus helped their listeners understand the issues. They were also the hardest work.

One of the huge advantages of broadcast as a news medium is the ability to add context to a person's words. The sound of their voice or their picture and habitat can tell us a lot about a person. Interviewing a farmer about farming in his best suit in the studio, for instance, would not be as accurate as interviewing him in the cowshed in his working clothes, but if he had just been elected the local mayor, then he might prefer to wear a suit and his mayoral robes in the mayor's parlour.

Quotes

What people say has a particular magic for the consumer, whether it is a local police officer, one of the victims of a rail crash, or the Prime Minister launching the latest government initiative. While what people say can be heard accurately on the TV or radio broadcast, this isn't the case in newspapers. Broadcasters need to be careful about taking quotes out of context or using them in a chronological order that is different from reality. To quote a politician as saying, 'There may well be a case for legalising cannabis, but I have to say that I disagree with it' gives a view of his political stance that is completely different from editing that comment to say, 'There may well be a case for legalising cannabis . . .'. To use it in this way might be an accurate repetition of what the politician said, but it is an unfair and untruthful representation of the politician's views. This kind of misrepresentation can also be done by changing the order in which sentences are said – something both TV and print have been accused of in the past. If a journalist is reporting an hour-long leader's speech at one of the political conferences, then reporting the whole thing would lead to no readers or viewers. Journalists have the right and the duty to offer the highlights as they see them, but they must be fair to the original intention of the politician.

Sometimes, however, print journalists may decide to improve someone's grammar. This is not a problem for broadcasters. The way the person speaks is part of their personality and tells us a lot about them, but often what is said in the heat of a situation might sound fine on broadcast, but looks terrible in print. Double negatives, repetition and malapropisms are just some of the problems with everyday speech that you might consider changing before quoting someone in print. It's our job to tell the world what they think and feel, not to make them look foolish. This particularly applies to someone for whom English is not a first language.

Another trick that is widely used by journalists, especially if the interviewee is being difficult and will not get onto the story, is to ask the interviewee, 'Well, would you say that: "..."' and use what they said as an original quote. If the journalist understands that putting the witness's view into the words of the journalist is to risk exchanging truth for a sharper soundbite, then it may be a fair exchange. It is a decision every journalist interviewing an inarticulate witness has had to make.

Interviewing minors

Interviewing children or vulnerable adults is another ethical minefield. Both the PCC and Ofcom warn journalists to interview a minor only with a responsible adult present, certainly if the story is about the child's own welfare or the welfare of someone they know. Having said that, children can make good witnesses if interviewed properly. They are observant and are better at seeing what is actually there. They are, however, keen to please and will often say what they think you want them to say. It is important not to ask leading questions and not to express interest if the answers seem to be leading in a particular direction. Remember that being interviewed by a journalist, particularly for 'the telly', can seem unbelievably glamorous to a child, and the risk is that they will try to impress the journalist with stories that simply cannot be true. Journalists also need to remember that there may be things the child does not want to admit to when being interviewed in front of the teacher or parent. If they were a witness because they skipped school or were playing somewhere they shouldn't, they may well lie to you about it rather than get into trouble. There is no real way round this but not to use the material. You should not try to interview the child without the parent or teacher.

Research and cuttings

No journalist should use press cuttings to put together what amounts to a fictitious interview. Even if you believe that all the quotes gathered by others and brought together in the press cuttings library are accurate, you can't be sure that the person hasn't changed their mind. What we say at one point in time is often not the same as what we say another time.

The PCC warned journalists about manufacturing interviews in its March 1992 report:

> Cuttings are an essential part of newspaper research, but too many journalists now seem to act in the belief that to copy from 10 old stories is better than to write a new one with confirmation by proper fresh enquiry. In one instance . . . a magazine admitted that because it had been unable to contact a woman who had been attacked by her husband some months previously, it wrote up the story on the basis of newspaper reports, inventing dialogue to put the story into the magazine's style. The result was an article which contained serious inaccuracies and was to a degree fictitious.
>
> (PCC report No 7 March 1992: 2)

10
Production

What happens to a story after it has been gathered is largely a decision for the editor, but whether you work for a newspaper, magazine, broadcaster or website, you need to have some idea of how your story might be used and therefore what final production will be required from you. Almost all reporters these days need to be able to file the story in some variant of text, video or audio, and although broadcasters still use professional crews for major coverage and send several reporters to report for different media, all too often these days a single reporter is expected to be able to file in all formats for whichever media employ them, and often to produce TV and radio packages ready for broadcast.

You need to think carefully about the type of story you are covering because that will alter how you cover it for each different medium. All journalists may need to file from the site of a story – in addition to discussing production methods, this chapter looks at the different ways of getting the story back to the office when returning yourself to produce and edit it is not an option, either because the office is too far away, you do not have sufficient time, or because you need to stay on the spot to continue reporting.

Filing the story

Speed is vital when sending text-based copy to your office. You may even need to file before you've finished the story. When this happens, it needs to be made clear to those receiving it that this is the case. Often – such as filing the first quarter of a football match – it will be obvious, but at other times it may not be. Filing the first part of a story on a major house fire and then later adding the quotes from an interview with the fire chief and the fire victims is a sensible thing to do for an evening paper or radio station around deadline, but the newsdesk needs to know that is what's happening so that they are ready to insert the material at the first possible opportunity.

Phoning copy

You may still find yourself phoning copy through to a newsroom from time to time, particularly if you work for a newspaper. Although it is becoming standard practice to find a wi-fi network or use a broadband dongle to access your news server direct or e-mail copy from your laptop, many offices still expect you to phone over urgent copy. It may also be that the broadband dongle is broken or some other technology deficit prevents connection. The one golden rule with technology is that if it can break down, it will, and usually at the most inconvenient time. If your run of disaster extends as far as your mobile phone, you may be obliged to use a public phone box.

In the early days of my reporting career, the traditional method of filing a story to a newspaper from outside the office was to find a phone box and read it over to a **copytaker** who typed the story into the office copy system. Often this was done from a notebook, with the reporter composing the story as he or she went along. Sometimes, if there was a bit more time available, the story could have been drafted in the notebook. Either way, if time is of the essence, don't re-transcribe quotes. Mark each quote in your notebook with a number and just put the number in your story. This will save quite a bit of time and allow you to get your copy in quicker. The mobile phone and laptop have made all this easier – but only when they work! If you do need to file copy, it will probably be to a newsroom secretary or colleague – no-one employs copytakers anymore.

Be polite, enunciate clearly and listen for their responses.

Read it out in a clear voice, broken down into sections of around five or six words at a time, not whole sentences. The copytaker has to remember what you have just said as he or she types. They will generally tell you when they have completed each typed section, to enable you to move on to the next. But each copytaker adopts his or her own style, so you have to be adaptable too.

Each time you reach a word with a capital letter, you must tell the copytaker and spell out the word to avoid mistakes. All punctuation must be dictated too, including full stops at the end of sentences plus the end of paragraphs.

Filing figures accurately and clearly is a crucial part of copy filing, whether someone's age, an amount of money, or the number of people in a crowd. The onus is on you to get it right and make sure the copytaker has taken it down correctly. Should you need to file a memo to the newsdesk or the subs, be sure you make this clear to the copytaker. File it separately and ask them to mark it clearly at the top as a memo – To: whoever; From: whoever. The worst possible mistake would be to file a confidential memo, with background information, that crept into the paper because it was added on to the end of a story.

If you need to file extra copy on the same story later in the day, tell the copytaker that it is *add-copy*. File your name at the top of the piece and ask them to name the file 'add-(whatever the original catchline was)'. For this reason it is very important to remember what catchline you used first time round. It will be a time-consuming task for them to seek out your first story to find it for you.

The following is an example of how to file copy:

Sentence to be filed:

'When Mr Arthur Smythe returned to his £95,000 luxury home in Wythington Avenue, Preston it was surrounded by a crowd of 300 protesters, waving placards with the slogan "End Animal Experiments".'

Method of filing:

'When Mr Arthur Smythe, cap A for Arthur – normal spelling, cap S for sugar, m-y-t-h-e [wait] returned to his pounds sterling, ninety five thousand, that's nine, five, comma zero zero zero luxury home [wait] in Wythington Avenue comma Preston, cap W, y-t-h-i-n-g-t-o-n Avenue, [wait] it was surrounded by a crowd of 300 that's three, zero, zero protesters, comma [wait] waving placards with the slogan [wait] open internal quotes, caps for start of each word, End Animal Experiments, close internal quotes, point, new **par**.'

   Spell out letters and figures that can easily be confused. On the end of a poor phone link, an 'S' may sound like an 'F' unless you say, 'S for sugar' or 'F for Freddie'. T and D are commonly transposed too, as are P and B, M and N. Nine and five are also easily misunderstood. Enunciate clearly and repeat if necessary. Copy-filing and copytaking is a time-consuming and exact art. But it's often the only method of transmitting a story in time for a deadline.

Electronic presentation

Most reporters (especially freelances) these days will be filing from a laptop by wi-fi or broadband, either direct to a news server or by e-mail to the newsdesk. If you send copy as an attachment, you need to be sure the file type is compatible with the system used by the newsdesk. Not all files are backward-compatible: Word 2007 files, for instance, can't always be opened in Word 2003. Unless the story is very long, you are probably better advised to send the copy as part of the e-mail message, leaving the newsdesk to cut-and-paste the copy across to their system.

E-mail is now easily available. It is possible to send group e-mails so that the same copy can be sent to several newsdesks – that may be useful to freelances filing on a non-exclusive basis – at virtually the same cost (and the same time) as sending one e-mail. In that case, remember to put your own address in the 'To' field and the newsdesk's in the 'Blind cc' field, so that they are not aware who else you have sent it to. The subject field is crucial here in trying to catch the news editor's eye. You want the newsdesk to use your story – not someone else's.

It's difficult to imagine being taken seriously these days as a freelance without having internet access on your mobile, allowing you to send copy or pictures from almost anywhere. If you are able to access a wi-fi connection, that's even better, giving you the opportunity to access the web for research. It's worth pointing out that logging into someone's unsecured wi-fi network might well be considered a criminal offence if the police can prove it. Nevertheless, some journalists have been known to file from their car, using a wi-fi network carelessly left unsecured in a nearby home. Even pictures, small audio and video clips can be sent over the net to a news server by broadband or 3G. Larger audio and video packages will probably take too long to transmit and you will probably take the packages back to the office still on tape or in the recorder, or use a satellite van with equipment designed for the purpose.

Mobile smartphones are now coming into their own as the all-purpose reporter's tool. Capable of recording good quality sound, they can now send audio back to the newsroom as a .wav file or MP2; a minute of good quality audio can be transmitted in only two or three minutes. The phones can also take pictures or even video suitable for a web page or even for transmission if the story is good enough to put up with low-resolution material.

Dealing with the office

Purpose-built news systems will alert the news editor to new copy and an e-mail will also alert the newsdesk. However, if copy is expected as part of a package, it might be wise to contact the news editor by phone to alert him or her to new copy and to explain what's going on. They also need to know where they can contact you in order to discuss any problems with the copy.

Breaking stories

Sometimes a story needs to be filed as it is happening. Sports stories, major disasters and other breaking stories mean having to ensure you get time away from finding the story in order to be able to file it or find yourself somewhere suitable in order to keep up a running report. If you are aiming for a newspaper or broadcast news bulletin, this is becoming more and more difficult as technology increases your ability to publish. Whether for a radio bulletin or for the voracious appetite of an online website or 24-hour news channel, you may have to make time to send over a report. That is easier now with mobile phones. Just turn away from the story and send your copy by phone. For radio and TV, that may well be done with a live link. A time will be arranged and at that time the bulletin will switch to your outside broadcast link and your words and pictures will be transmitted direct to the waiting public. For radio this can be done by phone, but TV still requires a more sophisticated link in order to send the video signal.

Although each bulletin needs to be treated as a separate, updated news item, you need to be sure that you repeat the essential information early on for people who have only just tuned in. The 7/7 bombings happened in daytime, so the first many people would have heard of it was on their radio in the car on the way to work, or from the main news bulletin on TV. On a story that's breaking as fast as this, a new **nose** or intro (the introductory paragraph of the story) is needed for those people who have already heard the news, but we don't want to confuse the new listeners, so the main information needs to be added early on in the story.

Broadcast

Coverage of a major story for broadcast will be organised by the newsdesk, with professional crews and satellite vans booked and sent to the site. Reporters will be detailed and all will be organised on a news production system such as ENPS. This coordinates reporters, production and crews and then logs material returned, keeping the newsdesk constantly updated on the progress of the story. Newsdesk is then able to use this information to form the running order for the news bulletin. As packages are put together, they are inserted into the running order with their length automatically totalling to give the news editor accurate information on the bulletin length, allowing the newsdesk to determine if more or less is needed. With a satellite van in place, the newsdesk is able to go live to that position for the reporter to give a live report. This may be for TV or radio or both. If the story is appearing on a number of bulletins, then a major broadcaster such as the BBC may well send one or more reporters to cover for TV, plus one for radio and one for the web report. Because information on ENPS, used by the BBC to manage its news input, is available to all staff, news editors on any bulletin, radio, TV or web, can use reports filed by reporters either in their entirety or edited – so no BBC reporter can be entirely certain where a report will end up. Of course they will produce different styles of report for video, audio or web, as these three media are very different in the way they present the news and what works best, and I will examine some of the differences later in this chapter.

Smaller news events will be allocated directly to a reporter on ENPS or whatever diary system your newsdesk uses. You will need to check during the briefing with the newsdesk what is expected. If you are working for a newspaper or website, you may need to take a camera or video recorder with you in order to get pictures or video to go in the paper or on the website. Radio reporters will always be required to take an audio recorder in order to get sound to augment the report. However, pictures or video may also be required to support the story on the website. TV journalists should remember to get sufficient basic information in order to be able to produce a detailed textual report for the website alongside any video and audio they record for their on-air story.

Each newsroom has its own system for booking out equipment and for booking such facilities as video or audio editing, and you will need to adhere to that. Pressure will always be on around deadline times, and you will be expected to use your editing time efficiently and quickly, so it is best to have a clear idea of what you hope to do from very early in the development process of the story so that you can put the package together quickly and effectively.

Audio

Radio and audio on the web create pictures through sound. The listener needs to be able to imagine the scene set by the background sounds. A pastoral story about spring lambs would not sound the same with a soundtrack of truck engines and pneumatic drills as with one of birdsong and baaing lambs.

Telling stories for audio and video is very different from the approach required for the written word. Newspaper articles can have longer sentences and a more formal approach. More detail can be inserted in the text because people's attention is focused more fully on the words than with radio or TV, and it is also easy for people to re-read a sentence if they are momentarily distracted. Radio and TV are more informal and require shorter sentences; the added facility for sound and pictures means that these should be used to their maximum potential in order to present the story. Why spend precious seconds describing the mangled remains of a car when a picture would show the scene much better? Why describe the agony of a mother whose child was cruelly killed in the crash when her tears would tell us all we need to know? Producing video and audio, whether for broadcast or the web, requires thinking about what you can show as well as what you can tell. By all means tell the viewer the *who*, the *when* and the *where*, but try to also show the *what*, the *how* and the *why*.

With audio you can also use the ability of sound to paint pictures in the mind, and you should attempt to tell the *what*, *how* and *why* of a story in sound. Radio is particularly good for alerting people to breaking news, and this style of radio tends to rely on voice alone for a brief summary of the story – often little more than a news headline. This can then be updated at the next bulletin, remembering to **lead** with the newest information. If the story is important enough, it may be appropriate to interrupt a programme for a news flash, picking up more detail in the next bulletin, possibly with interviews and/or other **actuality**, such as report from the scene or a phone interview with a witness. A live report from the scene can add atmosphere and colour, allowing the reporter to describe what is happening and talk to those involved.

The actuality can then be used to provide a news clip or to produce a longer edited item – either a **wrap** or a **package**. A wrap is usually actuality combined with reporter **voice-over** between the clips. A package will be a more sophisticated piece using actuality, reporter voice-over, **wildtrack** – the sounds at the scene – and other background actuality.

Recording on location

Reporting from a location allows the reporter to place the subject of the story, whether an interviewee or some form of action, in context to create a sense of the place and time in which the story is taking place that would be difficult to reproduce in any other way. Whether recording for audio only or for video with audio, the aim is to provide visual or audio clues and signposts that will add extra information about the story and help explain why a particular interviewee has been chosen.

Interviewing a doctor about the risks of swine flu and how the public should best prepare might be done in a consulting room with medical equipment, and with the doctor wearing a white medical coat. This immediately gives the viewer a sense that this is a medical professional who has the appropriate authority to give advice. For those who missed the introduction to the story, there is sufficient context for them quickly to understand what is going on. Familiarity is an important element of any news story and this should be borne in mind when choosing a location, as the careful choice of location can help to reduce the amount of description required. Next time you hear a story about your local area, try to work out from the description where it is; now see how easy it is to be reminded of a known location with just a few seconds of film or a still photo. Video is very good at these shorthand aids, adding support to the story.

Audio, whether to support video or run entirely on its own for websites or traditional broadcasting, needs careful handling. Listeners are much more easily distracted than those watching a piece of video. As viewers, we can appreciate even very poor quality video if it is telling a story. Clips from the camera phones of witnesses can be used to support a story even if the quality is terrible. The same is not true of audio. Listeners require quite a high standard of audio reproduction in order to make the effort of listening worthwhile. Booming, echoing sounds that are competing with background noise will soon lead listeners, whether on TV, web or radio, to switch off or over. So although choosing your location is important for video, you also need to take into consideration how audio will be handled.

When you choose your location, you need to consider a few points.

- Check the background noise – if it is too loud, it may become overly distracting and even drown out your interviewee, or oblige them to speak very loudly or shout. Roaring traffic, people working on noisy machines, racing car engines or overhead planes are all the sorts of noise you should consider – do you want them in, or are they too distracting?

- Is the location in a position that is too exposed to the elements; is wind noise going to cause interference?

- While you are recording, listen out for any background noise that could distract, sound odd or make editing difficult. Recording in the country for a piece about sheep farming will be enhanced by the occasional bleat, but a droning tractor engine or a ringing phone will not add to the scene, and you should move to a new location or re-record after the noise has been dealt with.

- Avoid recording in large rooms, they can add unwanted echo and lead to a poor recording. If this is the only place available then use a protected position against a wall or curtains.

If you want to emphasise the background noise in the sound track, then hold the microphone a little further away from the interviewee to allow the balance between their voice and the ambient sound noise to change in favour of the ambient sound. If the ambient noise is loud, or needs to be excluded, hold the microphone closer to the subject. Always record two or three minutes of wildtrack, as this can be added later to enhance the scene in a way that you can control. It allows you to repair bad edits, or to vary the level of ambient sound at different points in the story. It can also be overlaid on tracks where no such sound exists. This can be done to deceive – by laying a wildtrack of a railway station over an interview with a railway manager, for instance, even when the interview was done in a silent office; however, you would have to consider whether this is an aid to the listener or a deception and therefore unethical.

Actuality

Actuality is film or audio taken at the scene of an event (including interviews) that allows the viewer or listener to witness events. Actuality is vital to set the scene and show the viewer (in video or audio) *what* is happening, *where* the event is happening (the type of place, not just a geographical reference), and *when* (again, not a specific time, but whether at night, dawn or whatever). These descriptions of where and when are much more emotive than an address or time. However, you need to be careful about what is shown in actuality. Some scenes may invade people's privacy and should be handled with care. For instance, pictures taken at the scene of a major road accident should ensure they are not over-intrusive. A woman was filmed for the BBC1 programme *Front Line* at the scene of a major road accident in which one of her children died. She was filmed, in medium close-up, in a public place, but Ofcom found she had a reasonable expectation of privacy (because she was recently bereaved, and because she was injured) and that therefore the BBC breached her privacy.

Library material

When putting together packages for transmission, the reporter can access a whole range of material from the picture or film library. This will include still pictures of key public figures – politicians or showbiz celebrities. It will also include film of key events stored and indexed for future use. Film of ice breaking in the arctic or desert sand storms, for instance, could be used to illustrate stories about climate change. Graphics and computer-animated images have also increased, allowing maps, figures and statistics to be presented in a lively and engaging way.

Sound effects

Sound effects can add enormously to a piece for radio, but they need to be used imaginatively and with care. Good sound effects will add to the listener's understanding of the story, but inappropriate sounds or background music can become clichéd and distract or even offend. You also need to be careful that the sound balance still allows the listener to hear the interview and that sounds are not added that give a misleading effect about the story.

Graphics

Supers, **astons** or **captions**, as they are variously known, can be flashed up on screen to give an interviewee's name, profession or position; date; location; sources of material or other statistics.

Chromakey or **CSO** (colour separation overlay) is a means of electronically displaying still or moving pictures behind the newsreader. In the studio you will see only a very bright blue or green backdrop, which is replaced by the vision mixer with a graphic or a visual from a second camera.

Performance interviews

Many reporters these days need to film or audio record a performance interview. For TV and radio, this has always been the practice, but even newspapers and magazines now like to have clips of video or audio to augment stories. While the view that was current in the early noughties – that all newspaper reporters would be videoing all their interviews – has thankfully proved wildly optimistic because of shortage of time to edit and too few staff in newsrooms, all good reporters should be considering what to video.

Video interviews

In a TV interview, the aim is to allow the viewer to be an observer, but not to impinge on the action. The camera should be invisible, or certainly as discreet as possible while still allowing the interviewee to interact with the observer. The camera should frame them so that they can speak towards the reporter; making the observer a true observer, not the subject of the conversation. The interviewee should be talking to the reporter, with the viewer able to watch. They should not be addressing the viewer direct and excluding the reporter.

For a good interview, you should sit the participants almost opposite each other and close enough to hold a normal conversation. The interviewee can then look across the frame into what is known as the **looking space**, towards the reporter. The eyelines of the participants should match with the camera lens to ensure the viewer feels an equal part of the interview. Looking down would tend to distance the viewer or make them feel above what is going on; position the camera too far below the eyeline, and the viewer will feel dominated by the interviewee, alienating them from him or her. Check that there are no distracting elements in the background. Nude posters, flashing lights or TV screens all need to be covered or taken out of the picture. Choose a backdrop that suits the person and the interview: book-filled shelves for an academic, or a recording studio for a musician, for instance.

As with any good piece of television, the interview should involve action. Since the subjects are necessarily static, the impression of activity needs to be imposed by the edit. This is done by building the package up with a series of shots.

The first of these is an establishing shot or **set-up** shot. This can be almost anything that introduces us to the story and the participants. Your choice of visual signpost here will give the viewer the context they need to understand what is happening without requiring a long explanation from the reporter. If you were covering a story about food safety and were going to talk to an environmental health expert, then maybe opening shots in a kitchen making breakfast would be a good way to introduce the expert. A story about flu vaccines could start in clinic.

The interviewee will then be shown in medium close-up. This is a shot that gives a fair view of the interviewee without coming so close that it starts to feel intrusive. **Cutaways** can be added later to help cover the joins when editing. Although you might film for ten minutes, the final interview might only be a minute or even just a few seconds, and cutting bits of the interview would lead to the interviewee jumping around. By cutting back to the interviewer or some other element, such as the object under discussion, not only breaks the film and adds to the feeling of activity, but also hides the fact that the video is no longer a coherent, continuous exchange.

Radio interviews

Radio interviews aim to get the reporter and interviewee involved in a personal dialogue at which the listener is a guest – not eavesdropping, as both interviewer and interviewee are aware they are there, but not contributing either. They are merely listening to this shared experience. In order for listeners to get the best from the experience, the interviewer needs to get close in to the interviewee so that the microphone is placed close to the sound source. Most microphones work best at about 20–30 cm from the source. This distance allows listeners to avoid being overwhelmed by breathing or over-pronounced sibilants, but is close enough to pick up the sounds of the voices and minimise any background sounds. Of course, if you want to hear a little more of the background noise, just hold the microphone a little further away. You need to ensure you are comfortable, though, or there is a risk you will fidget, preventing both of you from concentrating on the interview.

The interview

There are different ways of approaching an interview, and it's important to establish what you are trying to achieve. The first questions the reporter should ask are: What do I want to know and how am I best going to get those questions answered? The old favourites of *who, what, where, when, why* and *how* will all require answering, but some more urgently than others. Different people will need to be approached, depending on what you want answered, and you will need to be certain you have the right person for the job.

If there has just been a plane crash, then you will want to find out *what* has happened, *who* it happened to, *where* and *when*. Later you will want to know *why* and *how*. Your first interview for such a story will be informational, but there are other types of interview, as below.

- *Informational* – the purpose of the informational interview is to provide information about a news event, often a breaking story.

These types of interview tend to be short and to the point, seeking to find an authority to give us definitive answers to the questions:

- *Who* did it happen to?
- *What* happened?
- *Where* did it happen?
- *When* did it happen?
- *Why/how* did it happen?

Once we know the basics of a story then we might want to go further and seek an emotional interview.

- *Emotional* – this type of interview allows us to share someone's personal experience. We are now going to talk not to an authority (someone in a position to tell us what is going on), but to someone actually involved in the incident. This might be a victim, or a relative, or perhaps even a rescuer. These types of interview can be powerful and revealing, letting the viewer know the enormity of what's happened and how horrific it is for the individual, but they also risk being intrusive and need to be handled sensitively. Ofcom, the broadcast regulator and the BBC editorial guidelines both warn about intruding into people's privacy at such times, either because they may be grieving for a loved one killed in the incident or because they were directly involved. However, if someone came away unhurt or with only superficial injuries, there is little risk of being over-intrusive. Even here, though, you should be careful you are not taking unfair advantage of them in a traumatising situation.

Moving further on with the story, we reach the time, possibly days later, when we need to analyse what's happened, probably talking to experts or to those interested in changing policy on the basis of the incident. It's then that we will want an interpretative interview.

- *Interpretative* – the interpretative interview will approach an expert or a campaigner attempting to analyse and explain what has happened. The interviewee might be a Civil Aviation Authority spokesperson attempting to explain their findings, or a head of a passengers' campaign group seeking safer flying. In both cases, the aim is to put the event into context and examine why or how it has happened and the possible implications.

Once the causes are clear and the various groups have proposed actions, we might move on to the adversarial interview.

- *Adversarial or accountable* – it is in this type of interview that the reporter needs to be careful to appear impartial. The purpose of the interview is to ask someone in authority – a politician perhaps, or the head of a big corporation or agency – to explain previous policy, justify why it failed in this instance, and explain how they intend to change things, or justify why they intend leaving them the same. The reporter may need to challenge what the authority is saying, and there is a risk that the interview might degenerate into a personal argument between interviewer and guest. You must remember that your job is to question. Intimidating or overbearing questioning may provoke the audience to feel the interviewee is being unfairly treated, regardless of whether the issues being raised are justified and in the public interest. The BBC's Eddie Mair is very good at this sort of interviewing, and is always worth listening to in order to study his technique. His questions are well considered, they are presented courteously, but he will press firmly and persistently if the question is not answered until he either gets an answer or it is clear the interviewee doesn't have one.

Put people at their ease

The performance interview is different from the research interview favoured by newspaper journalists because there is nowhere for the TV reporter to hide. He or she is there on our screen for all to see. The reporter needs to be in charge, challenging and questioning, but not intimidating or bullying.

While it might be fine for Jeremy Paxman to pressure politicians, it is not acceptable to do the same with ordinary people who do not have the experience and training of today's politicians. Listening to John Humphrys on the *Today* programme shows how this works. His approach to those who are inexperienced, ordinary members of the public is much gentler than to professional politicians.

Politicians spend their lives trying to get their message over, and all have media training these days or they won't last long. An ordinary person brought into the limelight by events rather than choice should be handled more carefully. Many people who are interviewed on television and radio may never have appeared on air before and have no idea what to expect. They can be nervous, or may come across as defensive, brash or even aggressive. Often potential interviewees who talk with ease over the phone or off-camera will freeze when the camera is switched on. It is the reporter's job to reassure them and to get the best out of the interview.

Remember to introduce yourself, and your crew, if you are working for television. You want the interviewee to trust you, so be friendly. It is important to judge each situation individually. Sometimes it is important to be friendly and informal, other times to be authoritative and professional, and if you're dealing with the personal or emotional interview, sympathy and sensitivity are vital.

A good interviewer will take control. They are the one asking the questions and they must be persistent and determined, but whatever the situation they must also always be polite and courteous. Explaining what is going on and why can help put the interviewee at ease and prevent them feeling quite so intimidated by the process.

It is important to discuss with the interviewee broadly what you will be asking them about, but be careful about over-rehearsing them. Often you will want to combine this with the research interview, as they will be telling you things about the story that are new to you. If they become over-rehearsed, they may cut out parts of their answer, thinking they have already told you about it, or start saying things such as 'As I said before' when in fact they haven't mentioned it on air. Before you start recording, reassure the interviewee that if they lose track of what they are saying, you can pause the interview and give them time to collect their thoughts. The radio reporter can also tidy up any coughs, stumbles or pauses in the edit. Of course, if the interview is live, it's best to warn them of that too.

Encourage your interviewee by maintaining eye contact, nodding and expressing sympathy or simply expressing interest in what they are saying, but not with audible or verbal expressions. The normal murmurs of approval we all use in order to encourage people to carry on talking could be misinterpreted as agreement in an interview, and in any case they become irritating and intrusive, cutting across what the interviewee is saying. Nodding or smiling approval off-camera will encourage the interviewee and confirm you are listening and engaged without you appearing to the viewer to be too involved.

Questions are important to ensure the interviewee tells the viewer what they need to know about the story. You may want to use the questions in the final edit, so keeping them simple is important for this reason.

Regardless of who you are interviewing, don't try to be clever with your questions or try to trip up the interviewee. The viewer wants to know what is going on, and if you ask questions to reveal that to them simply and straightforwardly, you will have done your job. Interview questions should be simple, clear, concise and to the point. If the question is long-winded or introduces too many issues at once, the interviewee will be confused and unable to answer. Make sure you ask open questions: what you want is explanation or comment, whereas closed questions prompt a yes or no response. 'Councillor, will the new speed restriction measures cut the number of accidents on the estate?' prompts a yes or no answer; but 'Councillor, *how* will the new speed restriction measures cut the number of accidents on the estate?' demands more information.

Sometimes you might want a definite yes or no answer, and want to prevent someone, a politician for instance, from making a verbose, prevaricating response. Then it makes sense to ask a closed question: 'Mr Brown, will you step down as party leader if Labour loses the general election next month?'

On the other hand, imprecise questions or those set too widely should be avoided, as the interviewee will not know where to start. They are likely to ramble and drift off the point. They also use up a lot of recording space and become difficult to edit: 'You're in favour of the health service, but think the government has messed it up – what do you think is wrong?' is likely to result in a politician presenting their election campaign, with very little usable material.

Avoid multiple questions, as the interviewee may forget to answer part of the question or deliberately choose to answer only part of it. You must also ensure you are actually asking a question and not making a statement of your own:

> *Reporter:* 'Mr Smith you're head teacher at St Thomas's Primary School. Only three years ago the school had a reputation for truancy, bullying and poor educational standards, today it's one of the best schools in the area. It's a remarkable transformation.'

> *Head:* 'That's true, but what is your question?

Once the interview is over, always remember to play back the last 15 or 20 seconds of the recording to make sure it is recorded and there are no problems. Thank the interviewee and continue to be polite and courteous.

Vulnerable groups

Broadcasters have a legal obligation to treat all their interviewees fairly, and all journalists should take that on board. While that would mean normally telling people who you are and who you are working for, it also means taking particular care when interviewing children or those with mental health problems, the bereaved or seriously traumatised, and those with serious illnesses, either mental or physical. Normal practice is not to interview children (that is under 16) about matters to do with their private life or welfare without consent of a parent or other person responsible for their care. The same may well apply to people in other vulnerable groups. There may also be some places where you will not be allowed to film. Women's refuges, for instance, would not normally allow filming on the premises or film the outside, revealing where it is.

Going live

There are some elements of TV and radio production that have not yet made their way onto the web and are probably unlikely to – at least in the normal course of events. Although it is perfectly possible to have a live transmission on the web, its lack of time dependence and ease of access at the convenience of the consumer means that live reporting is not what the web does best. Live reporting is likely to remain the key identifier of TV.

Live reports can be very useful, taking viewers to the scene and updating them. It gives a chance to interview on-the-spot witnesses or authority figures. When it works well, it can be excellent reporting. All too often, though, it is used as a device to fill time. Going live to a reporter who is based in the capital city of a country where an incident is happening, but who may be almost as far away from the incident as the presenter at home, does not necessarily add anything to the report. Too often, news editors go live to a reporter whose only information is what he or she has just been told by the newsdesk.

There are several types of live report.

The throw

The **throw** is where the presenter in either radio or TV goes live to a scene, taking an up-to-date report from the reporter there. Although this is normally done through a satellite van, allowing immediate transmission to the studio, 3G phones are now starting to move into this territory, allowing reporters to file live reports from around the world. The quality is not brilliant, and there is no real feedback, just a picture of the live screen on the phone.

Two-way

A **two-way** is when the presenter goes live to the reporter, in effect interviewing the reporter live on air about the situation. This needs to be used with care, because while it can make good TV, it can also make terrible TV. Going live to a breaking news situation where a reporter can describe what is happening in detail can be great. Who can forget the picture of John Sargeant being swept aside by Margaret Thatcher as she came to explain to the press how she was to continue fighting the election as Tory leader? But all too often, the two-way ends up in a version of: Presenter: 'So what's happening there?' Reporter: 'Not much I'm afraid.'

Learning more

The aim of this chapter has been to show how the news you have gathered can be put together to fit the production and distribution system you work to. Nearly all reporters now need to consider how they will deliver the news: as text, photographs, video or audio. However, TV and radio journalists will require more information about producing an excellent video or audio package than I can present here. There are several good books about on broadcast journalism and if you are intending to work mainly in TV or radio you should read one or more of them.

Bibliography

Beaman, Jim (2000) *Interviewing for Radio*, London: Routledge.

Chantler, Paul and Stewart, Peter (2003) *Basic Radio Journalism*, London: Focal Press.

Fleming, Carole (2009) *The Radio Handbook*, 3rd edn, London: Routledge.

Hudson, Gary and Rowlands, Sarah (2007) *The Broadcast Journalism Handbook*, Harlow: Pearson Education.

Ray, Vin (2003) *The Television News Handbook: An Insider's Guide to Being a Great Broadcast Journalist*, London: Pan Books.

And finally . . .

Throughout this text I have tried to discuss issues of ethics and good professional practice as they have come up, but it is important that you should have an understanding of the codes of practice and guidance notes issued by regulators and how they apply to the media in which you work. This means the Press Complaints Commission (PCC) Editors' Code of Practice, the Ofcom Broadcasting Code and the BBC Editorial Guidelines for broadcasters. Journalists working on websites linked to traditional media should follow the code/s applying in that medium, while journalists on websites that are completely independent would still do well to adhere to the general tenor of all the codes.

Organisations with Codes of Practice

Press Complaints Commission

A body set up and funded by the newspaper industry to investigate complaints brought by readers and to decide whether they have breached the industry's Code of Practice.

The PCC has a hotline for complaints. It will also answer queries from editors seeking advice on whether stories they wish to run breach the Code of Practice. The chair of the Commission is Baroness Peta Buscombe, a former Conservative Chief Whip. Its Code of Practice is agreed by a committee of editors, but the commission itself is made up of 16 members, the majority of whom are lay members not connected with the media in any other way. The journalist members are editors or senior journalists. Their Code of Practice is available at www.pcc.org.uk/cop/practice. html, and covers the following areas: Accuracy; Opportunity to reply;

Privacy; Harassment; Intrusion into grief or shock; Children; Children in sex cases; Hospitals; Reporting of crime; Clandestine devices and subterfuge; Victims of sexual assault; Discrimination; Financial journalism; Confidential sources; Witness payments in criminal trials; Payment to criminals; The public interest.

Ofcom

Ofcom is the regulator for communications in the UK. It regulates content on all broadcasts and on websites linked to broadcasters. It licenses all UK commercial television and radio services. It was set up under the Communications Act 2003 and its board is appointed by the Department for Culture, Media and Sport. It has statutory powers to punish broadcasters for transmitting material that breaches guidelines, but it has no power to prevent broadcasts. If a complaint is made about a broadcast, Ofcom will determine if it has breached the code, and if so it may levy a punishment that can include a fine or even suspension or removal of a licence to broadcast. Its Broadcasting Code (available at www.ofcom. org.uk/tv/ifi/codes/bcode) includes the following sections: Protecting the under-eighteens; Harm and offence; Crime; Religion; Due impartiality and due accuracy and undue prominence of views and opinions; Elections and referendums; Fairness; Privacy; Sponsorship; Commercial references and other matters.

At the time of writing, the Code was undergoing a review.

British Broadcasting Corporation

A corporation licensed by the government to provide audio and visual material by means of broadcasting or the use of newer technologies to fulfil its public purposes as identified in its Royal Charter. It is overseen by the BBC Trust, a body appointed by the Secretary of State for Culture, Media and Sport, and is responsible for ensuring broadcasting adheres to appropriate standards and represents the interests of the licence payer. The BBC is run operationally by the Executive Board, headed by the Director General. The BBC produces its own Editorial Guidelines that give excellent advice on ethical and some practical issues (www. bbc.co.uk/guidelines/editorialguidelines). The BBC also has its own journalism college, which has a really useful website that is soon to be opened to the public.

National Union of Journalists

The TUC-affiliated union for journalists in the UK. The NUJ has approximately 34,000 members in newspapers, broadcasting, magazines, books, PR and freelance journalism spread throughout the UK, Ireland and continental Europe. Office collectives are called chapels and are led by a Mother or Father of the Chapel.

It has its own Code of Conduct, agreed by the members. This is policed by the Ethics Council, a body that examines complaints sent to it by members or branches. If the Council finds a member guilty of breaching the Code of Conduct, it can reprimand the member or recommend to the National Executive Council that the person be fined up to £1000, suspended from membership or expelled. The Union's Code of Conduct has recently been revised and is available at www.nuj.org.uk/innerPagenuj.html?docid=25 along with union working practices.

International Federation of Journalists

An international association of journalism trade unions representing the views of members to the United Nations, European Commission and other national and supra-national bodies (www.ifj.org). The NUJ is a member. It has an international code of practice called the Bordeaux Agreement.

Other journalism organisations

Association for Journalism Education

A UK-based association of lecturers involved in journalism teaching (www.ajeuk.org).

British Society of Editors

An association of editors, mainly of newspapers, but also open to editors in broadcasting (www.societyofeditors.org).

Broadcast Journalism Training Council

A cross-industry body of broadcast employers' organisations, the BBC and the NUJ that validates broadcast journalism courses (www.bjtc.org.uk).

Campaign for Press and Broadcasting Freedom

An independent voice for media reform, the Campaign for Press and Broadcasting Freedom was established in 1979 as an association of individual campaigners and trade unions promoting policies for a democratic and diverse media (www.cpbf.org.uk).

Chartered Institute of Journalists

An organisation for journalists in the UK. It has approximately 800 members working mostly in newspapers, many of them stringers and part-timers (http://cioj.co.uk).

European Journalism Training Association

A Europe-wide association of schools of journalism in higher and further education. Represents approximately 60 schools throughout eastern and western Europe (www.ejta.nl).

The MediaWise Trust

A UK-based charity set up to help those who believe they are victims of an intrusive press. It aims to represent such people to the media and change how the media deal with such cases (www.mediawise.org.uk).

National Council for the Training of Journalists

A cross-industry body originally set up by the Newspaper Society, Guild of British Editors, National Union of Journalists and the Institute of Journalists. It is an independent charity with a board, composed mainly of editors, and it validates newspaper journalism courses and sets exams for the National Certificate in journalism (www.nctj.com).

Newspaper Publishers Association

A body representing the owners of national newspapers in the UK.

Newspaper Society

An association of provincial newspapers, lobbying on behalf of the newspaper industry as well as offering advice to individual newspapers. It has an excellent legal department (www.newspapersoc.org.uk).

Periodical Publishers Association

A body that represents publishers in the magazine field. It lobbies government and organises training for journalists and other staff (www.ppa.co.uk).

Press Association

A privately owned news agency providing national and international copy to provincial newspapers throughout the country on a fee-paying basis (www.pressassociation.com).

Glossary and acronyms

Actuality: Interviews or sound recorded on location.

Aston: A (brand) name for a type of electronic caption generator.

BJTC: Broadcast Journalism Training Council, a cross-industry body overseeing journalism training.

Byline: Name of the author.

Blog, blogging: Abbreviation of web logging – a form of diary or logbook kept on the internet, which is accessible to anyone who wants to view it. They can also comment on its contents. A useful way for reporters to interact with readers.

Caption: Words giving an explanation of a picture or graphic.

Catchline: A short phrase or title used to indicate the story content of newspaper or magazine copy (*aka* Slug).

Chromakey: Way of replacing a single colour with a second image or picture (*aka* Colour separation overlay).

Citizen journalism: Journalism carried out, usually online, by amateurs in their spare time.

Colour separation overlay (CSO): Way of replacing a single colour with a second image or picture (*aka* Chromakey).

Contact: Someone who provides information.

Copy story: News story for broadcast without accompanying interviews or audio.

Copytaker: Person who inputs copy dictated over the phone.

Copytaster: Someone who selects copy for publication.

Credit: Payment by a newsdesk for information or copy.

Cutaway: An editing shot that allows shots or speech to be edited without an unsightly jump cut.

Death knock: Visit to the recently bereaved.

Diary story: Routine news story usually based on planned forthcoming events.

Doorstepping: The persistent pursuit of an interviewee.

Down the line: Audio or video feed via an outside source or cable link.

Embargo: Instruction on press release not to use until a specific date or time.

Freelance: Self-employed journalist.

Freeze-frame: Single static image.

General view (GV): Wide shot to establish scene or location.

Hand-out: Written information from formal news sources.

Holding copy: Initial version of a story left by a reporter.

Intro: Introduction – first part of a story (*aka* Nose).

Kill: To decide not to publish part or all of a story.

Lead ('leed'): Main story on a page.

Looking space: Framing for interview that suggests the presence of the reporter.

Medium close-up: Shot framed on subject to show head and shoulders.

NCTJ: National Council for the Training of Journalists, a cross-industry body overseeing journalism training.

Newsdesk: News executives.

Nibs: News in brief.

Nose: The introductory paragraph of the story (*aka* Intro).

NS: Newspaper Society (employers' body).

NUJ: National Union of Journalists (employees' body).

OB: Outside broadcast.

Off-diary story: Story discovered by the reporter on his/her own initiative.

PA: Press Association.

Package: Report comprising interviews (and/or actuality and sound effects) separated by narrative links.

Par: Paragraph – as in, 'Give me six pars on that'. Usually around 30 words.

Phono: Voice report via the telephone.

Piece to camera: Information given by a reporter on location where the reporter directly faces the camera.

Reuters: International news agency specialising in financial and political affairs.

Rushes: Raw, unedited video tapes.

Set-ups: Sequence of shots used to establish or introduce an interviewee.

Side-bar: Story to the side of a main story, adding information or extra detail.

Slug: Copy identification information (*aka* Catchline). Formerly a slug of type.

Soundbite: Extract or snatch of interview or actuality.

Spike: To decide not to publish a story (used as a verb).

Splash: Front page main story given major display treatment.

Standfirst: Standalone piece introducing a story and often including a byline.

Still/still store: Still images, generally of leading politicians or celebrities.

Stringer: Supplier of copy or news tip-offs. Often a local amateur.

Sub: Sub-editor.

Subbed copy: Copy passed by a sub-editor.

Super: Title or caption superimposed or electronically generated over an image.

Talking heads: Expert contributors or authority figures.

Throw: Where the presenter in either radio or TV hands over to a reporter live at the scene.

Tip (tip-off): Information from a contact (named or anonymous) leading on to a story.

Two-way: Where the presenter interviews the reporter at the scene.

Up to the wire: Late edit, working right up to the point of transmission.

Voice-over: Commentary recorded over pictures.

Voicer: Explanation, details of story by a reporter.

Wallpaper: Generic shots used to overlay complex narrative.

Wildtrack: Ambient sound recorded on location.

Wire: Agency copy.

Wrap: Actuality combined with a reporter's voice-over.

Further reading

In addition to codes of conduct, many organisations offer guidance and advice on the reporting of issues from mental health and suicide to children and drugs abuse. The National Union of Journalists (NUJ), The MediaWise Trust and the Society of Editors try to help journalists by issuing advice from time to time that includes the best on all these subjects.

Guidelines can be obtained from the NUJ, MediaWise or the Society of Editors on the following issues: Writing about race; Disability; Children; Refugees; Drug abuse; Mental health; Suicide; Age discrimination; AIDS; Sexuality; Court reporting; Local government; ACPO [Association of Chief Police Officers] guidelines (www.acpo.police.uk).

Recommended books

There are plenty of books available about journalism, but some are more useful than others. Below is a short critique of several books that I have found to be particularly useful over the years.

Banks, David and Hanna, Mark (2009) *McNae's Essential Law for Journalists* (20th edn), London: Butterworths. This is excellent for print journalists but not so detailed about broadcast. It is worth checking that you have the latest edition as, inevitably, the law changes regularly. Because of this, websites can be useful and there are several that are designed to help journalists: the Society of Editors and the Newspaper Society are particularly good in this respect.

Blastland, Michael and Dilnot, Andrew (2007) *The Tiger That Isn't*, London: Profile Books. A very useful book looking at statistics and their use; particularly helpful for journalists. Based on the BBC Radio 4 programme *More or Less*.

De Burgh, H. (2000) *Investigative Journalism*, London: Routledge. A series of essays about investigative journalism.

Evans, H. and Gillan, C. (1999) *Essential English for Journalists, Editors and Writers*, London: Pimlico. A reprinting of Harry Evans's classic guide to writing for newspapers. A must on every journalist's desk, this accessible guide should help you to improve your writing style.

Frost, C. (2007) *Journalism Ethics and Regulation*, Harlow: Longman. A basic primer on the need for ethics in the media and how they are applied to the day-to-day professional lives of journalists. It also explains how the various self-regulatory bodies work.

Hicks, W. (1993) *English for Journalists*, London: Routledge. A good primer on English for journalists and others who want to be able to communicate well. Encourages a stylish and accurate approach to the use of English, without being dogmatic.

Hicks, W. (1999) *Writing for Journalists*, London: Routledge. A very good book on how to write news and features for publication. Mainly interested in reporting for newspapers and magazines, it does not cover very much for broadcast.

Hudson, Gary and Rowlands, Sarah (2007) *The Broadcast Journalism Handbook*, Harlow: Pearson. An indispensable book for those working in broadcasting.

Keeble, R. (2005) *The Newspapers Handbook* (4th edn), London: Routledge. This book offers sound advice on reporting and writing aimed specifically at newspaper journalists.

Markham, U. (1993) *Dealing With Difficult People*, London: Thorson. A very readable book that gives useful guidance on dealing with different types of people. While it is aimed at a general audience, there is much here that will be useful in any profession or trade that involves a lot of interaction with different types of people.

Morrison, James (2009) *Public Affairs for Journalists*, Oxford: Oxford University Press. An up-to-date account of the political workings of the UK and an essential guide for any journalist.

Northmore, D. (1996) *Lifting the Lid: A Guide to Investigative Research*, London: Cassell. A good introduction to some of the special skills of the investigative researcher.

O'Kane, B. (ed.) (1993) *Essential Finance for Journalists*, London: Price Waterhouse. Good advice and guidance on the financial maze that faces the journalist, whether dealing with company accounts, the stock market, or the personal finance nightmares of pensions, insurance and taxation.

Quinn, Frances (2009) *Law for Journalists* (2nd edn), Harlow: Pearson Education. A well rounded look at the law as it affects journalists, written in layman's terms. It is up-to-date, covering the Human Rights Act and the new Data Protection Act as well as the main sources of concern for most journalists: defamation, copyright and contempt of court.

Randall, D. (2007) *The Universal Journalist* (3rd edn), London: Pluto Press. A good all-round primer on reporting and writing. It covers the tasks of the journalist (mainly aimed at newspaper reporting) from start to finish.

Wilson, J. (1996) *Understanding Journalism*, London: Routledge. This also explores the kinds of issues journalists face in their everyday lives in an easy-to-read, well structured form, making it an easy-to-use reference book.

Internet sites
of interest

Government and politics

- Central Office of Information: **www.coi.gov.uk**. Press releases for all government departments.
- Department for Children, Schools and Families: **www.dcsf. gov.uk**.
- Department for Culture, Media and Sport: **www.dcms.gov.uk**.
- Department of Work and Pensions: **www.dwp.gov.uk**.
- Foreign and Commonwealth Office: **www.fco.gov.uk**. Government policy on foreign affairs as well as excellent up-to-date advice on travelling abroad and a reasonably detailed briefing on every country in the world.
- The Home Office: **www.homeoffice.gov.uk**.
- Ministry of Justice: **www.justice.gov.uk**. Information about the courts and justice.
- The Prime Minister's site: **www.number-10.gov.uk**.
- The Treasury: **www.hm-treasury.gov.uk**.
- UK Parliament: **www.parliament.uk** (ideal for parliamentary business, MPs, government ministers, *Hansard*, etc.).

All of the above allow RSS feeds, and carry policy changes and information as varied as visa requirements and benefit entitlements.

- Conservative Party: **www.conservatives.com**.
- Labour Party: **www.labour.org.uk**.
- Liberal Democrats: **www.libdems.org.uk**.
- Register of political parties and guidance about electoral law: **www. electoralcommission.org.uk**.
- UK National Statistics: **www.statistics.gov.uk**. Government statistics. This is a really useful site for seeking information to

underpin a story, whether employment statistics, population figures or energy prices.

- Information about local government and local councils can be found at: **www.local.gov.uk**.
- Information on quangos: **www.civilservice.gov.uk/Assets/Public Bodies2008_tcm6–6429.pdf**.

Organisations

- Companies House: **www.companies-house.gov.uk**.
- Insolvency Service: **www.insolvency.gov.uk**.
- The Suzy Lamplugh Trust: **www.suzylamplugh.org**.
- Trades Union Congress (has links to most union sites): **www.tuc. org.uk**.

Information

- AlertNet for Journalists: **www.alertnet.org/mediabridge/index.htm**. Another great set of tools designed to make life easier for journalists.
- BT phone directories: **www.bt.com**.
- Maps: **www.maps.google.co.uk**.
- Research Clinic: **www.Researchclinic.co.uk**. Carries a number of helpful research tools designed to support training courses, delivered by the BBC's Paul Myers.

Media

- BBC news and information (**www.bbc.co.uk**), including Editorial Guidelines (**www.bbc.co.uk/guidelines/editorialguidelines**).

Journalism sources

- Broadcast Journalism Training Council: **www.bjtc.org.uk**.
- Committee to Protect Journalists: **www.cpj.org**.
- EthicNet (a variety of different European codes of conduct): **www. uta.fi/ethicnet**.

- European Journalism: **www.journalismnetwork.eu** or **www.ejc.net**.
- European Journalism Training Association: **www.ejta.nl**.
- FAIR: Fairness and Accuracy in Reporting: **www.fair.org**.
- HoldtheFrontPage: **www.holdthefrontpage.co.uk**.
- International Federation of Journalists: **www.ifj.org**.
- Journalism UK: **www.journalismuk.co.uk**.
- The Journalistic Resources Page: **markovits.com/journalism/jlinks.shtml**.
- Liverpool John Moores University (journalism site): **www.jmu-journalism.org.uk**.
- The MediaWise Trust: **www.presswise.org.uk**.
- National Council for the Training of Journalists: **www.nctj.com**.
- National Union of Journalists: **www.nuj.org.uk**.
- Newspaper Society: **www.newspapersoc.org.uk**.
- Office of Communications: **www.ofcom.org.uk**.
- Periodical Publishers Association: **www.ppa.co.uk**.
- Pew Center for Civic Journalism: **www.pewcenter.org**.
- PR Newswire for Journalists: **www.newsdesk.co.uk**.
- Press Complaints Commission: **www.pcc.org.uk**.
- Reporters Sans Frontières: **www.rsf.org**.
- Skillset (broadcasting training organisation): **www.skillset.org**.
- Society of Editors: **www.societyofeditors.org**.

Local councils, organisations and businesses are usually on the net, and a quick search may well provide you with all the background information you need. For information on searching, see Chapter 4.

Bibliography

Adair, S. (1999) *Press and Broadcast Media*, East Grinstead: Bowker Saur.

Allport, G.W. and Postman, L. (1947) *The Psychology of Rumor*, New York: Holt, Rinehart and Winston.

Anthony, S. (1973) 'Anxiety and rumor', *Journal of Social Psychology* 40, 3: 597–620.

Argyle, M. (1969) *Social Interaction*, London: Tavistock Publications.

Argyle, M. (1988) *Bodily Communication*, 2nd edn, London: Routledge.

Bagnall, N. (1993) *Newspaper Language*, Oxford: Focal Press.

Banks, D. and Hanna, M. (2009) *McNae's Essential Law for Journalists*, 20th edn, London: Butterworth Heinemann.

Barker, M. and Petley, J. (1997) *Ill Effects*, London: Routledge.

Barron, F. (1969) *Creative Person and Creative Process*, New York: Holt, Rinehart and Winston.

Barthes, R. (1993) *Mythologies*, London: Vintage.

BBC (1999) *The Changing UK*, London: BBC.

BBC (undated) *BBC Editorial Guidelines*, BBC, London. www.bbc.co.uk/guidelines/editorialguidelines.

Beaman, J. (2000) *Interviewing for Radio*, London: Routledge.

Bell, M. (1998) 'The journalism of attachment', in Kierans, M. (ed.) *Media Ethics*, London: Routledge.

Blastland, Michael and Dilnot, Andrew (2007) *The Tiger That Isn't*, London: Profile Books.

Boyd, A. (1997) *Broadcast Journalism*, 4th edn, Oxford: Butterworth Heinemann.

Brett, M. (1988) *How to Read the Financial Pages*, London: Hutchinson.

Brighton, P. and Foy, D. (2007) *News Values*, London: Sage.

Calahan, C. (1999) *A Journalist's Guide to the Internet*, Boston: Allyn and Bacon.

Carey, P. (1999) *Media Law*, 2nd edn, London: Sweet & Maxwell.

Chantler, P. and Harris, S. (1997) *Local Radio Journalism*, Oxford: Focal Press.

Chantler, Paul and Stewart, Peter (2003) *Basic Radio Journalism*, London: Focal Press.

Corbett, B. (ed.) (1990) *Danger: Journalists At Work*, London: International Federation of Journalists.

Coupland, N., Giles, H. and Wiemann, J.M. (eds) (1991) *Miscommunication and Problematic Talk*, London: Sage.

Crone, T. (1995) *Law and the Media*, Oxford: Focal Press.

Curran, J. and Seaton, J. (1997) *Power Without Responsibility*, 3rd edn, London: Routledge.

Curtis, L. and Jempson, M. (1993) *Interference on the Airwaves*, London: Campaign for Press and Broadcasting Freedom.

Davies, N. (2008) *Flat Earth News*, London: Chatto & Windus.

Davis, A. (1979) *Working in Journalism*, London: BT Batsford.

Davis, A. (1988) *Magazine Journalism Today*, Oxford: Focal Press.

De Bono, E. (1977) *Lateral Thinking*, Harmondsworth: Penguin.

De Bono, E. (1986) *Six Thinking Hats*, London: Viking.

DeBurgh, H. (2008) *Investigative Journalism*, 2nd edn, London: Routledge.

De Fleur, M. (1997) *Computer-Assisted Investigative Reporting*, Mahwah: Lawrence Erlbaum Associates.

Dobson, C. (1992) *The Freelance Journalist*, London: Butterworth Heinemann.

Evans, H. and Gillan, C. (1999) *Essential English for Journalists, Editors and Writers*, London: Pimlico.

Feeney, R. (2000) *Essential Local Government 2000*, 9th edn, London: LGC Information.

Feldman, T. (1996) *An Introduction to Digital Media*, London: Routledge.

Fleming, C, (2009) *The Radio Handbook*, 3rd edn, London: Routledge.

Fletcher, W. (1992) *Creative People*, London: Century Hutchinson.

Fowler, R. (1999) *Language in the News*, London: Routledge.

Franklin, B. (1997) *Newszak and News Media*, London: Arnold.

Franklin, B. (ed.) (1998) *Making the Local News: Local Journalism in Context*, London: Routledge.

Franklin, B. (ed.) (2006) *Local Journalism and Local Media* (revised edition of *Making the Local News*), London: Routledge.

Franklin, B. and Murphy, D. (1998) 'Changing times: local newspapers, technology and markets', in Franklin, B. (ed.) *Making the Local News*, London: Routledge.

Fromkin, V. and Rodman, F. (1993) *An Introduction to Language*, Fort Worth: Harcourt Brace.

Frost, C. (2000) *Media Ethics and Self-Regulation*, Harlow: Longman.

Frost, C. (2007) *Journalism Ethics and Regulation*, Harlow: Pearson Education.

Fuller, J. (1996) *News Values*, Chicago: University of Chicago Press.

Gabriel, J. (1998) *Whitewash: Racialized Politics and the Media*, London: Routledge.

Galtung, J. and Ruge, M. (1997) 'The structure of foreign news', in Tumber, H. (1999) *News: A Reader*, Oxford: Oxford University Press.

Gans, H. (1980) *Deciding What's News*, London: Constable.

Garrand, T. (1997) *Writing for Multi-media*, Oxford: Focal Press.

Gluckman, M. (1963) 'Gossip and scandal', *Current Anthropology* 4, 3 (June): 309.

Goldie, F. (1985) *Successful Freelance Journalism*, Oxford: Oxford University Press.

Golding, P. and Elliott, P. (1979) *Making the News*, London: Longman.

Gudykunst, W. (1994) *Bridging Differences*, Thousand Oaks: Sage.

Hachten, W. (1998) *The Troubles of Journalism*, London: Lawrence Erlbaum Associates.

Halberstam, J. (1992) 'A prolegomenon for a theory of news', in Cohen, E.D. (ed.) *Philosophical Issues in Journalism*, Cambridge: Harvard University Press.

Harcup, T. (2009) *Journalism Principles and Practice*, 2nd edn, London: Sage.

Harcup, T. and O'Neill, D. (2001) 'What is News? Galtung and Ruge revisited', *Journalism Studies* 2, 2: 261–80.

Harris, G. and Spark, D. (1993) *Practical Newspaper Reporting*, Oxford: Focal Press.

Hart, A. (1991) *Understanding Media*, London: Routledge.

Hartley, J. (1982) *Understanding News*, London: Routledge.

Hausmann, C. (1987) *The Decision-making Process in Journalism*, Chicago: Nelson-Hall.

Henley, N. and Kramarae, C. (1991) 'Gender, power, and miscommunication', in Coupland, N., Giles, H. and Wiemann, J.M. (eds) *'Miscommunication' and Problematic Talk*, London: Sage.

Hennessy, B. and Hodgson, F.W. (1995) *Journalism Workbook*, Oxford: Focal Press.

Hicks, W. (1993) *English for Journalists*, London: Routledge.

Hicks, W. (1999) *Writing for Journalists*, London: Routledge.

Hoch, P. (1974) *The Newspaper Game*, London: Calder and Boyers.

Hodgson, F.W. (1993) *Modern Newspaper Practice*, Oxford: Focal Press.

Hodgson, F.W. (1998) *New Sub-editing*, Oxford: Focal Press.

Hoffman, A. (1992) *Research for Writers*, London: A&C Black.

Hopper, R. (1992) *Telephone Conversation*, Bloomington: Indiana University Press.

Houston, B. (1999) *Computer-assisted Reporting*, 2nd edn, New York: St Martins.

Hudson, G. and Rowlands, S. (2007) *The Broadcast Journalism Handbook*, Harlow: Pearson Education.

Huff, D. (1954) *How to Lie With Statistics*, London: Penguin.

Husband, C. (1975) *White Media Black Britain*, London: Arrow.

Jensen, K. (1998) *News of the World*, London: Routledge.

Jones, G. (1987) *The Business of Freelancing*, London: BFP Books.

Keeble, R. (ed.) (2006) *Print Journalism: A Critical Introduction*, London: Routledge.

Keeble, R. (2008) *The Newspapers Handbook*, 4th edn, London: Routledge.

Keene, M. (1995) *Practical Photojournalism*, London: Focal Press.

Kelly, John (2009) *Red Kayaks and Hidden Gold: The Rise, Challenges and Value of Citizen Journalism*, Oxford: Reuters Institute for the Study of Journalism.

Kieran, M. (1998) *Media Ethics*, London: Routledge.

Knapp, M. and Hall, J. (1997) *Nonverbal Communication in Human Interaction*, Fort Worth: Harcourt Brace.

Koch, T. (1990) *News as Myth*, New York: Greenwood Press.

Koch, T. (1991) *Journalism in the 21st Century: Online Information, Electronic Databases and the News*, Twickenham: Adamantine Press.

Laakaniemi, R. (1995) *Newswriting in Transition*, Chicago: Nelson Hall.

Lacey, N. (1998) *Image and Representation*, London: Macmillan Press.

Langer, J. (1998) *Tabloid Television*, London: Routledge.

Livingston, Charles and Voakes, Paul (2005) *Working with Numbers and Statistics: A Handbook for Journalists*, Mahwah: Lawrence Erlbaum Associates.

Lorenz, A. and Vivian, J. (1996) *News Reporting and Writing*, Boston: Allyn and Bacon.

Markham, U. (1993) *How to Deal With Difficult People*, London: Thorsons.

Matelsk, M.J. (1991) *TV News Ethics*, London: Focal Press.

McGuire, M., Stilborne, L., McAdams, M. and Hyatt, C. (1997) *The Internet Handbook for Writers, Authors and Journalists*, London: Folium.

McLeish, R. (1999) *Radio Production*, 4th edn, Oxford: Focal Press.

McNair, B. (1999) *News and Journalism in the UK*, 3rd edn, London: Routledge.

Milroy, L. (1980) *Language and Social Networks*, Oxford: Basil Blackwell.

Moeller, D. (1999) *Compassion Fatigue*, London: Routledge.

Murphy, D. (1976) *The Silent Watchdog*, London: Constable.

Negrine, R. (1994) *Politics and the Mass Media in Britain*, London: Routledge.

Niblock, S. (1996) *Inside Journalism*, Abingdon: Blueprint.

Northmore, D. (1996) *Lifting the Lid*, London: Cassell.

NUJ (2000) *Rule Book*, London: National Union of Journalists.

O'Kane, B. (ed.) (1993) *Essential Finance for Journalists*, London: Price Waterhouse.

O'Malley, T. (1994) *Closedown*, London: Pluto Press.

Paine, R. (1967) 'What is gossip about? An alternative hypothesis', *Man* 2, 2: 278–85.

Palmer, F. (1990) *Grammar*, London: Penguin.

Parsigian, E. (1996) *Proposal Savvy*, Thousand Oaks: Sage.

PCC (1991–2009) *Reports 1–80*, London: Press Complaints Commission. www.pcc.org.uk/cases/adjudicated.html.

Philo, G. (ed.) (1996) *Media and Mental Distress*, Glasgow: Glasgow Media Group.

Press Council (1953–90) *The Press and the People. Annual Report of the Press Council*, London: Press Council.

Press Council (1991) *Press at the Prison Gates*, Press Council Booklet No. 8, London: Press Council.

Quinn, Frances (2009) *Law for Journalists*, 2nd edn, Harlow: Pearson.

Randall, D. (1996) *The Universal Journalist*, London: Pluto Press.

Raudsepp, E. (1971) 'Try these six steps to more ideas', in Davis, G. and Scott, J. (eds) *Training Creative Thinking*, New York: Holt, Rinehart and Winston.

Ray, V. (2003) *The Television News Handbook: An Insider's Guide to Being a Great Broadcast Journalist*, London: Pan Books.

Reah, D. (1998) *The Language of Newspapers*, London: Routledge.

Robertson, G. (1983) *People Against the Press*, London: Quartet.

Rosenblum, M. (1993) *Who Stole The News?*, New York: John Wiley.

Rosnow, R. and Fine, G. (1976) *Rumor and Gossip: The Social Psychology of Hearsay*, New York: Elsevier.

Royal Commission on the Press (1949) *Royal Commission on the Press 1947–1949 Report*. London: HMSO.

Schlesinger, P. (1978) *Putting Reality Together: BBC News*, London: Constable.

Schlesinger, P. and Tumber, H. (1994) *Reporting Crime: The Media Politics of Criminal Justice*, Oxford: Clarendon Press.

Searle, C. (1989) *Your Daily Dose – Racism and the Sun*, London: Campaign for Press and Broadcasting Freedom.

Sellers, L. (1968) *Doing it in Style*, Oxford: Pergamon Press.

Sellers, L. (1968) *Simple Subs Book*, Oxford: Pergamon Press.

Shibutani, T. (1966) *Improvised News*, Indianapolis: Bobbs-Merrill.

Smith, G. (1986) *Local Government for Journalists*, London: LGC Communications.

Spark, D. (1998) *Journalists' Guide to Sources*, Oxford: Focal Press.

Stokes, J. and Reading, A. (eds) (1999) *The Media in Britain*, London: Macmillan.

Taylor, J. (1999) *Body Horror*, Manchester: Manchester University Press.

Tomalin, N. (1997) 'Stop the press I want to get on', in Bromley, M. and O'Malley, T. (eds) *A Journalism Reader*, London: Routledge.

Tumber, H. (1999) *News: A Reader*, Oxford: Oxford University Press.

Venables, J. (1993) *What is News?*, Huntingdon: ELM Publications.

Ward, G. (1997) *Mental Health and the National Press*, London: Health Education Authority.

Waterhouse, K. (1989) *Waterhouse on Newspaper Style*, London: Penguin.

Watson, J. (1998) *Media Communication*, London: Routledge.

Webbink, P. (1986) *The Power of the Eyes*, New York: Springer/Butterworths.

Welsh, Tom, Greenwood, Walter and Banks, David (2007) *McNae's Essential Law for Journalists*, Oxford: Oxford University Press.

Whitaker, B. (1981) *News Limited: Why You Can't Read All About It*, London: Minority Press Group.

White, T. (1996) *Broadcast News Writing, Reporting and Producing*, 2nd edn, Boston: Focal Press.

Williams, F. (1957) *Dangerous Estate: The Anatomy of Newspapers*, Cambridge: Patrick Stephens.

Williams, F. (1969) *The Right To Know: The Rise of the World Press*, London: Longman.

Wilson, J. (1996) *Understanding Journalism*, London: Routledge.

Winston, B. (1998) *Media, Technology and Society*, London: Routledge.

Yorke, I. (1997) *Basic TV Reporting*, 2nd edn, Oxford: Focal Press.

Index

academe 28
academic journals 28
academics 28
accommodation 93
actuality 171, 173
add-copy 165
advertisements 27
advertising revenues 8
Advertising Standards Authority 131
AIDS 84
Altavista 62
Andre, Peter 23
anniversary 39
archive 35
Arglye and Kendon 152
Argyle, Michael 103, 104
AskJeeves 63
Association for Journalism Education 4
astons 174
audiences 25
audio 170, 35
audio recorder 169
Audit Commission Act (England) 1998
   127
averages 67

background noise 35, 172
BBC (British Broadcasting Corporation) 20,
   53, 58, 74–76, 80, 109–112, 135, 136,
   169, 173, 178, 183
Bebo 31, 56
Beckham, David 74
Benjy the Binman 74
Blair, Tony 44
Blairs 141
Blastland and Dilnot 66, 67
blogging 1
blogs 58

BNP (British National Party) 56
body language 101, 152, 156
bookmarking 61
boolean algebra 63
brainstorming 38
Breen, Suzanne 110
bribes 75
British Medical Journal 28
British Society of Editors 124, 185
broadband dongle 165
Broadcast Journalism Training Council 4
broadcast 169
Broadcasting Act 1990 136
Brookes, Heather 47
BT (British Telecom) 88
building trust 100
Bulger, James 122
Buscombe, Baroness Peta 183
byline 3

caller hegemony 156
calls 32
camera/phones 36
Campbell, Alistair 18, 44
captions 174
chance 70
charitable and voluntary organisations 132
Chartered Institute of Journalists 186
chat rooms 59
China 16
citizen journalism 1
Clarke Kent 6
commercial organisations 129
Commission for Local Administration in
   Wales127
Committee to Protect Journalists 96
community groups 31
Companies House 72, 130

computer-assisted reporting 49
Conan the Barbarian 86
confidence 142
confidential information 141
consonance 17
contacts 20
contacts book 47
contempt of court 122
copyright 34
Copyright Designs and Patents Act 117, 138
copytakers 165
corruption 75
Cosmopolitan magazine 23
council meetings 125
council minutes 29
Counter-Terrorism Act 2008 113
CourtServe 120
creativity 36
credit crunch 11
Crockford's 46
Croggon, David 70
crowd sourcing 56
crown court 118, 122
cultural expectations 101
cutaways 175
cuttings 163

Daily Mail, the 23
Daily Telegraph, the 23, 51
Data Protection Act 49, 112, 114, 140
Davies, Nick 26
Day, Sir Robin 144
death knock 107
De Bono, Edward 38
Debrett's 46
defamation 136
Defamation Act 1996 138
De Fleur, Margaret 50
Delane, J 6
Denning, Lord 141
diary 25
directly elected mayor 126
directories 65
disaster, avoiding 135
doorstepping 108
Downing Street 27, 134
Drop the Dead Donkey 143

eaves-dropping 30
editorial guidelines 74, 107, 135
electronic presentation 167
Elphick, Michael 143

e-mail 52, 167
e-mail interviews 157
embargoes 82
ENPS (Essential News Production System) 80, 169
ethical matters 160
Ethics Council 185
ethics 32, 107
European Convention on Human Rights 123
Excite 62
eye contact 152

Facebook 31, 49, 56, 57, 87, 108
facial expression 34
father or mother of chapel (F/MoC) 132
female deficit 105
FHM magazine 21
filing the story 165
finance 71
Flat Earth News 26
Fleet Street 74
Flickmail 56
Flickr 56
football writers' association 19
Foreign and Commonwealth Office 90
Franklin and Murphy 26
Franklin, Bob 7, 26
Freedom of Information Act 2000 46, 51
freelances 19, 36, 77
Front Line 173
Frost, Chris 84

Galtung and Ruge 16
Galtung, Johan 16
Gluckman, Max 13, 24
Goody, Jade 8
Google 56, 59, 62, 63, 87, 146
Google Maps 56, 88
Google Satellite 87
Google Street View 112
gossip 13
GPS trackers 94
GQ magazine 87
graphics 70, 173, 174
Green River murders 51
Guardian, the 20
Gudykunst 101, 102, 105
guides 31

Habermas, J 102
Hamlet 137

Hansard 29, 54
Harcup and O'Neill 16
hard news 13
Harry 143
Hearing Aid Council 131
Henley and Kramarae 102, 105
Her Majesty's Court Service 120
Hetherington, Alastair 15
Home Office 125
Hopper 156
Hotbot 62
hotels 93
Hot Metal 143
House of Lords 138
Huff, Darrell 69
Human Rights Act 111, 123
Humphrys, John 178

IFJ (International Federation of Journalists)
    96, 185
India House 90
Information Commissioner 47
Ingham, Bernard 44
internet 52
interviewing minors 162

Jaspin, Elliott 51
Jordan, see Katie Price
Judicial Studies Board 124

Keeble, Richard 143
Keighley Times, the 23
Kelly Inquiry 44
Kelly, John 51
Kerrang 87
Knapp and Hall 85, 148

Labour party 44
Lancet, the 28
languages 93
laptop 167
library material 173
Loaded 21
Local Government Act 125
Local Government and Housing Act 2000
    126
looking space 175
Lycos 63

magistrates court 118
Mail on Sunday, the 141
Mair, Eddie 151, 178

Major, John 117
Malik, Shahid 113
Manchester University 70
Markham 148, 152
Marks and Spencer 60
Max Clifford Associates 8
McCartney, Paul 42
measurability 65
medium close-up 175
minimal response 106
misrepresentation 109
MMR vaccine 28
mobile smartphone 168
mode 67
moral rights 138
MPs' expenses 7
MSN (Microsoft Network) 62
muslim 104
Myspace 56

names and addresses 83
national press card scheme 95
National Statistics 71
National Union of Journalists (NUJ) 4, 65,
    75, 96, 107, 110, 111, 132, 185
NCTJ (National Council for the Training
    of Journalists) 4, 116
Nelson's Column 143
Netscape 62
Newham Council 27
news 12
news conference 78
newsdesk 1, 8, 36
newsgroups 58
Newsnight 144
Newspaper Proprietors Association 111
Newsroom 76
news server 167
Newspaper Society 111, 124, 187
news theatres 118
NGO (Non-Governmental Organisations)
    131
non-departmental bodies 131
non-verbal communication 34
nose 169
notebook 116

Ofcom 65, 82, 83, 107, 112, 114, 127, 162,
    173, 183
off diary 81
off-diary 22, 29, 81
office diaries 80

off the record 152
official sources 29
on diary 81
online 11
on the record 152
on the road 89

package 171
passport 92
Paxman, Jeremy 144, 178
PCC (Press Complaints Commission) 31,
    65, 75, 82, 82, 83, 84, 107, 109, 110,
    112, 114, 127, 135, 136, 157, 162, 163,
    183
PCC code of practice 109, 135
percentages 70
performance interviews 174
Periodical Publishers Association 187
personal contacts 30
personal safety 94
phone, mobile 168
phoning copy 165
photographs 111
pictures 33, 112, 135
PIN (number) 95
plagiarism 32
Plurk 56
portal sites 65
Posh Spice 74
Press Association 187
press card 95
press conferences 133
Press Gazette 124
press officers 43
press release 26, 41
Preston Crown Court 122
Price, Katie (Jordan) 23
Prime Minister 87
Princess of Wales 15, 98
print 10
privacy 173
privilege 137
problem solving 36
profile interview 145
promises 134
protecting notes 110
Protection from Harassment Act 1997
    172
protection of sources 109
proximity, touch and gaze 104
pseudocommunication 102
psychologists 101

Public Audit Act (Wales) 2000 127
public transport 89

quangos 131
Quinn, Frances 139
quotes 161

radio 10, 151
Radio 4 (BBC) 23
Randall, David 7, 25
Real IRA 111
recorders 115
records 28
reference book 46
Reporters San Frontières 96
reporting restrictions 124
Representation of the People Act 1983
    127
ringing back 157
rituals 104
rota passes 111
Royal Commission on the Press 15
RSS feeds 58
Ruge, Mari 16
rules of engagement 154
Rutherford, Ernest 70

Schlesinger, Philip 16
Scouts 31
search engines 62, 64
Seattle Times, the 51
set-up shot 175
Shibutani, Tamotsu 14, 103
Shipman, Harold 122, 124, 136
shorthand 116
Sinclair, John Gordon 143
social network 13
soft news 13
sound effects 174
source 41
Southampton University 70
Spider diagrams 37
spin doctors 43
Standards Board for England 127
Stock Exchange 129
stringers 77
sub-editors 77
Sun, The 23, 24
supers 174
surveys 67
Suzy Lamplugh Trust 94
Suzy Lamplugh 34

Swedish Press Ombudsman 116
swine flu 158, 171

taking notes 115
talking heads 36
Teeline shorthand 116
Telegraph, the 12
Television 10
territory 149
Terrorism Act 2000 113
Terrorism 113
Thatcher, Margaret 44
the throw 181
Thompson, Robert 122
Times, the 6, 139
Times Newspapers 139
Tip off 33
Today 178
topical 17
trade unions 137
travelling abroad 90
Twitter 31, 57

UFOs (Unidentified Flying Objects) 59
UK Press Card Authority 111
UN Declaration on Human Rights 123
unambiguity 17

Venables, J 12
Venables, John 17, 122
visas 90

Vogue magazine 87
voice-over 171
vox pop 145
vulnerable groups 181

Watergate 81
Webbink, P. 152
website 170
Who Wants to be a Millionaire? 150
Who's Who 146
wi-fi network 165
Wikipedia 55
wild card 64
wildtrack 171
Williams, Francis 6
Wine-writers' circle 19
witnesses 34
World Wide Web 52, 59, 61
wrap 171
www.192.com 55, 88
www.ask500people.com 57
www.journalismuk.co.uk 65
www.statistics.gov.uk 71
www.wikileaks.org 56

X-Files, The 86

Yahoo! pipes 65
Yahoo! 59, 62

Zoo Forum 131

Designing for Newspapers and Magazines

Chris Frost

Designing for Newspapers and Magazines examines how newspapers and magazines are produced. It offers guidance on how to produce attractive publications and how to tailor them to their target audience by advising on the use of colour, text placement, typography and images.

Designing for Newspapers and Magazines shows how a well-designed publication can provide a powerful platform for good journalism. Written by an experienced journalist and designer, the book details the elements of good design and provides instruction on how to get the most out of computers and computer-aided design. A final section examines a range of different local and national publications and explains the reasoning that underpins their design choices. *Designing for Newspapers and Magazines* includes:

- How to set up a new publication
- Planning an edition of a newspaper or magazine
- Typography and working with text
- Working with images and technical production
- Design pages and how to use colour
- Design and journalism ethics
- A glossary of journalistic and design terms

ISBN 10: 0–415–29026–0 (hbk)
ISBN 10: 0–415–29027–9 (pbk)

ISBN 13: 9–78–0–415–29026–5 (hbk)
ISBN 13: 9–78–0–415–29027–2 (pbk)

Available at all good bookshops
For ordering and further information please visit:
www.routledge.com

Writing for Broadcast Journalists, 2nd edition

Rick Thompson

'This is a superb book which combines the rare mixture of high quality information with humour. The style of writing engages the reader from the introduction and the experience and insight of the author occasionally makes it difficult to put down, a rare feature of a textbook. I would unreservedly recommend this book not only to those studying journalism but to students of language and all who use the spoken and written word as the 'materials' of their work.' – Barry Turner, Senior Lecturer, Nottingham Trent University and University of Lincoln

Writing for Broadcast Journalists guides readers through the significant differences between the written and the spoken versions of journalistic English. It will help broadcast journalists at every stage of their careers to avoid such pitfalls as the use of newspaper English, common linguistic errors and Americanised phrases, and it gives practical advice on accurate terminology and pronunciation, while encouraging writers to capture the immediacy of the spoken word in their scripts.

Written in a lively and accessible style by an experienced BBC TV and radio editor, *Writing for Broadcast Journalists* is the authoritative guide to the techniques of writing for radio and television. This new edition has a special section about writing Online News.

Writing for Broadcast Journalists includes:

- practical tips on how to avoid 'journalese', clichés and jargon

- guidance on tailoring your writing style to suit a particular audience

- advice on converting agency copy into spoken English

- writing to television pictures

- examples of scripts from some of the best in the business

- an appendix of 'dangerous' words and phrases to be avoided in scripts.

ISBN 10: 0–415–58167–2 (hbk)
ISBN 10: 0–415–58168–0 (pbk)
ISBN10: 0–203–84577–3 (ebk)

ISBN 13: 978–0–415–58167–7 (hbk)
ISBN 13: 978–0–415–58168–4 (pbk)
ISBN 13: 978–0–203–84577–6 (ebk)

Available at all good bookshops
For ordering and further information please visit:
www.routledge.com

Ethics for Journalists, 2nd edition

Richard Keeble

'Clear, comprehensive and challenging, *Ethics for Journalists* combines thoughtful reflection with practical skills. Every aspiring journalist – and many hardened hacks – should own a copy.' – Milan Rai, Joint Editor of *Peace News*

'*Ethics for Journalists* is brimming with intelligence and meets the gold standard of readability. This book is spectacularly well informed.' – Clifford Christians, Professor of Journalism, University of Illinois, Urbana, USA

Ethics for Journalist (2nd edition) tackles many issues which journalists face every day – from the media's supposed obsession with sex, sleaze and sensationalism, to issues of regulation and censorship. Its accessible style highlights the relevance of ethical issues for everyone involved in journalism.

Ethics for Journalists provides a comprehensive overview of ethical dilemmas and features interviews with a number of journalists, including the celebrated investigative reporter Phillip Knightley. Presenting a range of imaginative strategies for improving media standards, this second edition of *Ethics for Journalists* considers many problematic subjects including:

- representations of gender, race, sexual orientation, disability, mental health and suicide

- ethics online – 'citizen journalism' and its challenges to 'professionalism'

- journalistic techniques such as sourcing the news, doorstepping, deathknocks and subterfuge

- the impact of competition, ownership and advertising on media standards

- the handling of confidential sources and the dilemmas of war and peace reporting.

ISBN 10: 0–415–43074–7 (hbk)
ISBN 10: 0–415–43076–3 (pbk)
ISBN 10: 0–203–69882–7 (ebk)

ISBN 13: 978–0–415–43074–6 (hbk)
ISBN 13: 978–0–415–43076–0 (pbk)
ISBN 13: 978–0–203–69882–2 (ebk)

Available at all good bookshops
For ordering and further information please visit:
www.routledge.com

RELATED TITLES IN THE MEDIA SKILLS SERIES

Interviewing for Journalists, 2nd edition

Sally Adams with Wynford Hicks

Interviewing for Journalist (2nd edition) details the central journalistic skill of how to ask the right question in the right way. It is a practical and concise guide for all print and online journalists – professionals, students and trainees – writing news stories or features for newspapers and magazines, print and web.

Interviewing for Journalists focuses on the many types of interviewing, from the vox pop and press conference to the interview used as the basis of an in-depth profile. Featuring interviews with a number of successful journalists such as Emma Brockes (of the *Guardian* and of the *New York Times)* and Andrew Duncan (of the *Radio Times*), *Interviewing for Journalists* covers every stage of interviews including research, planning and preparation, structuring questions, the vital importance of body language, how to get a vivid quote, checking and editing material and suiting questions to face-to-face and web interviews.

Interviewing for Journalists includes:

- discussion of the importance of the interview for journalism

- advice on how to handle different interviewees such as politicians, celebrities and vulnerable people

- how to carry out web, telephone and face-to-face interviews

- hints on taking notes, shorthand and recording methods for both print and online interviews

- discussion of ethical, legal and professional issues such as libel, privacy, cheque-book journalism, off-the-record briefings and the limits of editing

- a glossary of journalistic terms and notes on further reading.

ISBN 10: 0–415–47774–3 (hbk)
ISBN 10: 0–415–47775–1 (pbk)
ISBN 10: 0–203–88885–5 (ebk)

ISBN 13: 978–0–415–47774–1 (hbk)
ISBN 13: 978–0–415–47775–8 (pbk)
ISBN 13: 978–0–203–88885–8 (ebk)

Available at all good bookshops
For ordering and further information please visit:
www.routledge.com

Multimedia Journalism: A Practical Guide

Andy Bull

Multimedia Journalism offers clear advice on working across multiple media platforms and includes guides to creating and using video, audio, text and pictures.

This textbook contains all the essentials of good practice that are the bedrock to being a successful multimedia journalist and is supported by an immersive website at **www.multimedia-journalism.co.uk** which demonstrates how to apply the skills covered in the book, gives many examples of good and bad practice, and keeps the material constantly up to date and in line with new hardware, software, methods of working and legislation as they change. The book is fully cross-referenced and interlinked with the website, which offers the chance to test your learning and send in questions for industry experts to answer in their masterclasses.

Split into three levels – getting started, building proficiency and professional standards – this book builds on the knowledge attained in each part, and ensures that skills are introduced one step at a time until professional competency is achieved. This three stage structure means it can be used from initial to advanced level to learn the key skill areas of video, audio, text and pictures, and how to combine them to create multimedia packages. Skills covered include:

- Writing news reports, features, email bulletins and blogs
- Building a website using a content management system
- Measuring the success of your website or blog
- Shooting, cropping, editing and captioning pictures
- Recording, editing and publishing audio reports and podcasts
- Shooting and editing video, creating effective packages
- Streaming live video reports
- Creating breaking news tickers and using Twitter
- Using and encouraging user-generated content
- Interviewing and conducting advanced online research
- Subediting, proofreading and headlining, including search engine optimisation
- Geo-tagging, geo-coding and geo-broadcasting
- Scripting and presenting bulletins

ISBN10: 0–415–47822–7 (hbk)
ISBN10: 0–415–47823–5 (pbk)
ISBN10: 0–203–86603–7 (ebk)

ISBN13: 978–0–415–47822–9 (hbk)
ISBN13: 978–0–415–47823–6 (pbk)
ISBN13: 978–0–203–86603–0 (ebk)

Comparative Media Law and Ethics

Tim Crook

Providing practical and theoretical resources on media law and ethics for the UK and USA and referencing other legal jurisdictions such as France, Japan, India, China and Saudi Arabia, *Comparative Media Law and Ethics* is suitable for upper undergraduate and postgraduate study, and for media professionals who need to work internationally.

The book focuses on the law of the UK, the source of common law, which has dominated the English-speaking world, and on the law of the USA, the most powerful cultural, economic, political and military power in the world. Media law and ethics have evolved differently in the USA from the UK. This book investigates why this is the case. Tim Crook also considers other media law jurisdictions:

- **Common law: A focus on India** – the biggest democracy in the world and largest middle class

- **Civil law: A focus on France** – the influential founder of the European Union and host country for ECHR at Strasbourg

- **Socialist law: A focus on China** – the country with the highest economic growth and largest population

- **Islamic law: A focus on Saudi Arabia** – one of the most influential sources of legal religiosity.

Tim Crook analyses media law, as it exists, the ethical debates concerning what the law ought to be, and the historical development of legal and regulatory controls of communication. Underlying concepts discussed include media jurisprudence – the study of the philosophy of media law; media ethicology – the study of the knowledge of ethics/morality in media communication; and media ethicism – the belief systems in the political context that influence journalistic conduct and content. Throughout, media law and regulation is evaluated in terms of its social and cultural context.

The book has a companion website at **http://www.ma-radio.gold.ac.uk/cmle** providing complementary resources and updated developments on the topics explored. If you need to compare different law and ethics systems, are studying international journalism or want to understand the legalities of working in the media in different jurisdictions, then you will find this an important and useful guide.

ISBN10: 0–415–55157–9 (hbk)
ISBN10: 0–415–55161–7 (pbk)
ISBN10: 0–203–86596–0 (ebk)

ISBN13: 978–0–415–55157–1 (hbk)
ISBN13: 978–0–415–55161–8 (pbk)
ISBN13: 978–0–203–86596–5 (ebk)